R:

CC

THE SHOOTING STAR

Denis Rake, MC
A Clandestine Hero of the Second World War

Also by Geoffrey Elliott

I Spy

From Siberia With Love

The Mystery of Overend & Gurney

Secret Class Rooms: An Untold Story of the Cold War
(With Harold Shukman)

Kitty Harris – The Spy With 17 Names
(With Igor Damaskin)

THE SHOOTING STAR

Denis Rake, MC
A Clandestine Hero of the Second World War

Geoffrey Elliott

Methuen

First published in Great Britain 2009 by
Methuen
8 Artillery Row
London
SW1P 1 RZ

www.methuen.co.uk

1 3 5 7 9 10 8 6 4 2

ISBN 978 0 413 77684 6

A CIP catalogue record for this book is available from the British Library.

Typeset by SX Composing DTP, Rayleigh, Essex

Printed and bound in Great Britain by Cromwell Press Group, Trowbridge

Contents

Illustrations

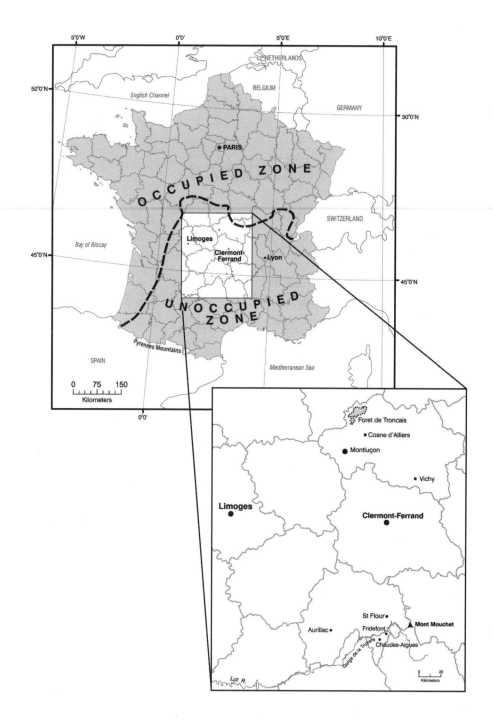

FREELANCE CIRCUIT'S FIGHTING AREA

Timeline

1901
22 May
Denis Rake born in Brussels

1914-1918
The First World War, the 'War to End Wars'; Denis and his mother
escape to Britain from Belgium

1929
October
The Wall Street Crash, start of the Depression Years

1933
January
Hitler becomes German Chancellor

1936
July
Civil War in Spain

1938
March
Germany annexes Austria

1939
March
Germany swallows Czechoslovakia

August
USSR and Germany sign Non-Aggression Treaty

September
Germany invades Poland
Britain and France declare war on Germany
1940
April
Germany invades Denmark and Norway

May
Germany invades France and the Benelux countries
Churchill becomes British Prime Minister
Evacuation from Dunkirk begins

June
Italy enters the war
German troops march into Paris
The *Lancastria* sunk off France, Denis Rake among survivors
De Gaulle flies to London
Germany and Pétain's Vichy Government sign an Armistice; France
sliced into Occupied and Unoccupied Zones

July
Special Operations Executive (SOE) created
RAF wins the aerial 'Battle of Britain' against the Luftwaffe

August/ September
First major German bombing raids – the Blitz on Britain

1941
April
Germany occupies Yugoslavia and Greece

June
Germany invades USSR

July
Denis Rake begins SOE training

October
Germans reach outskirts of Moscow but no further

December

Japan attacks US Fleet at Pearl Harbour. Germany declares war on US

1942
January
Wannsee Conference in Berlin plans 'The Final Solution to the Jewish Question'
U Boat offensive against Atlantic convoys starts

May
Rake lands secretly in France for SOE

June
Battle of Midway
Germans in Tobruk

October
British defeat Rommel's Afrika Korps at el Alamein

November/December
Allied landings in North Africa, Germans march into the Unoccupied Zone of France on anniversary of the First World War Armistice

1943
January/February
German defeat and capitulation at Stalingrad

May
Germans lose Tunisia
Denis Rake returns to London from French and Spanish jails

July
Allies invade Sicily

September
Italy surrenders

1944
May
Denis Rake returns to France to join the FREELANCE mission

June

'D-Day' Normandy landings
Allied forces in Rome

July
Wehrmacht officers fail in attempt to assassinate Hitler

August
FREELANCE embroiled in heavy fighting
Paris liberated

1945
March
Allies cross Rhine

April
Hitler commits suicide

May
Germany surrenders

August
A-Bombs dropped on Hiroshima and Nagasaki

September
Japan surrenders

1946
January
SOE disbanded; Rake works briefly for SIS in Paris

1968
Rake's Progress published

1969
Denis makes cameo appearance in *Le Chagrin et la Pitié*

1976
12 September Denis Rake dies

1

The Hills are Alive

'Hello, duckie. What are you doing there? Picking yourself a grave?'
The voice is English, the delivery arch. An odd question to ask anywhere, all the more in France a month before the D-Day landings in
June 1944, high up in the foothills of the Massif Central. And an
unusual setting, alongside the low drystone wall of a cemetery, north
of the hamlet of Chaudes-Aigues.

Down in the valley a German Fieseler spotter aircraft, nicknamed
the Stork for its long fixed undercarriage legs, drones in lazy circles,
as it hunts for Resistance hiding places, reminding us that we are in
the middle of a war. The bright sun has not yet taken the edge off
the chill in the air, and the woman sitting on the cemetery wall is
shifting with impatience and cold. She looks to be about 30-years-
old, on the plump side, with shoulder length dark hair. She is
clutching a bulging handbag.

In that back-country setting and at that stage of the war, petrol-
engined cars are rare and also menacing, since they are the vehicle of
choice of the Gestapo and their French police collaborators. Most
transport is horse-drawn, and the few vehicles to be seen are the
gazogènes powered by a combustible mix of carbon monoxide,
nitrogen and hydrogen generated by Sabatier-Decauville or Berliet
charcoal burners, usually wedged clumsily in the boot or sometimes
carried on a small rear trailer. But the woman waiting on the wall
(born Nancy Wake, now Nancy Fiocca, but using the cover name
Helene for security reasons) knows that the low-slung Citroën she
heard approaching, its gears grinding at every sharp bend in the road
is in safe hands. Its sole passenger who saunters over from the car
with his flippant, even fey, enquiry, is a youthful 'forty something',
slightly built, of medium height with light brown, wavy hair and

grey-green eyes. His name is Denis, born Denis Rake but in many years on the musical comedy stage and in cabaret, usually billed as Denis Greer. Nowadays his bogus French identity card says he is *Denis Rocher*. Nancy knows him from their time together at a top-secret mansion in England, remembered by its guests as 'The Mad House', where she nicknamed him 'DenDen'.

He walks with an almost imperceptible limp. Dressed in worn blue canvas jacket and trousers, he would not stand out in a crowd of local farmers in the local bar, except that he is carrying a battered suitcase. Both speak fluent if accented French but with each other allow themselves the luxury of English. She knows full well why she has had to hang around for days waiting for him to appear: he has been having 'a last fling' with a boyfriend. But she did not want to spark a row. So she hugs him, kisses him on each cheek in the French style, *bisou bisou*, and laughs: 'DenDen, you darling, how lovely to see you. Where on earth have you been?'

'Oh, my dear, I've had such a time, hundreds of Germans chasing me all over the place,' he fibs. If we weren't in a war zone, we might wonder if we were watching the curtain go up on one of those breezy musicals in which Denis sang and danced in 1930's London.

Telling herself that his excuse is just another 'cock and bull' story, she shrugs. They move on to Chaudes-Aigues, Denis carrying his suitcase, which conceals a weighty British-made wireless set, Nancy clutching the handbag which holds thick rolls of French francs and a list of sabotage targets. Now that its wireless operator has finally turned up the FREELANCE mission of Britain's Special Operations Executive (SOE) can begin doing what it was sent out from England to do.

None of it is easy, much of it is deadly dangerous. They have to gain the confidence of the local Resistance leaders, find out how many men they have, and what supplies they need. With D-Day imminent the Resistance effort needs to be ratcheted up to full fighting peak so that as the Allies land and press across France, the Germans can be stabbed in the back, their movements of supplies and reinforcements harassed, delayed and disrupted by blowing up railway lines and roads. Convoys will be ambushed by men who appear from nowhere and then vanish back into the woods. London has to be asked to arrange the airdrop of supplies to remote sites that Nancy has scouted out, around which the mission and their Resistance allies will hover night after night to help guide the dropping aircraft. They will also make sure that everything is collected and properly shared out, and all traces of the night's work are obliterated.

Much of the action Denis and FREELANCE will see is on and around the Massif Central, an outcrop of ancient volcanic peaks, deep gorges, tiny villages, rushing rivers, hot springs and narrow roads. It is a territory that Denis will soon come to know as a landscape where danger and death lurk, where villages are sacked and burned, where sudden fire fights and the shriek of German dive bombers shatter the illusory quiet of the forests.

In the twenty-first-century most of the tourists have little or no idea about what happened here more than sixty years ago. They flock in to hike, to ride, to sail on the lakes formed by post-war damming of those once rushing rivers, to swim and enjoy the views, the food, the peace and quiet. Today the main risks to life and limb are not shells or tracer bullets but bungee-jumping, amateur rock climbing or tangling with one of the heavy trucks which grind at high speed through the narrow streets of the small towns on their way to Spain.

Back in 1944, the village of Chaudes-Aigues is safe, as far is it can be in those fevered days. A single road leads up from the market town of St Flour. The once-daily bus is operated by the Resistance, who make sure only trustworthy locals are allowed on board. Sentries hidden in the hedgerows whistle early warnings of any other approaching vehicle. News travels at the speed of light, so by the time Denis and Nancy arrive at the four-storey house at the top of the main street to meet the local Resistance chief, Henri Fournier, excited villagers are already starting to head there too. Their boots and clogs clatter on the cobbles as they mill up from the square, along the stream on the left-hand side, past the communal iron spigots out of which gushes rust-tinted water, almost too hot to touch, from a spider's web of underground springs from which the ancient village gets its name.

The locals are quick to boast that 'Aigues' has its roots in the Roman 'aquae' and 'ayga', the word for 'water' in the ancient Occitan dialect of southern France. The crowd moves on uphill past the hotel and the small 'Établissement Thermal', where aching joints can still be bathed today in the hot, mineral rich waters.

Fournier, a hotelier 'charming to everyone except his wife', who is given to nagging, has come to Chaudes-Aigues with his family and his savings to get away from the war, but now finds himself in charge of a small Maquis group of 200 or so men, some of whom are jammed into his living room and crowded on his staircase waiting for Denis to work his magic with the radio and call down boxes of boots, guns, ammunition, and bundles of cash from the sky, courtesy of the legendary 'Secret Service' in London.[1]

Also there is the 'organiser' or officer in command of FREELANCE, John Hind Farmer, known to the French as *Hubert*, a self-effacing soldier whose French is noticeably classical, more Molière than Montparnasse. He is drawn and tired, worrying he may have an ulcer. As Denis sets up his equipment, and squints at the cabbalistic coding instructions on a tiny square of celluloid, he resembles a Siberian Shaman about to perform a sacred ritual, an impression he fosters by asking a gawping farmhand to act as acolyte in laying out the aerial wire and then insisting that the room is cleared before he begins the final secret rites.

In a few minutes he announces that the message has been sent, champagne is unearthed from the cellar and opened with a flourish and everyone crowds back in for cheers, kisses and hugs. Only Denis, Nancy and John Farmer know that Denis has misread the signal square and transmitted at the wrong time; his message has literally vanished into thin air. No matter, it will be sent tomorrow at the appointed hour and within days the night sky will fill to the swell of RAF engines, the swish of falling parachutes, and the thump of their loads. FREELANCE is in business. It will prove a complicated and bloody one. They are a long way from home.

As Denis transmits he has no idea that in a village close to SOE's

[1] *Sometime in 1943 the Corsican word Maquis, meaning hillside brush, became the collective noun for the Resistance, and Maquisards for its men; quite why is a linguistic puzzle*

radio hub in Bedfordshire, England is doing its best to be English, war or no war, and a cheerful Peggy Clark is being crowned as the Land Army's 'May Queen', making her way with a garland of flowers in her hair, through a double line of sturdy jodhpur-clad 'Maids of Honour' brandishing scythes and pitchforks.

The ranks of the Maquis are growing daily, mostly with the young men who don't want to be shipped off to forced labour and an unimaginable fate in Germany. There are also local farmers, a sprinkling of ex-officers, escaped French and Polish prisoners of war, Spanish Civil War exiles, and some who are simply freebooters. When the Maquis descend on local towns waving guns and demanding tobacco, food, and fuel, the dividing line between men of honour and bandits is sometimes hard to discern.

They live scattered over the Massif in abandoned farms, isolated stone barns and cattle shelters, in forest rangers' huts, in logging camps, empty Youth Hostels, sometimes under canvas or in mountain caves.

Around them is their invisible 'support network', French men and women who go on with their day to day lives in the towns and villages. There are many ways they can help: as doctors, treating wounded or handing out spurious certificates of ill-health to help young men avoid forced labour, as town hall clerks rubber-stamping authentic identity and ration cards, as policemen passing on early warnings or turning a blind eye, as couriers and drivers, all the time hoping they will never attract Gestapo attention; malicious neighbours currying favour as German informers are as great a threat as the police.

Not every French citizen is yet ready to rise. Some are understandably terrified of reprisals against themselves or their families. Even at this late stage as the tide of war turns, some still feel it safest to 'sit on the fence'. And some are working directly as undercover agents for the German intelligence and police services. Life for those embroiled in the Resistance, whether French or British, has direct echoes of the fog of terror which enveloped persecuted English Catholics in the sixteenth century.

'Someone rings at the front door a little more insistently than usual, so he can be put down as an official. Immediately, like deer that have heard the voice of hunters and prick their ears and become alert, all stand at attention, stop eating and commend themselves to God in the briefest of prayers; no word or sound of any sort is heard until the servant reports what the matter is . . . it can truly be said of them that they carry their lives always in their hands.'[2]

Though 'Maquis' is a collective noun which implies a cohesive coordinated organisation, and though there have been increasingly successful efforts to bring its various factions together, there are still deep differences in political outlook and allegiance, in opinions about strategy, and the inevitable clashes sparked by the egos and personal ambitions of fiery individual leaders.

The Maquis are brave, but outnumbered and outgunned, short of food and money, hence the essential role of FREELANCE in assessing their needs, communicating these to London through Denis's nimble fingers, orchestrating the supply drops, and training the flood of raw recruits in how to use their deadly new toys. Even their rudimentary training is scant defence against an enemy, who will throw at them battle-hardened troops, heavy guns, tanks and armoured cars, and air support. The Germans have spotter and attack aircraft and also gliders to drop troops onto the hilltops in almost silent attacks. They have clawed back a little of the 'home team' advantage through the Milice, a paramilitary police force of some 25,000 Frenchmen, who swagger around in blue berets, blue jackets and brown shirts but are even more dangerous when they are in plain clothes, infiltrating a crowd or sitting casually in a café.

Some are Fascist fanatics, some petty criminals for whom enlistment meant reprieve, but many are just ferret-faced misfits and outcasts who see helping the Germans against their fellow countrymen as their own way to avoid forced labour, and are seduced by the promise of regular wages and guaranteed food rations.

Once recruited, they are moral lepers with nothing to lose. 'Terrorists' (the Maquis) are their prime targets but Jews and Freemasons are also grist to their mill. One group stands to pocket

[2] *Letters and Memorials of Father Robert Perse, cited by Hutchins; see Bibliography*

500 francs for every Jew they catch, 1000-2000 for a prisoner of war or someone evading forced labour, and a mouth-watering 150,000-200,000 francs for a regional Resistance chief. They are more of an immediate threat than the Germans because they know their countrymen and their countryside so well. Their German puppet masters would also dearly like them to get their hands on British agents like the FREELANCE team; if they should, it would mean torture for the agents, and a long and most likely fatal journey to a concentration camp. Around this time, unknown to Nancy Wake, several of SOE's heroic women agents are about to begin such a journey.

As the Maquis build, so the German Commander in Clermont Ferrand, the 58-year-old veteran General Fritz von Brodowsky watches, assesses the intelligence brought in by Section IV 2 A of the German secret police in Vichy and Clermont Ferrand, which specifically targeted the Resistance, and by the Milice, or beaten out of Maquis prisoners, and makes his plans.

Nancy Wake is a remarkable woman and her story has deservedly been told and retold.[3] But what about Denis Rake? What vaulted a cheery charmer from the chorus of long forgotten West End shows like *Mercenary Mary* into the cross hairs of a German gun sight, into the middle of a battle that will be remembered with pride as one of the epic moments in France's four year fight to regain its honour – a true '*pièce de résistance*'.

---

[3] *Nancy Grace Augusta Wake, now Mrs Nancy Forward, 1912-, AC, GM, Chevalier de la Légion d'Honneur, Croix de Guerre with two Bronze Palms and Silver Star, Medaille de la Résistance, US Medal of Freedom with Palm, NZ RSA Badge in Gold. A true heroine*

2

That Sinking Feeling

The short answer is that Denis Rake volunteered, twice.

At the end of September 1938 Winston Churchill's predecessor as Prime Minister, Neville Chamberlain, thought he had reached an agreement with Hitler at Munich which he and a sizeable coterie of supporters saw as a guarantee of 'Peace for our time' but which realists knew was a gesture of appeasement which had only delayed the inevitable. Soon afterwards, Denis, evidently a realist, had written to the War Office, registering himself as a fluent French speaker who wanted to make himself available as an Army interpreter if, or when, war came.

The letter must have stayed close to the top of a Whitehall filing cabinet. The day war was declared, on 3 September 1939, just short of a year after the sad farce of Munich, a 'telegraph boy' knocked on his London front door to hand him a buff envelope. Denis remembered it all the more vividly because even then a Sunday delivery was unexpected. (The express messages known as 'telegrams' were sent via the Post Office, the text printed out in capitals on narrow paper strips pasted onto a dun-coloured backing sheet. They are now relegated to display cases in museums of postal history, as are images of the smart boys who delivered them, wearing a peaked cap, and a neat navy blue jacket with a brass badge proudly displaying their official serial number.)

Denis's message ordered him to report to a Royal Army Service Corps depot in Croydon. It turned out not to be the forbidding brick barracks which he had apprehensively expected, echoing to bellowed orders and the rhythmic crunch of metal-studded boots, but a 'funny little dance hall', from which he emerged, bewildered but proud as Sergeant Interpreter Denis Rake of The Royal Army

Service Corps.[4] He must have been one of the few British servicemen of any generation since the Boer War who took pleasure in the thick khaki serge blouse, the trousers which would prove almost impossible to press neatly because of a deep pocket, strategically sited by some maverick tailor right across the left thigh, the orthopedically challenging black boots, a brass-buckled webbing belt and anklets, and either a 'fore and aft' cap or a beret resembling a cowpat modelled in blue felt. Indeed he was so pleased that he claimed to have rushed back to London to have his picture taken by his friend, the fashionable photographer Anthony Buckley.[5]

It was, Denis later remembered, 'the most marvellous photograph I have ever had taken in my life'. Anyone (including the present author) who has had to wrap, buckle and button himself into the chafing embrace of Army battledress, will be surprised that it gave Denis such joy. In fact he may just be mixing memories, something to which he was prone, as we shall see. Enquiries of the distinguished Mayfair studio, now Anthony Buckley & Constantine, which has continued Buckley's business and holds his archive, revealed that they did indeed have two photographs of Denis. They were not though in the version he remembers, but far more impressively as a Captain, later in his SOE career, comfortable and cool in barathea, tailored in all likelihood by Messrs. Gieves & Hawkes at No. 1 Savile Row, outfitters to officers, for two centuries, among them Lord Nelson and the Duke of Wellington. He looks every inch the soldier, or more precisely, an actor revelling in the role of a soldier, which is after all what he was.

A few days later Sergeant Rake sailed from Avonmouth to the French port of Nantes. It was the time of the so-called 'Phoney War', that false lull, the calm before the real storm broke. His first few months there were spent on mundane interpreting between a

---

[4] *Searches in Croydon records and military archives have thrown up nothing matching Denis's description. The author's post-war memories suggest he may have had in mind the Civic Hall in Crown Hill, a long open hall ringed by balconies, a short walk from East Croydon station, well suited to accommodate trestle tables piled with clothing, berets and boots, and more readily commandeered by the Army than privately owned premises*

[5] *Buckley began his career in 1937, and became a frequent Royal photographer in the 1960s and '70s. He died in 1991. A collection of his work is in the National Portrait Gallery*

resolutely English-speaking Army and the monoglot local people. Then came a lonely spell at Biscarosse on the fringe of the vast pine forests of Les Landes, south of the Gironde estuary, sitting around waiting to work as an interpreter for an Australian Pioneer battalion who were to set about timber felling in the vast pine forests. Before they arrived (it might have been an interesting encounter) the 'Phoney War' ended and reality set in.

Just over twenty years since the end of 'the war to end all wars', a conflict which had left its mark on Denis as a boy, European soil was again soaking up young men's blood. The British Expeditionary Force, flung across the Channel to slow the Wehrmacht's advance, was in desperate retreat. Between 26 May and 4 June 1940, 338,000 soldiers had been evacuated from the beaches at Dunkirk. On 14 June a triumphant German army entered Paris, the tramp of jackboots echoing under the Arc de Triomphe. Two days later the Third French Republic, enfeebled, socially and politically sundered, was in its death throes, and Marshal Henri-Philippe Pétain, hero of the 1914-18 war and now at the improbable age of 84, newly appointed head of a newly established 'French State' announced to a devastated nation in a voice quivering with emotion that he was reaching out to Berlin to agree terms for an Armistice. It would be signed just over a week later.

Alone in the Landes Denis was ordered to use his initiative – there was no organisation to help him, to get himself back north to Nantes, the rendezvous for British troops and civilians scrambling to get out of France. There he found 'all hell let loose', a mood close to panic, everyone desperate to clamber on to any car, truck, horse-drawn cart, bicycle, railway goods wagon or cattle car, to get to the Atlantic port of St Nazaire. There, in a smaller scale version of the Dunkirk evacuation, they were to rendezvous with a hastily assembled flotilla, which would take them back home in a move codenamed 'Operation Ariel'. Monday, 17 June 1940 was a bright and sunny day, which would end in one of the more appalling tragedies of a war, which was to have its fair share of them.

The largest vessel there was the *Lancastria*, built in Glasgow in 1922 as a passenger liner designed to carry 1,785 people and which had spent much of its life as a cruise ship in the Mediterranean. Now gutted and reconfigured as one of His Majesty's Transport Ships, her official carrying capacity had been increased to 3,000.

No one will ever know for sure how many managed to scramble on board that afternoon. How could anyone keep count in that torrent of weary, panicked bodies, soldiers, airmen, civilian parents trying to stay calm and their screaming, terrified children? One account claims that by 1 p.m. there were 6,000 on board, and that by the minute, countless more scrambled up the nets hung over its sides, clinging as best they could onto their rifles, gas masks, kitbags and suitcases. By any measure the *Lancastria* was grossly overloaded. In the end there may have been as many as 9,000 desperate souls on board, daring to believe they were on their way to safety. One of those crushed and jumbled together on the deck was Denis Rake.

At about 4 p.m., a warning siren began to moan. Denis saw German aircraft circling – a later account says they were a pair of twin-engined Junkers 88, one of the Luftwaffe's most versatile fighter-bombers. He watched transfixed as one screamed into a dive, which seemed bound to end with it smashing into the deck. It pulled out at the last second, and as it did so, released two bombs from the racks underneath its wings. One of them plummeted straight down the *Lancastria*'s funnel and blew out its heart.[6] The ship shuddered, rolled agonisingly slowly from side to side, and began to sink like a dying Leviathan in a welter of steam, spouts of oily water, flickering flames and hopeless shouts for help. Those trapped below decks had almost no chance. There were few lifeboats and almost no time to lower them. Denis and hundreds of others crammed together on the deck took the only way out; they leaped like khaki lemmings into the sea.

Like so many of his comrades, Denis could not swim (it was later claimed that this was a major factor in the terrible casualty toll) but he jumped hand in hand with 'a very nice man called Sale whom I knew'. Sale kept him afloat and helped him to a life raft. Denis never saw him again. A swarm of fishing boats and smaller naval vessels

---

[6] M*emories differ as to whether the bomb did fall down the funnel, or whether the many who thought it did were deceived by terror into an optical illusion. It barely matters*

pulled out 2,447 survivors, Denis among them. He was hauled on board HMS *Berkeley* (a newly commissioned Hunt Class escort destroyer, which would itself be a casualty of the Allied raid on Dieppe in 1942).

Assuming there were at least 6,000 people on board, of whom some 2,500 were rescued, the likely casualty total is more than double the 1,522 who went down with the *Titanic*. But they at least live on in films and folklore. No orchestra played as the waters swallowed the *Lancastria*; its rusty ribs lie deep off the French coast, commemorated by a gull-splattered orange marker buoy swaying at the site and a memorial on the St Nazaire sea wall. No wonder that Winston Churchill ordered the Censor to suppress news of the tragedy; there was enough bad news as it was. It was not until 26 July 1940, after the *New York Times* had broken the silence, that its London namesake published its first report of the disaster, datelined 'from a South West Port, 19 June, Delayed By Censor'.

By that time Denis had been discharged from hospital after recovering from the *Lancastria* ordeal. In another of those twists of fate which challenge the imagination of anyone who has not been caught up in the cogs of the Service machine, he found he had been transferred to the Royal Naval Reserve, swapping his khaki serge for a Petty Officer's blue flannel, and posted as an interpreter to HMS *Pollux*, a minelayer based in Portsmouth with British officers and a crew drawn from de Gaulle's Free French supporters. He recalls that he was on board the vessel itself when it hit a mine (a classic case of being hoist by one's own petard). The records show *Pollux* still afloat in 1944, so the damage was probably only minor but though it made a good story, coming on the heels of the *Lancastria* disaster it cannot have done much for Denis's health and state of mind.

He found himself with time on his hands, and undaunted by his experiences, started to fuss about how he could do more to help win the war; to be seen to be 'doing your bit' was a wartime phrase.

Had he been a Nazi spy, rather than a shell-shocked middle-aged musical comedy actor looking for a new challenge, the indiscreet chatter he overheard in a Portsmouth pub one August evening would have been gold dust. As it was, when he heard a bevy of RAF pilots braying that a secret organisation was being put together to parachute men behind German lines, and that being able to speak good French was an essential qualification, he decided to see where the rashly dropped clue led. He took the train to London to see his friend 'Burnett-Brown', who knew many influential people and 'a great deal about most things', and who explained that the pilots had been talking about the Special Operations Executive, or SOE.

Though it had its origins in earlier, shadowy components of the British undercover underworld[7], SOE was officially established in the deepest secrecy about a month after the *Lancastria* tragedy. Its primary mission in Europe was to help bring about victory with no holds barred, through sabotage, subversion and above all the building, arming and training of resistance movements in German-held territory which would rise as a powerful secret army when one day the tide turned and the Allied forces liberated the European mainland.

Without a first name, closer identification of Denis's well-informed source is impossible. An elderly Burnett-Brown was at the time Surveyor to one of the oldest and richest City livery companies and a senior Mason (he succeeded the King himself as 'Provincial Grand Master' for Middlesex in 1937). His son, who died in 1966, commanded a Territorial Army regiment in the course of a distinguished career and might be a more likely candidate. However, later on in his story Denis speaks of Burnett-Brown being 'on an anti-aircraft gun in Hyde Park', which does not fit with either of these intriguing possibilities.

Wherever he fitted in, 'Burnett-Brown' was, in twenty-first century-speak, 'wired'. He obviously knew enough about SOE and enough about Denis to discourage him strongly from having anything to do with it. Depending on what he knew of Denis's life up to this stage, he may well have had a point.

Born in Brussels and claiming an opera diva as his mother and a tubercular journalist from Bristol as his father, sent away as a child to join a Continental travelling circus, chorus boy in a succession of

---

[7] *The historian Elizabeth Sparrow traces its roots as far back as William Pitt's Alien Office, set up to spy on France after the Revolution*

West End musicals, embroiled at various times in relationships with a British diplomat, and a Greek Prince, Denis hardly fitted the stereotype of the clean-cut Secret Service hero from the pages of John Buchan, Captain of School, dashing all-round sportsman dispatched with a gruff farewell by his monocled monosyllabic Chief to bury himself in the bazaars of Baluchistan.

But Denis persisted and Burnett-Brown drafted a letter for him to sign. He clearly believed that taking the highest road of all was the best route, since Denis's SOE personal file has a handwritten note which shows the source of the recommendation to SOE as 'The Secretary of State for War via the Marquess of Carisbrooke'. The dates are not clear, and as three ministers held the Secretary's post in 1940 we do not know whose office passed the letter along.

In the midst of the 'anti Boche' hysteria whipped up by the British press, as 'feral' in the First World War as some of its targets claim it is today, the Marquess, a grandson of Queen Victoria, agreed at King George V's request to give up his title of 'His Highness Prince Alexander of Battenberg' and to change the family name to 'Mountbatten'. In return he was created Marquess of Carisbrooke, Earl of Berkhampsted and for good measure, Viscount Launceston. He was a man of considerable distinction, prominent at Court, in charities and on major corporate boards.[8]

He served in the First World War and in the Second World War he became an officer in the RAF Volunteer Reserve. Though no mention of him can be found in the main literature, he may well have had links with SOE in a liaison capacity, and he would certainly have been on amicable terms with some of its 'top brass'. He was also Senior Master of the United Grand Lodge of Antient [sic] Free and Accepted Masons, and though no link with the fuzzily-glimpsed Burnett-Brown can be found, it is possible that Masonic broad-band connectivity was at work; otherwise it seems on the face of it improbable, if only given the social dynamics of the time or, for that matter, today, that a Marquess should take the trouble to help Denis catapult from the back row of the *No, No, Nanette* chorus into a

[8] *Alexander Albert Mountbatten Carisbrooke, GCB, GCVO, 1886-1960*

frontline role in a super-secret wartime organisation. Though it was little more than a mile from the Marquess's London home at Kensington Palace to Denis's pre-war digs off Gloucester Road, in social terms the gulf was as wide as the Atlantic.

Though Denis's route into SOE (however it was contrived) could fairly be said to be unconventional, the same could be said for many others; the highways and byways that led to its discreet Baker Street front door were as diverse as its people. Men and women in the armed forces who were seen to have backgrounds and language skills that might make them good material were interviewed so discreetly that many did not know until they were in training the perilous nature of the work they would be asked to undertake.

Senior soldiers, business men and City bankers nodded and winked at one another on the 'old boy' circuit. There were enigmatic introductions in the bars of St James's clubs. The City solicitors Slaughter and May seconded several partners. Some in the senior echelons, especially its Middle East HQ in Cairo, were less conventional. One dismissive judgement claimed that among them 'many displayed an enthusiasm unrestrained by experience, some had political backgrounds which deserved rather closer scrutiny than they ever got, and a few could charitably only be described as nutcases . . .'[9]

At the field level, SOE's widely-spread nets brought in many young men and women often from conventional backgrounds possessed of quite extraordinary courage. Their bravery in the face of the enemy, and in too many cases looking into the blank eyes of an executioner, is beyond praise and any attempt at comment leads simply to cliché. Inevitably the nets trawled so widely that they also snagged a few candidates cut from even more exotic cloth than Denis: a gold prospector, an explorer, a man who sold contraceptives in Bucharest, a pimp, a princess, a prize-fighter, at least one safe-cracker, a self-confessed confidence trickster who vanished with his operational funds, a 'South of France playboy', several committed Communists, a former soldier in the French Foreign Legion, a

[9] *Elliott p. 42*

washing powder salesman from Zagreb, a Hollywood stuntman and an acrobatic double act from the circus.[10]

Denis's entry into SOE and his indefatigable work in its service raised the same issue, namely the criticism levelled at SOE for failing to check the background of some of its recruits with sufficient care. Its security and an institutional mindset made it reluctant to concede operational or human errors, often in the teeth of strong evidence to the contrary. It is fair to comment by way of balance that every major clandestine service has had its share of miscreants, flaws and failures. Over the years SIS, CIA and the FBI, not to mention the former KGB, have all experienced disastrous hostile penetrations. Though it scored a major wartime success 'turning' German agents through the Double XX System, Britain's security service, MI5, among the more vocal critics of SOE, was simultaneously being leached of some of its innermost secrets by the epicene traitor Anthony Blunt. At the same time one of the key day to day conduits in SIS for much of MI5's liaison on counter-espionage was another Soviet 'mole', Kim Philby.

Errors of organisation and judgment, the cutting of corners, were all the more likely in SOE, kick-started to cut against the grain and do new and nasty things, things that other longer established members of the intelligence community felt were their rightful 'turf'. Thus while criticisms made with the benefit of hindsight about SOE's shortcomings, real though many were, and its frequent unwillingness to face up to them, a trait exhibited by many others when problems arise, they do not diminish what Denis and so many others achieved against all odds.

---

[10] *See e.g. Foot, and Butler, p. 28*

3

Chagrin

It was all a long time ago. Few if any of those who were directly involved are left to tell their stories. So we fall back upon legwork and paperwork: tours of the area over which Denis and FREELANCE fought and scrambled to safety, the crumbling Château de Fragnes, the rainy streets of Chaudes-Aigues and Montluçon, curling pages of many wartime files, biographies and autobiographies, a major film, a minor TV appearance, letters, pre-war West End playbills, opera house archives, a Society photographer's files, and sheet after sheet of faded newspapers whose headlines tell of distant, sometimes bloody, sometimes golden days.

Official and narrative histories provide much context. Here accounts of events as seen through French eyes are an important counterweight; though it has understandably taken on an English patina, the story of SOE in France still reverberates as an impassioned and complex passage of French history bitterly experienced and bloodily acted out by the French themselves.

But what first prompted the idea of telling Denis's story, of presuming to become curator of his memory? First, seeing and hearing him in the Marcel Ophuls film, *Le Chagrin et la Pitié*, (*The Sorrow and the Pity*). This is the controversial cornerstone of Resistance chronicles. It takes a chilly look back, appropriately in shades of black, white and grey, at the reality of occupation and Resistance, compromise and collaboration, bravery and betrayal in and around Clermont Ferrand. Its portrayal of France and the French is said to have so disturbed the authorities when it was first shown in 1969 that it was kept off French TV screens until October 1981, when 15 million viewers watched.[11]

---

[11] *It also prompted Woody Allen to crack after taking Diane Keaton to see it in the movie 'Annie Hall', 'Gee, those Resistance fighters were brave, you know. Having to listen to Maurice Chevalier sing so much . . .'*

Some of what Denis has to say to us through the camera we will weave into the story later, but when one knows the background it is riveting to see him transmuted onto the screen, white haired, neat, a cat purring contentedly on his lap, a man of gentleness and charm, his French impeccable, though not perhaps a hundred per cent Gallic in intonation, (by then he had been too long in England), his English just a shade prissy.

Above all, he seems vulnerable, flattened, probably a reflection of the bouts of mental and physical ill-health he went through in the immediate post-war years. There is none of the joie de vivre, the gift of laughter, which so struck those who met him during the Second World War. It is of passing interest, at best, that in talking about his war years, Denis describes himself as having been a homosexual '*à ce moment là*', i.e. 'at that point in time', a phrase it is hard to construe other than as a suggestion that with old age what Ophuls delicately termed his '*tendances*' had by then, somewhat dimmed.

More importantly, though it goes unsaid in the film, is that it is far more closely related to Denis's second operation, the FREELANCE mission, than appears at first sight. Some of the Resistance person-alities who appear are among the men of the Maquis who were Denis's brothers in arms. They were almost Central Casting stereo-types of the French farmer, who were filmed seated sturdily and disputatiously around a table while their aproned wives hover in the doorway and dutifully replenish the bottles of *vin du pays*.

Their leader, the man whom SOE and Denis knew (and we shall come to meet) as the indomitable and sometimes intractable *Colonel Gaspard*, is seen talking proudly about the harm he and his colleagues had inflicted on the Germans, although it is not made clear that part of what he is describing relates to the bitter fighting around Mont Mouchet in 1944, in which Denis and the FREELANCE team were to make their important contribution. There is nice irony in the fact that just twenty-five years after the fighting, the film shows us *Gaspard* in his real identity as Emil Coulaudon, a burly businessman seated comfortably behind the wheel of a large Mercedes. He is going about his work of marketing Dutch televisions to a new generation of French consumers, embodying in miniature (and despite everything) the essence of the European Economic Community. This was a vision of the twentieth century Continent espoused by many of the Vichy collaborators he so loathed, as an important justification for cohabiting with Germany.

The film's production must have overlapped with the writing of Denis's autobiography; indeed in an early example of what modern advertisers call 'product placement', at one point the camera lingers for a second on a proof copy of *Rake's Progress* published in 1968. Though it has been long out of print, I managed to track down a copy in the wilds of the secondhand book trade. It proved tantalisingly unreliable.

His publishers[12] cannot be blamed for failing to resist the tempting choice of the title, or the irritatingly whimsical dust jacket proclaiming it as *The Gay and Dramatic Adventures of Major Denis Rake MC, the Reluctant British War-Time Agent*. '*Reluctant*' (as we have already begun to see) is extremely unfair. In its old-fashioned meaning, '*Gay*' is also wide of the mark since, though Denis could certainly charm and amuse, sometimes outrageously, his story is essentially that of a fragile and lonely man, though without question a brave one.

However, his editors might be more squarely criticised for an apparent lack of supervision, which allowed him to leave many loose ends dangling, and to gloss over several key facts, names and dates. Some of the errors and omissions may be matters of Denis's discretion. Many are just mistakes of the sort we are all prone to make when peering back down the dusky elm-lined cemetery avenues of memory.

Taking 'gay' in its modern sense, his book is for its times also a frank, even matter of fact, avowal of his homosexuality and his various liaisons, or at least, those that seemed to have mattered. Though he was driven by the urge to prove himself as brave as other men and his relationships often ended with a tinge of sadness, and in one case, tragedy, there is no feeling that he was 'uneasy, timid and melancholy' about his orientation in the sense, for instance that

---

[12] *The eclectic, prolific and occasionally headline grabbing oeuvre of Leslie Frewin Limited deserves a chapter in any study of post Second World War British publishing*

the brilliant writer Colm Tóibín describes his own feelings.[13] Almost to the contrary.

The book's publication came close on the heels of the 1967 Sexual Offences Act, which after a decade of acrimonious debate finally passed into law the main recommendation of The Wolfenden Committee Report, that 'homosexual behaviour' between consenting adults in private should no longer be a criminal offence.

Though the law thus became somewhat less oppressive, British public opinion, or at least the opinion of Middle England, wherever that might be, was still a long way from regarding that 'behaviour' as acceptable, and magistrates initially defined 'private' narrowly. So, to declare himself, as Denis did, still took some courage.

In a sense the Anthony Buckley photograph might be a metaphor for Denis's autobiography. It is a stylish triumph of the portrait photographer's art: Denis the suave soldier. However when the negative, not reproduced here, is held up to the light, we can see that while much depended on the empathy between Buckley and his sitter, the pose, and the lighting, the end product has been subtly embellished in the studio basement. Denis's image has been retouched by the studio 'finishers' with pencil and airbrush, removing bags under the eyes, and wrinkles on the forehead, and artfully shading the jaw line, even adding back a shirt cuff that had slid up his sleeve. So what we see is certainly Denis, but not quite 'warts and all'.

It is also interesting that Denis did not use this photograph in *Rake's Progress*. Maybe he felt it was just too much of a stereotyped pose. He preferred the image of himself in his brief spell as an RNVR Petty Officer. With his coat collar turned up and a cap jauntily on his brow, he was the sort of cheery cove you might have met in a smoky wartime saloon bar, light years away from the distinguished 'Army and Navy Club' profile captured by Buckley.

The book took me to the more measured but all too brief account of Denis's story included by Marcus Binney [see bibliography] as a chapter in his enthralling book about several clandestine heroes. But

[13] *Toibin, p. 2*

the tipping point, when a full scale effort was too compelling to ignore, was when I happened upon a recording made by his mother in 1931 of a couple of songs from Offenbach's *Orpheus in the Underworld*. Through the inevitable background hissing and scratching, she sings in a light, clear, almost girlish soprano. As with almost everyone to do with Denis, her precise role in his life, even her identity, is unclear. Nonetheless, one began to think of them both as real, lifted off the printed pages into the mind's eye and ear.

The trail then led to another and, up to a point, more reliable source. The cache of SOE personal files on Denis, and other agents, is now in the UK National Archives. Denis's own file contains many key facts about his personal background and his missions, which are omitted from, or fudged in his autobiography and many documents of importance, especially the debriefing reports written after his first mission to France, the citations for his various decorations and perhaps most important in terms of understanding the man within the modest and self-mocking shell, the positive appraisals of his cheerfulness and courage made during his SOE training by a series of hard-boiled instructors.

But even the personal files have to be treated with some care. Though the SOE archive remains an extraordinary and copious resource, it is the residue of a positive orgy of destruction. The first of the two episodes was a bonfire in Cairo in 1942, sparked, literally, by apprehension that the Middle East and Balkan records might fall into the hands of the advancing Germans. The second episode was a conflagration in Baker Street in 1946, over whose origins conspiracy theorists still debate.

But these episodes were probably insignificant by comparison to the later bouts of official 'weeding'. These were designed to remove anything that a handful of often insouciant vetters concluded was ephemeral, and thus taking up valuable storage space, such as anything that was personally embarrassing to the subject of the file or their family, or material which described actions Government would prefer to disavow. The archive passed into the care of SIS, which presumably overlaid its own introspective criteria on the weeding process, and by one estimate, between August 1946 and

May 1947, the equivalent of 119 filing cabinets full of papers were destroyed. Further heavy culling in the 1950s, physical moves, and much reshuffling of papers in an attempt to introduce a new classification system, have taken their cumulative toll.[14]

Thus while not false or misleading, what is left may well be nothing but the truth, but may not be the whole truth. As one example, (although it is tempting to take at face value the personal details which someone enters on an official form) in Denis's case there is no evidence that what he told SOE about his background was ever checked, despite glaring inconsistencies or 'facts' which cried out for follow up. In any case, in many organisations some things are simply never put on paper. When they are, memoranda of meetings or conversations record what was said as filtered through the static of the writer's personal sound system. And even if carefully teased out by a skilled debriefing officer, SOE agents' first hand accounts of what actually happened in the field are bits and pieces grasped from the whirling memories of those who have been under immense stress; this is certainly true in Denis's case.

One of the more vexing questions both in the reports which remain on the files and in the recollections of Denis and others, is timing. Just when did things happen and were they a matter of days or of weeks? How much time did Denis or other agents spend on the Riviera, in Paris or in Lyons? How long did his romantic fling in Paris last? Understandably no one kept careful notes in a leather-bound Smythson's of Bond Street diary.

Messages to and from the field, which might have included more specific information, and given invaluable context were among the first items to be consigned to oblivion, and with the efflux of time and the erosion and conflation of memories, accounts published years later inevitably contain elisions of events and differ from one another in points of detail. The present author has been told more than once, that when they got together to reminisce many years later, SOE agents (who had either been in the same firefight or who had scrambled away through the woods together from a German

[14] *See, e.g., Murphy p. 214*

patrol) found that they had often starkly different memories of actions in which they had participated shoulder to shoulder.

In any event SOE was not given to meticulous record keeping. Writing after the war, Maurice Buckmaster, who ran its French Section, took some pride in his aversion to paperwork '. . . the more . . . one undertook, the less attention one could pay the actual job itself . . . people wonder why we never kept proper files and they jump to all sorts of wild and preposterous conclusions; the reason is simply that when you have worked every night till somewhere between three and five in the morning, you feel little desire to tabulate the results of the day in order to earn the gratitude and admiration of some hypothetical historian of the future'.[15] MI5 had a different view, commenting acidly in 1943 on 'the peculiar system of records prevailing in SOE'.[16]

One aspect of Denis's story presents a particular dilemma. In his memoirs, probably out of tact and a sense of the moral climate of the time, he either did not name, or altered the names of, the men with whom he had relationships that were important to him. These include 'the British diplomat', 'the Prince,' the German officer 'Max' and the Transylvanian born SOE agent Alex, even though they were all by then dead. But when matched against the files and further research the shadows masking those oblique pen portraits do clear away sufficiently to allow us to put names to two of them, and make a reasoned though not definitive speculation about a third.

But what good is it to 'out' someone all these years later? To say that they are long dead, so it does not matter, is a lame excuse. A more compelling reason is that Denis himself was the first to tell us about the relationships and to stress how much they meant to him, so that if we want to do him justice by telling his story in full, it does not seem unfair to try to reach behind his obfuscation.

Even the other SOE memoirs in which Denis appears are not infallible sources. Their authors are telling their own story not his, and a narrative that is on the face of it frank can, with the best of intentions conceal genuine or selective lapses of memory, attempts

[15] *Buckmaster p. 83*
[16] *Knight, p. 4*

at self-justification, even a barb or two, all the more when it has been whetted on the grindstone of a ghost writer or a commercially minded editor. And most personal accounts of SOE experiences were written without access to the long-concealed files. Anyone who has tried to make a statement even a short while after say, a traffic accident, knows all too well how soon details get lost or blurred.

So though we have these several starting points none of them alone leads us to the whole story. The multi-coloured, ragged strands need to be plaited together.

In doing so we need to take into account a cautionary note on the draft debriefing report on Denis's initial mission into France (a note which incidentally supports the point about the accuracy even of official records), since it recommends that 'special care should be taken in pruning [the report] before circulation' because it gave leads to the names of other SOE agents.

It was written by Maurice Buckmaster, whom we have just quoted on the matter of SOE records. He wrote: 'It must be borne in mind that Rake is an actor by profession and that some of the more theatrical passages in his report *may* have been unconsciously exaggerated. I think this should be borne in mind when assessing them. Rake is an exceptionally courageous man because he has screwed himself up to overcome his natural timidity and in the process is apt to become dramatic about his exploits. I do not for one moment however suggest that the substance of this report is anything but true and I think it reflects very creditably on his guts.'[17]

Or, as put rather more eloquently by Shakespeare into the mouth of King Henry V, 'Old men forget, yet all shall be forgot, but he'll remember with advantages what feats he did that day.' However, it remains the case, as a veteran SIS officer once remarked to the present author, that 'even when you have all the facts, you may still never know the truth'.

---

[17] *In a letter on another subject in his PF Denis says he later saw this comment of Buckmaster's on a file in the SOE Registry and implies he does not disagree with it!*

4

The Daring Young Man on the Flying Trapeze

His story begins with mystery and muddle, nicely spiced with romance and ambiguity and in the background, that girlish soprano voice.

We introduced it with the opening line of Rafael Sabatini's 'Scaramouche' because it seems to catch part of the essence of Denis: 'He was born with a gift of laughter and a sense that the world was mad.'

That picaresque romance, later filmed with Stewart Granger in the title role, has other coincidental parallels with Denis's story: vexed questions of parentage, aristocratic connections, multiple identities, France in revolutionary turmoil, life on the run. The hero even joins a troupe of strolling players and reveals real acting talent. But Denis's life was in so many ways stranger than fiction or Sabatini's imagination.

Denis claimed that he was born in the rue de Commerce in Brussels, right at the heart of the city, on Sunday 22 May 1901. But he qualifies even this rather basic fact by saying that there was always some uncertainty about the day and the year and that he had relied on his mother for the information. If the date is correct, it reminds us that he was within a few months of being a child of the Victorian era. So, as the dangerous central events of his life unfolded, he was not one of SOE's dashing young adventurers, but an actor already on the cusp of middle age. It is characteristic of him that more than once when he filled out SOE forms he claimed Paris as his birthplace; maybe he thought it sounded more glamorous.

Though he remembers vividly that his father's life was being drained away by tuberculosis, (when Denis was born, the disease was still a scourge in the Western world), he does not bother to give us his father's first name. He only tells us that he came from Bristol, that his mother (Denis's paternal grandmother) had been born a Fry (and thus a member of one of Britain's prominent Quaker clans) and that his father's family owned 'Rake and Tuckett', a leather tannery in Bristol. Also according to Denis, his father worked in Brussels as 'correspondent for the *Times*' but he omits the definite or indefinite article.

The personal file helps by putting a name to the anonymous father. He was Francis Joseph Rake, born in Bristol in 1870. As to his role with the *Times*, the one time 'Top People's' newspaper has no record of him today. A random walk through its columns in the early 1900s suggests that there were several categories of Belgian contributor: 'Our Special Correspondent', 'Our Brussels Correspondent', 'Our Own Correspondent' and finally 'Our Correspondent',[18] the category to which we can surmise Francis Rake belonged, and who today would be classed as a 'stringer', paid by the published word rather than with a regular wage.

Stringers cover everything from local politics to an international Sugar Conference, and a New Year's Day in 1901 which 'was not marked by any incident of a noteworthy character', a report rivalling in its leadenness the 'dullest headline' competition between *Times* sub-editors in the 1930s, won by the polemicist Claud Cockburn[19] with the line 'Small Earthquake in Chile – Not Many Dead'.

As to the family tannery, Bristol records show either out of forgetfulness or perhaps out of unconscious filial pride Denis had reversed the names – it was actually 'Tuckett and Rake'.

Had John Galsworthy, the chronicler of British upper class mores,[20] turned his attention to tradesmen, the Rake family saga might have made interesting material. We can trace the story of the Rakes, through the mercantile directories and census returns of

---

[18] *A gradation echoed in Evelyn Waugh's sardonic classification in 'Decline and Fall' of British preparatory schools as ' "Leading School', "First Rate School, "Good School" and "School"—frankly "School's" pretty bad'*
[19] *1904-1981, inter alia prime mover of 'The Week', a well informed pre Second World War political newsletter*
[20] *1867-1933, author of* The Forsyte Saga

the late nineteenth century. They were an initially prosperous family in the leather trade who moved from tanning (the messier and smellier end of the business) to wholesaling, selling dressed hides as well as the bark and 'valonia' (a by-product of acorns) needed by other tanners. Tucketts and Macgregors come and go in various partnership combinations. In 1867 Denis's paternal grandfather Joseph Rake had enough standing in the Bristol area to be listed in *Morris' Directory of Clergy, Gentry and Private Residents*. By the time of the 1881 census he has gone, and his widow and young son are in Brighton, where she is running a 'private school'. By 1883, the leather warehouse has been sold to the local tobacco giants Wills, and in 1891 the assiduous census takers find Denis's father and grandmother in a Paddington lodging house.

Though Denis believed that his paternal grandmother was a Fry, and the records show that at least one Rake did marry into a branch of the Bristol cocoa and chocolate dynasty, a direct connection is hard to see; the marriage certificate of Francis Rake's parents show Denis's grandmother was a 'Sarah Windham', daughter of a local corn merchant.

Just who Denis's mother really was, is a major, and far more romantic enigma. In his version she was from Wales with the 'uncompromising Welsh name of Llewellyn though there was a strong French streak in her ancestry'. She was 'attached', as he puts it, to the centuries old *La Monnaie Opera* in Brussels and became well known as an opera singer in England and on the Continent using the professional name of 'Madame Emma Luard'.

First, and as a minor disconnect, the correct spelling is 'Luart'. Second and more puzzling is that Emma Luart, or to use her full name Emma Victorine Luart (spelled 'Luwaert' in Flemish documents) was a real person, not a stage persona. She was the second daughter of 'M. Victor Luart of Brussels' and studied singing at the Brussels Conservatoire. She went on to have an important career, and earn her own entry in the *New Grove Dictionary of Music and Musicians*.[21] The Offenbach recording which came our way is just

---

[21] *See J.B. Steane in Bibliography*

one of several which can still be heard today through the imperfect wonders of digital re-mastering. But when he filled in a form for SOE Denis gave his mother's name as 'Margaret Llewellyn *Jones*', (rather than 'Llewellyn'). He added that she was born in Meifod (a tiny village in Montgomeryshire, in the lee of Mount Snowdon; in 2003 the Meifod valley was the site of the Welsh National Eisteddfod).

To confuse things even more the General Register Office records show that when his father Francis Joseph Rake married at a London Registry Office on 19 September 1891, giving his occupation as 'commercial traveller' and his address as 528 Oxford Street, Marylebone, his bride was a 21-year-old Margaret *Morgan* Jones, daughter of a Paddington grocer.

The Welsh are rightly renowned for their gift of song. Even so it would take a considerable stretch of the imagination to see a girl from Meifod, let alone a Paddington grocer's daughter, reborn as a Brussels opera star. Unless of course we move into the world of fiction and fantasise that she had been hypnotised and re-engineered into the role by some Belgian Svengali as another 'Trilby', in a Druidic echo of George du Maurier's celebrated 1890s Gothic romance.[22]

Further reinforcement that the two women were not one and the same comes from Emma's handwriting, seen in several letters which survive in the archives of *la Monnaie*. It is wholly 'Continental' and angular, without the slightest resemblance to the round, copybook script, which would have been painstakingly taught to pigtailed girls in the Victorian village school in Meifod, or for that matter a Board school in Paddington.

But to round off the case, Emma Luart's date of birth is consistently documented as 14 August 1892. Denis implies that he never saw his birth certificate, and relied on what his mother told him. But if we take his autobiography as correct, and he was born in 1901,[23] this would rule out Emma conclusively, in the absence of a

[22] *George du Maurier, 1834-1896, cartoonist, artist and author. 'Trilby' written in 1894 is said to have inspired 'Phantom of the Opera'. Those who wish to stretch their imaginations to breaking point may note that du Maurier had studied in Paris and Belgium and that his English wife was also named Emma!*
[23] *Though an entry on a 1944 SOE form corrected in a clerkly hand implies that he was born in 1898*

physiological miracle worthy of a Special Correspondent's urgent telegram to the *Times.*

And yet if we look from Denis's photograph to Emma's there seems to be a likeness. We are left guessing. Maybe Emma simply lied about her age; she would not be the first prima donna to do so, though the fib would have to have been on a bravura scale. Maybe someone told Denis that if he admitted that his mother was not British it might make it more difficult for him to get clearance to join SOE.

Margaret Jones, whatever her middle name, was born in 1870, and based on age alone is a more logical candidate for Denis's birth mother. Denis's autobiography makes the briefest mention of an elder sister who was 'sent away' at an early age. If this were a novel, we might speculate that Francis Rake did indeed marry Margaret, and that he brought two children, Denis and the elder sister, in his wake when somehow, somewhere, he met and was swept off his feet by a young, glamorous Emma. This theory might explain what we shall soon see as Emma's less than maternal instincts.

Even so, what took him from life as a commercial traveller in London to scraping a living as a newspaper stringer in Brussels? Was he spurred by love, by ambition, or was he in the classic Victorian and Edwardian tradition of the 'remittance man', a Bristolian scape-grace sent abroad and encouraged to stay there by regular payments from home? Were he and Emma even married? Was he really Denis's father? There were some in SOE who gossiped that Denis was the illegitimate son of a British nobleman but this is as likely as not to have been a rumour Denis himself could have started in a mischievous moment.

In the end it is impossible to connect the dots, and the only point in even speculating is to question the likely effect this confused background had on Denis himself and the compelling role that women with strong personalities were to play in his life.

We shall be running ahead too far if we sketch out Emma's full and successful working life now. But when trying to make sense of Denis's dysfunctional, almost unbelievable, childhood, the key point is that whatever the family's real story (and even the most outwardly respectable families have episodes or characters in their history that they prefer to airbrush into oblivion), Emma was a beautiful and talented woman whose career came first, second and third. Children would have had no place in life's headlong rush into the spotlight. Denis's elder sister, whom he does not name, had been sent to England before he was born, and he himself was disposed of in a way that would read like a grim fantasy conceived by Roald Dahl, had Denis himself not described it in rather positive terms. When he was just three-years-old (or according to the personal file, four-years-old), a 'friend' of Emma's, perhaps on the receiving end of many theatrical moans and much lace handkerchief wringing about how little Denis was always in the way, came up with a solution.

Before we finally throw in the towel on the motherhood mystery we may as well glance at one more intriguing lead that Denis tosses us. He names the problem-solving friend as 'Mrs Morgan'. Is that just an irrelevant, half remembered fact, a Freudian confusion, or is it a hint at the truth, a repressed memory of the shadowy presence of Margaret *Morgan* Jones somewhere in the Brussels household? There is no way of knowing. Whoever she was, Mrs Morgan, as Denis recollected, worked for a Mrs Jarrett, who was in turn in charge of the eighteen strong troupe of child performers in what he remembers as 'Sarazini's Travelling Circus' (the correct name is 'Sarrasani').[24]

Why not pack Denis off to join them, Mrs Morgan suggested? Emma jumped at the idea, and off Denis toddled, his hand nestling trustingly in Mrs Morgan's fingers. He soon become a 'tumbler', turning lithe somersaults across the sawdust-strewn ring or spot-lit by a carbon-arc lamp in white shorts, a blue jersey and silver-buckled shoes, grinning out at the crowd, balanced at the apex of the human pyramid that was one of the Circus set pieces.

A present-day reaction to this strange tale, somehow made even chillier by Denis's throwaway line that these tiny children had to

---

[24] *Started in Dresden in the late 1800s as a troupe of 'dogs, monkeys, a bear and a pig' by 1902 it was advertising itself as 'the biggest and most elegant' Big Top Circus in Europe. It is now a complex entertainment empire still run by the Sarrasani family*

wash their own clothes every night, is conditioned by what we know or can imagine about the psychological stun grenade which explodes when infants are wrenched from home. Denis should have been deeply unhappy, wanting desperately to run back to his family, scarred for life.

So it comes as a surprise to read his recollection over half a century later, that the Circus people were 'terribly kind'. It was 'a glorious life, more like a game. I was very happy in my childhood', and these were years in which he developed self-discipline and self-reliance. But a little later in his narrative he is more equivocal, giving us a glimpse into Emma's chilly heart with the casual comment that had he not fitted in to the circus, he would probably have been sent to a children's home. He notes ruefully that her selfishness had deprived him of the 'love and affection which play such a large part in a child's development' (he does not mention his father).

Later on in his narrative he reflects that he 'really hardly knew my mother. She was a strange woman, very like Nancy Wake, very beautiful,[25] very amusing . . . a lovely sense of humour'. Superficially these were storybooks, magical days, the stuff of dreams. What the songwriters called 'the smell of the greasepaint, the roar of the crowd', were the back-cloth to lion tamers, magicians, dwarfs, bare-back riders on plumed white horses,[26] fire-eaters, clowns, a top-hatted, pot-bellied whip-cracking ringmaster and the free-ranging company of other children. They may have seemed carefree in retrospect but it is hard to avoid the conclusion that underneath all the fairytale fun, the sense of being an unloved outcast must have left deep wounds.

Mrs Jarrett did her best; she fussed over him and taught him to read and write and to do elementary arithmetic. That was it as far as his formal education went; put in an English context there were no headmasters in mortar boards and gowns, no prefects, no houses or

---

[25] *Nancy Wake, the SOE heroine for whom Denis served as wireless operator in the Maquis mayhem of 1944 has already been mentioned briefly above. A fuller picture of her, and some explanation of why Denis might have made this comparison, will need to wait until its proper place later in the story*

[26] *By trial and error long before Sarassani the community of riders had fixed forty-two feet, now standard for all circus rings, as the diameter which combined maximum benefit from centrifugal force with the greatest visibility for the audience*

house colours, no morning assembly, no team games, no half terms, no school trips, and no exams. 'School' is and was a period enjoyed by many, and grudgingly tolerated by others. But it is hard for anyone who went through any variant of a formal education, whether English, French or Belgian, to imagine what life would have been without that *centre of gravity*, that day to day certainty.

True, Mozart was only five when he and his sister began touring the courts of Europe showing off their talent to the periwigged Princes and prelates. But for good or ill he had his father at his side, and had a home he could think of as his own, however little he saw of it. Even Sabatini's Scaramouche was privately and thoroughly educated until he was 15-years-old, and then sent to Law School in Paris.

In his middle-age SOE would send Denis to various secret establishments that it called 'schools' but the curriculum there had nothing to do with the 'three R's.' It was all about how to use plastic explosive to maximum destructive effect to de-rail trains, how to kill with knives, guns, and matchboxes, how to strangle a sentry, how to resist interrogation, how to use codes, pick locks, and various other black arts about which today's schoolboys can only fantasise while flexing their prehensile thumbs to barrel their way through the bombs and bodies of the latest computer game.

In July 1914, Denis was close to home, in Antwerp, where impatient children and their patient parents were queuing in the sun to buy tickets for the Sarrasani 'big top'; the gaily painted caravans and animal cages had coincidentally come to rest there as part of their European *perpetuum mobile*. Neither the crowd nor the circus performers would have given much thought to the possible after-effects of what at the time had seemed no more than another paprika-fuelled burp of Balkan indigestion.

Just a few days earlier, on 28 June, Archduke Franz Ferdinand and his wife had been shot dead by a Serbian nationalist student as they drove though Sarajevo. To the consternation of statesmen and diplomats, let alone the millions toiling in factories or in their fields, the assassinations and the game of political liars' poker which followed escalated fast, and tipped the world into an abyss of slaughter. On 28 July Austria declared war on Serbia. On 1 August Germany announced it was at war with Russia, and on the 3 August, France. On 4 August, Britain itself joined the conflict, which at various periods has been referred to triumphantly as 'the Great War', fallaciously as 'the War To End Wars', and nowadays more sensibly as 'the First World War' or 'World War I'.

Like Nellie the Elephant in the 1950's song, Denis prudently decided to pack his trunk and say goodbye to the Circus; he went home to his mother in Brussels, just thirty miles away. Whether Emma was pleased to see him we don't know, but she was worried enough about what lay ahead to tell him not to go back. She must also have been concerned about Francis whom the 'White Plague' had by then consumed to the point of putting him in a hospital bed in the Nursing School and Clinic in rue de la Culture. It was run by Edith Cavell, iron-principled daughter of a Norfolk clergyman. She had first come to Brussels as a governess in 1889 and went back to England to train and work as a nurse. She returned to the Belgian capital in 1907 as Matron of the first school for nurses, which was not under the wing of one of the religious orders; it had a small clinic as an annex.

Denis assumed his 1960s readers would not need reminding about her, nor indeed the quirk of world politics that would see Belgium invaded and ravaged by the Kaiser's army, while neighbouring Holland remained precariously though profitably neutral, making the frontier between them an important barrier. Both these strands come together in his story, along with his first, guileless, diversion into the undergrowth of secret intelligence, a diversion in which his father and Emma also played a role.

Denis's impressions of the Occupation were those we would expect of a 13-year-old boy: the first grey-uniformed German troops arriving in the city on 20 August, from the direction of Waterloo, some ten miles to the south, the sandbagged gun emplacements that sprouted overnight on street corners, biplanes wheeling and diving over the city, machine guns chattering in an aerial 'dogfight'. How odd that we can share at least one of those impressions, captured close to a century ago on a clip of grainy newsreel now floating on the Internet, and see the Kaiser's soldiers through Denis's eyes, in their spiked '*pickelhaube*' helmets, peering around them more like sightseers than conquerors as they parade past the City Hall. It is tempting to try to spot a young Denis somewhere in the background but there are almost no Belgians in sight.

Reflecting the grimmer realities of occupation seen through adult eyes a refugee wrote in the *Times* after reaching London that Brussels had become 'a dismal city of silence. Anxiety fills the hearts of thousands and thousands and the fear of spies keeps their mouths closed. Only the conquerors talk aloud.' Unemployment was high, food was running short, galleries and museums were shuttered, and cafés and coffeehouses had to close at 9 p.m. 'The deserted streets are poorly lighted and ring from time to time with the heavy and disturbing tramp of patrols.' But Brussels suffered far less than some of the smaller Belgian towns such as Andenne, Seilles and Tamines, where on the pretext that they were being attacked by civilian snipers, the Germans are said to have rounded up and shot hundreds of civilians; those who did not die in the volleys of rifle fire were bayoneted. The mediaeval buildings of the university city of Louvain were blown up and torched, and the manuscripts, books, artworks, the accumulated wisdom of many centuries in its ancient library, were scattered to the west winds.

In Dinant, where Denis appears later, German soldiers allegedly shot over 600 civilians (including a 3-month-old baby) and laid waste to the town's centuries old heart. The carnage was no doubt much exaggerated in the British press – then as now ravished nuns and xenophobia sold more newspapers than small earthquakes in Chile, and did more to sway neutral opinion in Britain's favour. But whatever the real scale of the brutality in Belgium, it was perpetrated by 'ordinary' German soldiers and their officers, not the psychopathic SS thugs of later years.

In a chilling portent of things to come a quarter of a century later, Hugh Gibson of the US Consulate, heavily involved in negotiating the passage of food supplies for the starving Belgians through the British blockade, remembered the Kaiser's General von Luttwitz declaring vehemently that 'the Allies are at liberty to feed the

Belgians. If they don't, they are responsible for anything that may happen. If there are bread riots, the natural thing would be for us to drive the whole population into some restricted zone like the Province of Luxembourg, build a barbed wire fence around them and then leave them to starve in accordance with the policies of their Allies.'[27] Foreshadowing another tactic which they would apply with far greater rigour in France in the Second World War, (with the powerful unintended consequence of creating a nucleus of objectors who joined the Resistance), the Germans trawled from house to house for young Belgian men who were shipped back to forced labour in Germany.

A post-war summing up[28] reminded its readers that the Belgian people 'suddenly and utterly crushed by the horrors of invasion, betrayed of their independence, treated with terrible harshness by the German army, had lost all courage, morale and hope' but not quite all courage, as we shall see. The seeds of resistance were quick to sprout.

Thousands upon thousands of Belgians fled to England as the Germans tightened their grip on the conquered country. Among them were British wounded and soldiers who had been captured in the early turmoil but had managed to make their way to safety. How they 'managed' takes us back to Brussels, the early days of British secret intelligence efforts in Belgium, to Nurse Cavell, and the Rake family, and to a story many aspects of which Denis would find himself reliving as a clandestine agent in the Second World War.

Denis remembered that soon after the Germans marched in he began to carry letters almost daily between an American neighbour of his mother's, a Mrs Assernacher, and a Mr Van der Ooft (more probably 'Hooft'), who lived on the other side of the city and was 'in charge of some transport organisation'. Much as would happen in the Second World War, initial British espionage efforts were muddled,[29] with several different organisations cutting across and even competing with each other, and other Allied services. But Denis's

[27] *See Gibson, Bibliography*
[28] *See Gay and Fisher in Bibliography*
[29] See e.g. Paper *by Lt Col Drake, in Bibliography*

understandably hazy memories and what we know of those efforts suggest that he may have been playing his first 'stage' part as the juvenile lead at the dress rehearsal stage of what would soon become a well-reviewed spy drama, produced by the War Office's own intelligence service.

In today's world of cyber-wonders, human espionage still has a key role to play. But most raw intelligence is vacuumed up on a massive scale by computerised surveillance of emails, text messages, cell phone calls, bank account and credit card transactions, airline bookings and Internet encounters. CCTV cameras sweep the streets while high above the clouds satellite-mounted cameras and tiny remote controlled drones film everything that moves, whether it is a scurrying rabble of terrorists or a retired merchant banker peacefully fishing for trout by a Wiltshire chalk stream. So watching German trains chuff and clatter along European railway lines seems positively quaint today. But in the First World War it was vital. There were reports on the number of carriages, how many were goods vans and how many carried soldiers, how many horses, whether there were howitzers on the flatcars, what were the unit badges of the troops on board. This was all augmented by bills of lading and traffic telegrams purloined or copied by Belgian railway workers at the risk of their lives. All these were key fragments of the mosaic from which the British General Staff built their picture of where and on what scale the Germans were concentrating their men and artillery.

The main train-spotting efforts of LA DAME BLANCHE circuit and the Luxembourg operations run by British intelligence from a narrow side street in central Paris[30] did not get into full swing until later in the war. However Denis's reference to 'some transport organisation' suggests that something was already being done on these lines in and around Brussels. But it was not to last. After a few weeks as a messenger boy, Denis, rewarded with a slice of homemade chocolate cake by Mrs Assernacher every time he came to call, was stopped by a German officer who asked him for the envelope that he suspected he was carrying. Taken to the Kommandatur, Denis convinced the

---

[30] *See e.g. Tammy Proctor and also Janet Morgan in Bibliography*

Germans that he had no idea what was in the envelope; he was an innocent lad running an errand for one of his mother's friends. They let him go, but Mrs Assernacher and van der Hooft were arrested. Denis comments that Emma backed up his story, telling the Germans she herself had no idea what her friend was up to. He adds that 'to this day I don't know whether she did or not'.

Sifting through his tangled comments about life in Brussels, we can be reasonably confident that she did, since one of her other friends in the city was a British intelligence officer. He appears first in Denis's narrative as an anonymous but influential diplomat on the staff of the pre-war British mission, who helped Emma at two critical points in those risky years. Only as we turn the pages do we find his name, Maurice Jeffes, renowned as a figure of some intelligence. Denis does not comment on him, but we know that Jeffes had spent some of his school years in Brussels, where his father was British Consul, before serving as a military intelligence officer in the First World War and joining SIS in 1919. Nominally he served most of his career in the Passport Control Organisation ('PCO'), the 'cover' adopted for SIS in a bid to give a veneer of British diplomatic status to SIS stations overseas. He later became its Head.[31]

Whether or not Emma and Jeffes had a professional relationship, they had another interest in common. The index of the *Times* throws up the coincidence that as a young man Jeffes was also an aspiring singer, though his aspirations did not take him far. His solo debut at the Aeolian Hall in London in 1912, when he was in his mid-twenties, was reviewed in terms that were at best lukewarm. Though he had a 'serviceable baritone', the *Times* reviewer sniffed on 23 February, there was 'a lack of variety in his singing which is instantly apparent when he ventures upon anything requiring energy, strong rhythm or sustained power'. (Half a century later a rather different commentator, the duplicitous Kim Philby, remarked snidely of Jeffes's contribution to a study of the post Second World War structure of SIS: 'I do not suppose that he himself would have claimed to be more than a capable if colourless

---

[31] *Maurice Jeffes, 1888-1954 CMG 1939, awarded the King Albert of Belgium Medal for 'works of a charitable and humanitarian nature' in the First World War*

administrator'. Philby could not resist the further jibe that 'colourless' was a figure of speech. In the inter-war years a travel inoculation by a negligent SIS doctor had given Jeffes's face a permanent tinge of 'strange purplish blue'.

In the meantime, Denis's father Francis was lying ill in Nurse Cavell's clinic. It was soon overwhelmed by wounded British soldiers. Medicine and even cotton wool ran short. She put out an appeal for old sheets and as the tattered bundles arrived, Denis, in and out of the clinic almost every day to see his father, was put to work with other children shredding them to make absorbent pads. Meanwhile Edith Cavell had turned her practical eye and her Christian energies to the war, and what she could do to help. Legend has tended to typecast her as an agent of British intelligence, the vestal counterpart of the promiscuous 'Mata Hari', the Dutch born 'exotic dancer' who allegedly spied for the Germans.[32]

In fact Nurse Cavell's mission[33] was not espionage but rather to shelter and pass on escapees to safety via Holland. The clinic was the nodal point of escapelines run by rather blue-blooded Belgians with 'outstations' near Mons and close to Lille; yet another precursor of the Second World War, though in those later years, the lines would run mainly over the Pyrenees into Spain. At a later date Denis would find this out for himself.

But to cross the frontier, evaders needed papers. Denis tells us that the ailing Francis had 'discovered' a talent for forging signatures. (It is unkind, but we might wonder whether something on these lines had led to him moving to Belgium in the first place.) He was soon put to work by Edith Cavell, scrawling an imitation of the signature of Brand Whitlock, the US Minister in Brussels, on false American travel papers – America was then still neutral.

The operation was too large: some 200 soldiers passed through the clinic in just two months. It was also too insecure to last. On 5 August Edith Cavell and others were arrested. This occurred after the Germans had caught one of the Belgian organisers, the architect

---

[32] *Born in Margaretha Zelle in Holland in 1876, executed by the French in 1917*

[33] *See e.g. Proctor op. cit*

Phillippe Baucq, red-handed with a stack of copies of the underground newspaper *La Libre Belgique*.[34]

She made no attempt to dissemble (some said she was morally incapable of telling a lie) and signed a confession that was to prove her death warrant. It is hard to judge from the printed word, but on the face of it, the Whitehall reaction seems from the British press accounts to have been rather less than robust; no tightening of the blockade screw, no threats, no Germans seized as hostages. The American Brand Whitlock, an author turned lawyer, whose Methodist family had been prominent in the movement to abolish slavery, tried his best to reverse the decision but the German Military Governor, Baron von Bissing, was Prussian and unyielding. Nurse Cavell and Baucq, squares of white lint pinned to their chests as aiming points, were shot at dawn by a platoon of edgy German reservist soldiers on 12 October 1915 at the Tir National rifle range in Brussels.

There is no evidence to suggest that Denis's father also faced the firing squad; had it been true it would have been a story Denis could not have resisted telling. The worldwide fury which echoed from that volley of shots did even more harm to Germany's already black reputation and is said to have accelerated US entry into the war and boosted British army recruiting. This led one conspiracy theorist, R.W. Rowan,[35] to claim in 1938, that the British Secret Service had been approached by a French intermediary offering to arrange Nurse Cavell's escape for £1000. Rowan argued, convincing himself but few others, that Whitehall had rebuffed the approach ostensibly because the price was too high, but in reality because they were already banking on the immense propaganda value of her death.

Nurse Cavell lives on in our collective memory as a heroine, a legend and a martyr. Deservedly so, though it is refreshing to note

[34] *In the summer of 1919, a Paris Court Martial heard the case of Gaston Quien, 'a man of no scruples, idle and debauched' accused of betraying Nurse Cavell to the Germans. He had penetrated the escape line posing as a doctor, and given his German masters a full picture of how it worked. Though even the prosecution conceded he was not the only informant involved, he was sentenced to death. Whether this was carried out is unclear, since six of the seven judges recommended mercy. He had been identified to the French by British intelligence, who had uncovered his name in their efforts to unravel what had happened*
[35] *See Bibliography*

Denis's comment that for all her nobility he had found her 'a rather terrifying, very tall, severe, hard woman'.

Denis does not tell us when in October someone warned Emma that she too needed to leave, or risk being interned, but the warning cannot have been unrelated to the Clinic debacle. Others had the same idea; the *Times* reported that between 7 and 10 October alone 10,000 refugees had crossed the Channel to Folkestone and on 11 October five ferries brought almost 5,000 more.

Advised by or through Jeffes about which trains and routes they should follow, she and Denis crossed the heavily patrolled and electrified Dutch frontier, not without incident and risk. Unbeknown to Denis, this was to serve as a taste of what he would find himself doing some thirty years later with SOE.

They found berths on a British destroyer to Dover (again suggesting some official assistance) and arrived in London where a new chapter of Denis's erratic life was to begin. Back in Brussels, he tells us laconically, his father died soon after Edith Cavell's execution. From the family home, then in the Brussels suburb of Uccle, to the aspidistras and lingering aroma of boiled cabbage of 'a boarding house in Westbourne Grove', on the outer fringes of Bayswater, is a journey to be measured in more than just miles.[36]

For a start, Denis spoke better French than he did English (though presumably with an accent and the vocabulary differences that a Parisian ear would have condescendingly detected in an instant as Belgian). He knew so little of London and England that he must truly have seemed a foreigner in his father's country. But Emma had brought her rings, bracelets and necklaces wrapped in a handkerchief, so that she and Denis (who does not mention his sister) were better off than those refugees who had left their money and valuables behind in the scramble to flee, and who spent weeks in makeshift accommodation at Alexandra Palace in North London, then a 'pleasure resort'.

As the *Times* reported, the women and girls slept on rows of cots in the concert hall in the shadow of the giant Willis Organ,

---

[36] *We are done with speculation about Denis's parents but feel compelled to record that '20 Westbourne Grove Terrace' was the home of the elusive Margaret Morgan Jones, the grocer's daughter*

temporarily silenced by the war. Men and boys occupied bunks on the boarded-over skating rink. Others were sent off, bemused and disorientated, to Cardiff, Birmingham and other provincial centres. To this extent they understood why they were suddenly at war, and the Kaiser had become the embodiment of evil, the British public felt in those early days that their Army's primary aim was the liberation of Belgium, and reparations for the suffering of its people. So their response to the refugees was initially at least warm-hearted, though some good souls were taken aback when they handed round jugs of tea on the crowded trains from the Channel ports, only to find the Belgians rejecting it in bewilderment and asking plaintively for '*Café*'.

Committees and Commissions were formed to give earnest attention to the refugees' plight. Appeals were launched, Society hostesses gave fund-raising balls, and lesser lights organised suburban bake sales. Some ingenious mind even fostered the creation of a Belgian 'enclave' around a munition's plant in County Durham, in which the community was subject to Belgian law, patrolled by Belgian gendarmes and amply supplied with Belgian beer to compensate for the bracing climate of the north-east coast. But the goodwill did not last. Some refugees felt that Britain had not done enough to save their country in the first place, while British workers grumbled, as ever, about refugees taking British jobs.

For her part, highly strung as well as restless and ambitious, Emma took to yelling abuse at any German servants, waiters or others trapped in England by the war who happened to cross her path, a reflex which caused Denis some embarrassment. But she soon decided it was her duty to raise morale by singing to the British troops in their holding camps around the country. But what to do with her pubescent and precocious son? Once again he was in the way. Presenting him as one hundred per cent Belgian, Emma persuaded one of the Refugee Committees to take her '*petit mignon*' under its wing, give him bed and board at its hostel in Woburn Place, in London's Bloomsbury, and find him something useful to do. There a kindly Miss Rate and a perhaps more ambiguous Portuguese diplomat, Mr Lem, took an interest in him, taught him English and found him a daytime job which put him on the first square of a lifelong game of social and personal 'Snakes and Ladders'. Even perhaps right at the top of a ladder, since the one time circus tumbler found himself working at 43 Belgrave Square, home of Lord and Lady Aberconway, then one of the highest peaks in the mountain range of London society, now the Turkish Embassy. As the Major General sings in Gilbert and Sullivan's *Pirates of Penzance*, 'It sometimes is a useful thing, To be an orphan boy.'

Laura Aberconway probably brought more money to the marriage, based on her family holdings of the mundane but essential china clay, than her husband, though he built industrial interests of some size. Born in 1854 she was far from the social butterfly suggested by her annual routine. Her year would consist of the summer 'season' in Belgrave Square, winter in the magnificent setting of Château de la Garoupe near Antibes, with its one hundred white marble steps leading down to the sea, and spring at her Bodnant estate in North Wales. Here she and her son created magnificent gardens, whose blooms won prize after prize at London flower shows and exhibitions. None of it diluted her political and public activity. She was an ardent Liberal and a fervent and out-spoken supporter of women's rights. (She probably would not have appreciated the well-meaning tribute to her when she died at the Château in 1933, that she had 'the ready grasp and courageous power of decision that enabled her to weigh big problems with the brains of a man'. But she might well have been amused that by complete chance la Garoupe would make a brief but key appearance in Denis's first perilous Second World War adventure.[37])

Denis became her errand boy. One can almost hear it: 'My dear, just too divine. This little Belgian boy. So eager to please. So *charmant . . .*' But war had turned Lady Aberconway's London life upside down. She had a son at the Front (who would be killed in 1917) and she converted 43 Belgrave Square, once the venue of glittering balls and white tie and tails dinner parties, into a hospital for wounded officers. There was much to be done, most of it by her, down to presiding over the dinner table, heavy with Bodnant

---

[37] *It is now reputedly owned by a Russian 'oligarch'*

blossoms and carving the joint (which suggests the officers may have been closer to 'convalescent' than seriously wounded). She needed a 'gopher' and silver polisher.

Denis, keen, sharp-witted and with a ready smile, fitted the bill admirably, to the point when, with her interest in his future aroused, she decided he should 'learn a trade' and sent him off to train as a wireless operator. It was a skill much in demand. Messages tapped out on a Bakelite and brass key (a device which looked rather like a fancy desktop stapler) in the dots and dashes of Samuel Morse's code were the only way for governments, newspapers, commercial and banking houses and shipping lines to move data rapidly around the world.

His editors allowed Denis to get away with naming the training school as 'the Earls Court College of Cable and Wireless something Ltd.' [sic] but research has shown that it was nothing in fact to do with the company of that name, but a strictly commercial venture. Based at 226, Earls Court Road, the London Telegraph Training College advertised regularly for pupils both before and after the First World War, holding out 'splendid opportunities for youths aged 16 to 25 with commencing remuneration of £120 to £150' at the major telegraph and cable companies. Sometimes the advertising bait was dangled directly in front of 'Parents and Guardians' which may have been what caught Lady Aberconway's eye. Denis seems to have stayed the course, even though, as he says, he 'could not spell "cart"'. He thus acquired the second skill (the first being his fluent if Brussels-flavoured French) which was to make him such a good catch for SOE all those years later.

The war rolled towards its close in mud, blood and futility. Back in Germany all the major theatres and music halls had been mobilised in a desperate bid to boost public morale. The highlight of the Sarassani Circus contribution was 'Torpedo Los' ('Fire the Torpedo'), a spectacular show with a cast of 500 and watched by thousands, its complex technical effects climaxing in a mock Zeppelin bombing raid on London. In Brussels the occupying forces, anxious to demonstrate in the face of rather compelling evidence to the contrary that they were as cultured as they were tough, had brought their own operas to *la Monnaie*. They imported

Richard Strauss himself to conduct his *Rosenkavalier* and subjected audiences to a full cycle of *The Ring*. Some might have preferred to take their chances in a Zeppelin raid.

When the Armistice came, at the eleventh hour of the eleventh day of the eleventh month in 1918, Emma was again in a hurry, this time to get back to Brussels and re-launch her career. With the help of Maurice Jeffes, she and Denis were among the first refugees to return. She went her way, back to the opera stage, and to a new husband, a fact mentioned nowhere in Denis's account, a lacuna which those interested in psychology can pick over at their leisure. On 13 March 1919 in Brussels she married a Captain J. Montgomery of the 7th Dragoon Guards, a gentleman whose only appearance in this story is the brief formal announcement which appeared in the *Times* a week or so later.[38]

Sentimentalists would hope it was a love match, cynics might argue that it might have had more to do with regaining or perhaps gaining (the announcement makes no mention of a previous marriage) the security of a British passport; we shall never know.

Also in 1919, Denis's fortunes took him to the little Belgian town of Dinant. It is sheltered under the cliffs on a bend of the River Meuse, some sixty miles from Brussels. Dinant was one of the cities ravaged by the trigger-happy Germans in the early days of the war in reprisal for some gestures of defiance which by the standards of the twenty-first century insurgents were relatively minor. For reasons which are impossible to fathom (maybe Emma or Jeffes had pulled strings) and in what capacity it is even harder to envisage, Denis was given a job in the closing stages of the massive US-led international effort to feed and support the populations of German occupied territories. This effort foreshadowed the post Second World War Marshall Plan but is today undeservedly forgotten.[39]

---

[38] *Montgomery, about 38-years-old when they married, saw service in the Boer War, and later qualified as a German interpreter. As a PoW in Germany in 1917 he was alleged to have attacked a German sentry. Though his brother officers swore he had done no more than be 'perhaps somewhat injudicious in his language', no doubt putting his German skills to good use, Montgomery was sentenced to a year in a German jail, but this was waived under the provisions of the Hague Convention, a gesture inconceivable today*

[39] *Over the four years of the War, vigorously headed by a future US President, Herbert Hoover, the Commission for Relief in Belgium, which also covered northern France, pumped in aid, mainly food, worth $5 billion in current values*

It is hard to imagine that in his later SOE days Denis did not look back on the shooting of Edith Cavell, the rubble of Dinant, and the miseries of the victims' families as a reminder of the grim practical consequences of crossing the Germans, be they the Kaiser's troops or the Nazis'. But for now he was off on a different square of his lifetime 'Snakes and Ladders'. He was 18-years-old or so if we go by his 1901 birth date, and by his own account 'quite good looking and physically attractive' when he plunged into an affair with a married British diplomat stationed in Brussels, who was also working on the relief operations. If Denis's comment had been confined to Emma it would be understandable. But it seems slightly unfair to Mrs Jarrett at the Circus, to Miss Rate in London's Woburn Place, to Lady Aberconway and indeed others, that he should describe the diplomat as 'the first person who showed me any real affection . . . A warm intimate relationship developed between us that all of a sudden gave everything in my life a meaning. I went to live with him'.

Though the relationship had to be more discreet when the diplomat's wife later joined him *en poste* in Brussels, it continued happily if intermittently. Denis does not name the diplomat, but the personal file gives the clue. In a form he filled in for SOE, he included in his record of past employment that he had been 'Private Secretary to R.F.H. Duke in Brussels and Athens'. Reginald Franklin Hare Duke would have been around 30-years-old when, assuming he is the unnamed diplomat, he and Denis met amidst the rubble and misery. The son of a clergyman, Duke had joined the Board of Trade from Oxford and spent the First World War as General Secretary of the *Commission Internationale de Ravitaillment*, a component of the Relief Commission. In 1919 he was appointed Commercial Secretary at the Brussels Embassy. He had married in 1913 and had a distinguished career; he was awarded the CBE and a host of foreign decorations.

Though the relationship continued, Denis gave up reparations to return to the sawdust ring. From its name, the Cirque Royale, which is actually a venue in the centre of Brussels, seems to have been based in the capital rather than a touring troupe. Here he claims to have had an even more extraordinary role, as assistant to 'Paulmann the

Magician', the centrepiece of whose act was hypnotising humans and animals alike, a skill now largely confined to politicians. He then learned that his friend was being posted to Athens and would not be accompanied by his wife. It is fair to suppose that she had probably had quite enough of being the third person in a sham marriage, the sidelong sympathetic or knowing glances of her fellow wives, all that whispering. His friend then asked the obvious question would Denis like to come along instead? Though he might have formally employed Denis as his 'Private Secretary', of which there is no indication in the Foreign Office List, and which would have taken some explaining away, it seems more likely that the title was confected later by Denis to rationalise the relationship.

Here again time slides confusingly, since Denis dates the move to 1920 whereas Duke first appears in the Foreign Office List for Athens in 1922. He served there as Commercial Secretary, First Grade, at an annual salary of just over £1000 and a local allowance (together perhaps equal to around £120,000 today). Given the scars the war had left on Greece it is likely that Duke's mission would have been on the same lines of reconstruction and relief as his work in Belgium.

Denis leapt at the chance of another ladder to climb. By then he had discovered that he had a decent singing voice, he auditioned successfully to join 'an international company', which had been booked to perform in Greece. It is hard to imagine that in those difficult years there would have been much of an audience for musical comedy even in Athens, let alone in the barren Greek hinterland. Although the 'company' is now untraceable it might well have been a 'concert party' hired to entertain British troops. In one sense it was a wasted journey. He and the diplomat fell out, not least because Denis thought the latter, now given to being 'brusque' and 'wounding', had found someone else.

But another big step up the social ladder was right ahead. Just a fortnight after the breakup Denis's singing at a reception at the British Legation caught the ear, and the eye, of a 'Prince', whom he does not identify. He does not tell us whether his diplomat friend was in the audience in his white tie and tails, sulking or pointedly ignoring him, when the Prince strolled up to the piano and joined Denis in song, or when at the end of the soirée the Prince drove Denis away in his car. How high the eyebrows must have risen, how tongues must have wagged, how merry the sniggers behind the lace fans. (Duke was posted to Budapest in 1926; he died in 1929, when he was just 41-years-old. His service in Athens is not mentioned in the *Times* obituary published on 17 June 1929.)

Set up by the Prince in an apartment on Kefissia Street, close to the Royal Palace, Denis could afford to give up the stage and to ignore the realities of the Greece outside his shuttered windows, for a while. He enjoyed a retinue of discreet servants, had plenty of pocket money and lived a life of figs, fountains and fine linen. But the world outside would soon intrude, and even the world inside had its abrasive moments, as the Prince was given to mood swings and fits of violence.

Like the story of France in the 1930s and '40s, the tragic and complex history of the Balkans and Asia Minor in the early twentieth century is a subject which deserves a far fuller exposition than we can give it as mere background to an intriguing part of Denis's life story. For English readers, Compton Mackenzie's *Greek Memories* give the flavour of the country's politics in the early years of the First World War. As an added bonus it says so much about the British Secret Service operations in which he was engaged there that he was prosecuted under the Official Secrets Act and the book was 'suppressed'. At a higher level of political intrigue the backstairs machinations of the Greek-born arms merchant Basil Zaharoff, on behalf of Whitehall, and above all, his own financial interests, is another fascinating sidebar to Greek history of the period though not central to Denis's story.[40]

Denis's Greek adventure had its roots in the First World War too. Greece's King Constantine was thought to be pro-German, a not unreasonable judgement as he was married to the Kaiser's sister. But his popular Prime Minister Venizelos[41] favoured backing the British and French Entente on the pragmatic grounds that he was sure they

---

[40] *See e.g. Alfrey and Lewinsohn in Bibliography*
[41] *Eleftherios Venizelos, statesman, diplomat and politician, 1864-1936*

would win. King Constantine tried to keep his country on a path of 'even-handedness', a path which led to escalating tensions with the Entente representative in Athens, the arrogant French General Sarrail. In June 1917, Sarrail forced King Constantine into exile, along with his eldest son, Crown Prince George, a great-grandson of Queen Victoria.

The King's younger son Alexander, took the shaky throne, and within a month Greece had joined the Allied cause.

The 1918 Armistice did not bring it peace. Greece's glories, its ancient civilisation, its ambitions, were now overlain by poverty, bitter struggles between Royalists and Liberals crusading for reform, with the Army an ever-present background threat. Half a century of regional wars and revolutions had brought little or nothing except dead and wounded. A new fight with a resurgent Turkey under Kemal Ataturk, surreptitiously but substantially backed with Zaharoff gold, was to end in defeat, massacres, massive 'ethnic cleansing' of Greeks from Turkish territory, and a deep sense of national shame. On 26 October 1920 King Alexander died from sepsis after being bitten by a pet monkey in the Palace grounds.[42]

Constantine returned, but the groundswell of popular support which greeted him soon dissipated and he was ousted and permanently exiled after a military coup in 1922 led by Colonel (later General) Plastiras, the one character in the whole imbroglio whom Denis names. On 28 September 1922 Crown Prince George became King George II of the Hellenes, but as a figurehead 'under the control', as a later *Times* commentary puts it, of the Plastiras junta, who treated him with 'studied neglect'. In an echo of what Denis was to remember, the Plastiras junta 'maintained a censorship to protect themselves but allowed full rein to propaganda against the monarchy'. An abortive Royalist counter coup gave the junta the opportunity to strike at the monarchy.

King George left the country again on the night of 18 December 1923, after the Generals resolved that his 'Glucksburg dynasty is a national stigma which should be blotted out' and that 'the

---

[42] *Athens being then and now a cauldron of gossip, rumours flew that Republican plotters had injected the monkey with a deadly bacillus before letting it loose in the gardens*

forfeiture of the Crown by the dynasty is a national necessity'. The Athens Correspondent of the *Times* commented sardonically that 'undoubtedly the Greeks are a greedy people. Other countries have been satisfied with one revolution during the last decade or so, or have abstained altogether from this form of activity, but Greece within the past fourteen years has had four revolutions and is now looking out for a fifth.'

One world-weary Greek King quipped that the essential equipment for that role is a suitcase, but these cycles of Hellenic royal exile, return, referenda and 'rebanishment' are not of relevance for us except to the extent that they might help us identify the 'Prince'.

Denis's version is discreet, indeed, appropriately for its setting, Delphic. He gives no dates, which makes the story harder to unravel. Nevertheless, setting against his broadly brushed, even airbrushed, narrative, what we know of the aftershocks which were regulating Greek political and Palace life, there is no reason to believe that he simply made the whole thing up, though he may again have embroidered the emotional aspects.

Denis tells us that the country's troubled political situation 'conspired to place the Prince in a role more exalted than he had expected, hoped for, or indeed wanted'. As for Plastiras, 'It was he who had promoted the Prince and it was he who was soon to be the agent of his downfall.' The relationship was arousing gossip, envy and hostile anti-Royalist press comment, with Denis targeted, as he remembered, as 'the spoiled English favourite of royalty'.

There is no suggestion that Denis spoke or read Greek so we have to assume he was relying on others to tell him what was being said. Nor do we have any way of knowing whether he was referring to mainstream newspapers, or as seems more likely, ephemeral and polemic broadsheets. From the outset of the First World War, first the Germans, quickly followed by the Allies, spent lavishly to suborn the Greek press in favour of their respective causes. The tradition of a biddable press continued into the troubled 1920s, so that attacks on Royalty through Denis or for any other reason could have been orchestrated very easily by any one of the many players in that high-stakes game.

The attacks reached a level at which Plastiras 'suggested' that Denis leave Greece, which he did, the 'Prince' saying goodbye with the gloomy comment that Greece would soon have no further need of his own services either and that 'when he was dismissed' he would meet Denis again in Venice.

It is then fair to conjecture that for George, ascending the throne in 1922 was the 'role more exalted than he had . . . indeed wanted,' which Denis ascribes to the unnamed Prince. Is it in fact King George expressing a clear-eyed view of his destiny when 'the Prince' tells Denis that he would soon be dismissed? On the face of it both phrases seem to fit the facts summarised above. But neither of the reports to London from the Athens Legation published in the compendium of British diplomatic papers of the time, nor a quick sample of histories of modern Greece and of mainstream newspaper archives give any hint of scandal underlying the brutal political manoeuvrering.

Did Denis and the Prince meet in Venice? In 1921 George had married Elizabeth, eldest daughter of the King and Queen of Romania, and when he left Greece again in December 1923 contemporary press reports speak of him departing on the Greek steamer *Daphne* for Romania rather than Venice, the Queen crying on the dockside at Piraeus.[43]

[43] *Not long before all this, the ubiquitous Basil Zaharoff had been given a Royal reception in Bucharest by Romania's glamorous Queen Marie in a bid to swing his, and British influence behind King George and keep him on the throne. This bravura display of a mother-in-law's energies swayed Zaharoff but he could not persuade Venizelos, and George's fate was sealed, at least for now*

5

'All the World's a Stage'

But the train ride from Baneasa Station in the Romanian capital Bucharest to the Santa Lucia terminal in Venice, where Denis says he was waiting, is a matter of not much more than a day. The fourteenth century Gothic architecture, galleried marble halls and unobtrusive white-gloved service of the Danieli Hotel (then known as the Royal Danieli) in Venice, with its breathtaking view over the Bacino San Marco,[44] can usually be counted upon to bring the magic back to any flagging relationship. This time they failed to work. The 'difficult times' he had been through had re-ignited 'the Prince's' mood swings, and though Denis claimed his own feelings were still as strong, the endless bickering was too much to bear. He packed his bags and left for London. From this point 'the Prince' drops out of Denis's story, save for an improbable exchange in a Spanish internment camp in 1943, So there's little more to add.

From 1924 King George spent a large part of each year in England and five years later it had become his home. We have two accounts of his life there, one pieced together from the contemporary Court and Social columns of the *Times*, the other written in 1955 by an English author, E.E. Tisdall, who seems to have followed Greek Royal affairs with informed assiduity. Neither suggest George was anything more than a sociable, well liked if rather complex character.

Tisdall writes that George and his queen settled in the manor house of a Surrey village, where the ultra-anglicised king played the role of country squire to perfection. In parallel, the Court columns

---

[44] *The Danieli has changed hands more than once in the intervening years and its guest records from the 1920s have long since disappeared*

of the *Times* show him lunching and socialising with his royal relatives at Buckingham Palace and Balmoral. They record his presence at Ascot and every other landmark on that still glittering social scene: Cowes, the grouse moors, Royal garden parties, Highland Gatherings, house parties, charity concerts, air displays, the full gold-braided gamut of Royal weddings and funerals. He even took part in a debate at the Oxford Union and initiation in 1930 as a Freemason. It is a feature of virtually every report that George is on his own; his queen might as well not exist.

Tisdall offers a possible explanation and another perspective, though he cites no sources. He suggests that the queen was in poor health and preferred her quiet life in the country (though some press reports imply that she may have spent more time back home in Romania). In his view George's public persona was 'only half the story'. He also 'harboured a secret penchant for horseplay and whimsicalities [sic] such as cooking unusual dinners at his friends' abodes'.

Though in public King George could come across as serious, Tisdall comments that he was 'equally a figure at those wilder unconventional extravaganzas which were a feature of the smart young set of the time'. (The *Times* made the same point more succinctly and tactfully in a later profile of King George, noting that he 'has been described as "very gregarious"'.)

In Tisdall's words he began to lead 'a double life, only one half of which he shared with his wife, and this way of living began to emphasise the incompatibility between them which led to a separation and a broken marriage'. At a hearing in Bucharest in 1935, from which the public were excluded and which the King did not attend, Elizabeth was granted a divorce on grounds of desertion. The *Times* reported that the Romanian censorship took 'elaborate procedures' to suppress any details; there were no children. (This was apparently the first time in European history that a queen had divorced a king.)

All this only tells us that King George had a withered marriage, that he liked a good time and that as a younger man he may have run with a 'fast set' in the small hours. He was not alone. Many memoirs and novels of the time tell us that night after night politicians, diplomats, *le haut monde* and *le monde lancé* glided (without guilt or damage to their reputation) backwards and forwards across whatever line separated the respectable from the louche, from White's to the Gargoyle in Soho and back again to a Mayfair breakfast. Read in the context of Denis's version of events, Tisdall's account might be construed as more delicately nuanced than it appears at first sight but there is no reason not to take it at face value.

A few months after the divorce in 1935, the giddily spinning wheel of Greek fortune brought King George back to the throne to preside over the authoritarian regime of General Metaxas. And by 1936, if not earlier, he had taken another rather royal step and acquired a mistress. In August that year he was able to introduce her to another Royal paramour when the then King Edward VIII (later the Duke of Windsor) called on King George in Corfu during the course of a holiday cruise on the steam yacht *Nahlin*. It was a voyage that grabbed headlines everywhere (except for the discreetly muzzled press in England) because King Edward's principal guest was the controversial American divorcee Wallis Simpson, later his Duchess. One of Edward's aides snootily described the yacht, chartered from Lady Yule, as 'fitted out like a Calais whoreshop', a comment suggesting a spell of wild oats sowing in his youth, but it was certainly luxurious.

Among the socialites who made up the merry party were the actress Lady Diana Cooper and her diplomat husband, Duff. Seeing King George again after a long gap, she thought that he had 'lost five stone and some of his affability'. His life was 'very sad' despite his relationship with his mistress Mrs Jones, the 'exceedingly good looking' former wife of an Army officer. Much like the beleaguered Prince sketched by Denis, she thought that King George had no one whom he could trust or take advice from, and 'not one personal friend'.[45]

When the Italians invaded Greece in April 1941, with the Germans close on their heels, George came to London after a narrow escape from Crete. Whether or not he was in London when Denis

[45] *Cooper p. 182*

was pushing to get into SOE, we cannot tell, but it is clear he and his advisers were closely in touch with the British Cabinet and SOE. Greece was vital for the Balkans and the fate of the Middle East, so that resistance to the Germans and its future political direction were key issues (not the first time SOE had its knuckles rapped for mixing the two). George returned to Greece in 1946 after a plebiscite in favour of the monarchy. He died in Athens on 1 April 1947.

So in conclusion, though the early parallels are tempting (and we recognise that Denis's account can be plausibly overlain on some real events), there is nothing in what we know that proves, or for that matter disproves, the speculation that George and 'the Prince' were the same man.

This perplexing regal *tour d'horizon* has allowed us to run ahead of Denis. His own return to London brought him back in contact with Emma Luart. The First World War had not kept her confined to touring England singing to soldiers. She can be tracked through newspaper reports and advertisements (did Denis ever see them?), which show that between 1914 and 1917 she was a frequent star performer at the French Theatre in The Hague; Holland was still neutral territory. Her many roles included Mimi in *la Bohème* and Cio Cio San in *Madame Butterfly*. When Denis was first dallying in Athens she was delighting the audiences back at *la Monnaie* in Brussels. In 1922, around the time of the Plastiras coup, she began what one commentator calls 'an extraordinary career' with the *Opera Comique* in Paris.[46]

Emma sang the title role in Delibes' *Lakmé* and trilled her way through the operatic repertoire from *The Marriage of Figaro* to *The Tales of Hoffmann*. For Emma the applause, her appreciative curtsies, and the conductor's respectful bow as he kissed her hand, never stopped. It is hard to match the dates but around the time Denis's life with the Prince was fraying, she was basking in the bouquets and cries of 'encore' from her audiences at Nice, at the Monte Carlo Opera (a season notable for her appearance along-side the celebrated Irish tenor John MacCormack in the first

[46] *Or Salle Favart, in the Place Boieldieu, created in 1714 as a venue for French opera in contrast to the then prevailing Italian variety*

performances outside Russia of Modest Mussorgsky's *The Fair At Sorochintsy*), the Kursaal in Ostend, and major theatres in France and Belgium.

During the years between the two World Wars, she found time to get to London, which is where Denis tells us that after his tremulous retreat from Venice, she gave him the advice that would frame his own career during the years remaining before the Second World War.

Contrary to the counsel Noël Coward would give the mythical Mrs Worthington in his 1935 song ['*Don't put your daughter on the stage Mrs Worthington . . . the profession is overcrowded and the struggle's pretty tough . . .* '], Emma pushed Denis towards the theatre, taking the briskly chauvinistic view that if he could sing well enough for the Greeks, he must be good enough for the English. 'They know nothing at all about music.'

Somewhere in her early career, a London impresario, Herbert Clayton,[47] had given Emma a small part in *The Toreador*, which Denis says was performed at Daly's Theatre, in Leicester Square, the cradle of British musical comedy.[48] It does not matter to our story, but a quick run through the available records and the mismatch of dates suggests that her appearance must have been in a revival, maybe outside London, since *The Toreador* actually opened at the Gaiety in Aldwych in 1902, where it ran for nearly 700 performances, with Clayton in the title role. Emma now asked him to find something for Denis. At that time Clayton was putting together a company to tour the provinces with *Suzanne* a now forgotten musical comedy, a small role in which called for an actor who could sing in French. This was the first rung on the ladder which over the next fifteen years would take him from a repertory theatre in Plymouth, to the bright lights and 'high camp' buzz of the West End stage.

Denis's luck was in. Ours too since this role is the only trace we can find of Denis on a playbill. *Suzanne* opened at the Palace Theatre, Plymouth on 31 December 1923, and went from there on

[47] *1876-1931, began his career in the chorus of* The Circus Girl
[48] *Built in 1893, demolished 1937, now a cinema complex*

a successful tour, though the closest it came to the West End was the Chiswick Empire and a perhaps more raucous audience at its sister theatre in Shepherds Bush. The leading lady had perhaps wisely chosen to shed her real name of Gwladys [*sic*] Hay-Dillon (under which she had written at least one radio play, *Flower of A Thousand Nights*) and billed herself as 'Edriss Coombs'.

Listed among the 'Additionals' in the role of 'Theodore' is Denis, who was also using a stage name, in his case Denis Greer. Its origin is surprisingly straightforward for a man whose life was so complicated; by the end of his SOE service the list of cover names and aliases on his personal file reached beyond the imagination of any writer of espionage thrillers. (They included Justin, Roland, Dieudonné Requet, Rocher, Juniper, Receiver and, rather oddly, Slacks.) Greer, as research in the General Register Office has shown, was nothing more exotic than the middle name of his paternal grandfather. Quite why he preferred it to 'Rake' with its swash-buckling resonance, is another missing piece in the colourful jigsaw of his life, lost to sight under the sideboard.

Those fifteen years had their highs and lows, cheers and boos, rows about money and who was billed where on the posters, fleeting romances and tempestuous fallings out, and a gritty slog round the provincial theatres which were then an integral part of the British cultural fabric. Almost every city and market town from Aberdeen to Yeovil had its 'Grand', its 'Theatre Royal', its 'Hippodrome', nearly all now smashed by the wrecker's ball or converted into cinemas and 'leisure centres'. Plymouth's ornate 'Palace' (where Denis got his start) has gone through a similar downward spiral of closures, ever more tawdry reincarnations and reopenings until it was finally shuttered in 1983. It would have given Denis a giggle to know that one of the last live shows, in 1981, was the drag artist 'Danny la Rue in Review'.

For the audiences, the provincial theatres were an escape from the drudgery and humdrum into enchantment and dreams. For the players, they meant railway journeys at the cheapest possible 'off-peak' Third Class fares. These journeys ended in smoky factory towns, trudging wet streets, cardboard suitcases in hand, in search of a boarding house whose front door, so often embellished with diamond patterns of stained glass, did not display the warning notice 'No Theatricals'. Actors' lodgings were all the same: a communal linoleum-tiled bathroom with a gas-fired geyser oozing noxious fumes as it fought all odds to heat the water, whilst the next in line impatiently rattled the door handle; over the wash basin a hand-written notice asked guests to 'Please Leave the Bathroom as You Would Wish to Find It'.

After the show was over, and the takings had been counted, there would have been brown ale and ham and cheese sandwiches, curling at the edges like the bathroom linoleum, in steamy cafés or in pubs foggy with the fumes of cheap tobacco. On occasions there would be a few stage-struck fans fluttering in the background. Denis makes an oblique reference to this period in his personal file, noting that he has 'a good knowledge of almost every large town in England, Scotland and Wales'. Replace the brown ale with rough red wine, and add in the threat of the Gestapo, and we have something close to the peripatetic life Denis was to know on his first mission as an SOE officer in war-torn France.

Eventually Dennis graduated to London's West End. There was plenty of work. A random snapshot of newspaper listings in the mid-1920s shows fifty theatres in the capital, against just eight 'Picture Theatres'. (Around the same time, the *Times*, reporting the opening of a powerful new radio transmitter in the Midlands, agreed that 'broadcasting has come to stay'.) But when we look at the records of the shows in which he tells us he appeared, it is like searching for the Invisible Man, made even more complicated by the fact that Denis, true to form, muddles his chronology and is a touch imprecise about his roles.

For instance Denis tells us that he 'played the lead' in a musical called *Mercenary Mary*. Herbert Clayton, who had first set him on the acting road, and a partner brought the show over from America and opened it in Glasgow for two weeks in September 1925, before moving it to the London Hippodrome. There it had only a moderate run of 262 performances, after it left the *Sunday Times* reviewer 'swooning with boredom' at this 'exposition of ludicrous senility'.

But neither the complete run of the comprehensive *Play Pictorial* cast lists in the Special Collections Library of the University of Kent nor research in the Theatre Archive of the Victoria and Albert Museum bear out Denis's claim.

The most likely explanation is that Denis was in the chorus doubling as understudy to A.W. Baskomb, who is listed as the leading man, and stepped into his shoes on several nights or at matinees when the great man was ill or wanted a night off. He may well have joined the cast late, since he also appeared in *No, No, Nanette*, the last weeks of whose run at the Palace Theatre overlapped with the first stretch of *Mercenary Mary*. The staying power of a pair of the *Nanette* melodies, 'Tea for Two' and 'I Want to be Happy', have helped it long outlive *Mary* in the theatrical repertoire.

When Joseph Coyne and Binnie Hale let themselves loose on 'I Want to be Happy', the rather bewildered *Times* reviewer, who was careful to put inverted commas around 'jazz' noted that the 'atmosphere was charged . . . the orchestra stood up and joined in . . . and eventually the audience wanted to join in too . . .' We cannot find Denis listed in this programme either. Nor is there a mention of a totally unconnected character who is anecdotally claimed to have been in the same chorus line, Jack Hewitt, a boyfriend of the louche garlic-chewing Soviet 'mole', Guy Burgess.

In 1929 Denis understudied Bobby Howes, already well on his way to becoming a stalwart of British musical comedy (his career would run until the 1960s) when he starred with Binnie Hale in *Mr Cinders*. It was a version of the fairy tale that some in the audience with an interest in sexual psycho-dynamics must have found especially intriguing, since 'Prince Charming' is a 'young and forceful woman' while the man in the title role is played as a meek menial.

As war came closer, Denis was somewhere in the 200 strong cast of Ivor Novello's spectacular *The Dancing Years*, which opened at the Drury Lane Theatre on 25 March 1939.[49]

Set in Vienna before and after the First World War, its first half

---

[49] *Ivor Novello, 1893-1961, singer, actor, composer and playwright who became one of the most popular stars on the British stage. Unabashedly gay, it was cattily said of him that 'as well as delighting thousands of women on stage he gave pleasure to a number of gentlemen off it'*

struck the *Times* reviewer as a 'sumptuous entertainment which may be offered as an antidote to present realities', though after the interval he found it became a touch too sentimental.

Denis does not tell us how he lived 'between engagements'. 'Resting' is a fact of life for all actors, whether Garrick Club grandees or lesser lights like Denis. Those with star status and money in the bank could just stay at home, breaking the day with a convivial lunch at the Club or the Café Royale. The less successful lived off their dreams, waiting for the next 'casting call' telegram from their agent or for an interesting opportunity to show up in the small ads in the theatrical trade press. In the mean time they scratched a living working in shops or restaurants, domestic service, entertaining at children's parties, anything to bring in a pound or two for the rent and shillings to feed the greedy gas meter in the bedroom.

Denis's personal file, though nothing in his own account, says that he 'had a hotel in Queens Gate, 1927-39', though since he seems never to have been asked, it is not known whether he owned it or simply managed it. What sort of hotel it was is also unknown. The 1930s Post Office listings for London show that Queens Gate was much like it is today, home to a broad range of hotels large and small, but there is no mention of a 'Greer' or 'Rake'.

He also refers in his book to appearances 'in cabaret' from time to time. But since we cannot trace him in the main theatre programmes, we did not expect to find him in the much narrower world of hotel and nightclub 'cabaret'. This less transparent part of the entertainment world employed legions of dancers, singers, jugglers, acrobats, chorus boys and girls and the names on billings of the period seem as confected as some SOE aliases. 'Dora Stroeva', 'Gaudot, Leo Bill and Toto', 'Rennee Riano', 'the Foushee Sisters', 'les Zengas', 'O'Hanlon and Zambouni' and 'Nitzka Kodolban' surely conceal more conventional, even suburban personalities. In contrast 'A. Nilson Fysher' sounds more like a composer of church music or a dubious headmaster in the mould of Waugh's *Dr Fagan*.

All of this supposes that Denis operated in the conventional world of cabaret. His wartime roles in France suggest that he might have been equally at home in the furtive 1930s nightspots, which catered for the gay community, and might have included 'the Jamset' and 'the Caravan' in Endell Street, 'Billie's' in Little Denmark Street or the not so fictional 'Blue Grotto', its entrance between 'a disreputable newsagent and a disreputable chemist', to which the epicene Anthony Blanche drags an understandably skittish Charles Ryder in *Brideshead Revisited.*[50]

Then comes the surprise, the script tripwire that film director Alfred Hitchcock called 'the McGuffin', though here it does not advance the plot. In fact it brings us to a blank wall. Filling in the 'marital status' box in an SOE questionnaire, Denis declares that he is a 'widower'. When he married and whom, and indeed why, given all the circumstances, we sadly have no idea. Nor is there any clue of what happened to her.

Moreover, there is no record of anyone asking for further details. Was she perhaps the owner of the Queens Gate hotel? Had Denis lied about a wife in a bid to muffle lifestyle enquiries in a blanket of sympathy? Much later in his story, when he was on the run in Vichy France, a tart with a heart of gold offered Denis her consolation free of charge as a contribution to the war effort. His response, as he recalled in his memoirs, tells us much of what a marriage, if there was one, might have been like: '. . . for a few minutes her quite genuine offer, even her keenness, frightened me more than the nightly visits of the police to the [French] hotel'.

But buried in the fading typewriter print of the personal file is another small surprise. In describing to SOE debriefers a nasty moment in enemy hands, which crops up later in the story, Denis lists what he had in his pockets, including 'his son's picture'. There is no other mention of this either in the personal file or his book, and we need to remember that Denis identified his next of kin as his sister. So if there was a picture, was it just a piece of a deceptive paper trail confected to shore up a cover story? Or had Denis married a lady with a son he had come to think of as his own?

[50] *Houlbrook p. 81; though the photograph of a deserted Caravan reproduced by Houlbrook (p. 13), probably taken after a police raid, portrays a singularly cheerless little cellar, with scarcely room for the 103 people arrested there after a police swoop in 1934, let alone for the 'divers scandalous, bawdy and obscene performances [leading] to the manifest corruption of the morals of His Majesty's subjects alleged in the* Times *report to have taken place; Billie's (p. 73) has all the allure of a teashop in Oban on a rainy Sunday*

As with his own background, it is too easy to stray into the realms of the fiction-writer. Our curiosity has to go unsatisfied, though it seems inherently more likely that the 'widower' claim was indeed a diversionary tactic, and that the 'son' too was an invention, a figment of SOE imagination. The fascination of Denis is that one can never be sure.

Denis makes no mention of Emma in this period, but riffling through the 1930's newspapers we find her as busy as ever. Initially she was at *la Monnaie* in Brussels, and then the *Opera Comique* in Paris playing Mimi again, the heroine Marie in Donizetti's *La Fille du Regiment* and starring in operas by Massenet and Charpentier.

Denis left the Novello production in June 1939 and 'went to Juan-Les-Pins', he tells us without further explanation. What a crescendo of a summer it was. The end of peace and the end of a way of life, the last plangent notes of the Jazz Age, were just months away. Most of that fateful season's visitors – as many as ninety per cent in Monte Carlo itself – were British. The clotted cream of Mayfair café society, namely Ministers, Members of Parliament, newspaper magnates, and a phalanx of industrialists, the 'hard-faced men', who in Prime Minister Stanley Baldwin's words, '. . . looked as if they have done very well' out of the last war and expected to clean up handsomely in the next. Never mind that the British tone was diluted by raffish Latin American playboys, jewel-encrusted ladies of the night, Hollywood stars and starlets, Russian Grand Dukes, and minor royals from the footnotes of the Almanach de Gotha.

Whatever their passports, and some prudent folk had more than one, all had a lot to look forward to, at least in the short term. So did all the other pilot fish who fed off them, the hoteliers, barmen, jewellers, pimps, casino croupiers, dance band musicians, restaurateurs, and discreet peddlers of morphine and cocaine. There were so many places to go, to see and be seen – the Val d'Esquieres tennis tournament, the Cannes regatta, the motor boat race down the Rhone and along the coast to Cannes, the invariably spectacular wave-clipping finale of the Deauville-Cannes air race, a water ski tourney, charity balls, and dinners under the stars. Provençal peasants might have muttered darkly about ill omens when on

25 June in the midst of massive thunderstorms the night sky was set alight by the purple-pink glow of the phenomenon known as 'St Elmo's Fire' and three eight foot fireballs shot across the heavens over Nice. But what did peasants know? It was time to enjoy, to eat, drink, be merry and work on the suntan.

Where Denis fitted in, who he was with, he does not tell us, merely recording that he returned to London in the last days of August. He was cutting things fine. On 3 September 1939, Prime Minister Neville Chamberlain told his country that Britain found itself at war with Germany again, this time a Germany under the control of a far more formidable and infinitely more savage state machinery than that of the Prussian Kaiser. By some ill-fated last-minute misjudgment the star-spangled opening of the very first Cannes Film Festival had been deferred from 1 September to 10 September. By this time audiences had fled, the Festival was cancelled and the simple pleasures of *The Wizard of Oz*, and the more robust sagas of *Stanley and Livingstone* and *The Four Feathers*, would have to wait for another day, another venue. In Malcolm Muggeridge's nostalgic summing up '. . . strangely, sadly and rather foolishly, the Thirties drew to a close'.[51]

It was a war that would soon bring Denis back full circle to the Riviera in less glamorous but far more dangerous circumstances.

All because of those two letters. The first, offering his services as a French speaker, had plunged him into the maelstrom of the *Lancastria*. The second, the letter his worldly friend Burnett-Brown dictated, introducing him to SOE, was about to launch him on a long and even more dangerous road.

---

[51] *Muggeridge p. 318*

6

Join the Club

It was the summer of 1941, in a London already devastated by the Blitz, blacked out at night except for searchlight beams probing the sky, and grey by day, broken glass crunching underfoot, grit and smoke heavy in the back of the throat. Curving Georgian façades, shop fronts and modest suburban streets were punctuated by water-logged bomb-sites. It was a time of ration books, gas masks and quiet despair hidden by the proverbial 'stiff upper lip'.

The ability to remain unflustered by chance encounters is an important element in a secret agent's makeup. Rake the (minor) actor seems to have displayed appropriate *sang froid* when, in response to the Burnett-Brown letter, he was summoned for his first contact with the secret world. He found himself in an anonymous office in Northumberland Avenue, just off Trafalgar Square, shaking hands with Major (later Lt Colonel) Lewis Gielgud, elder brother of the (major) stage star, John.

Lewis Gielgud was well suited by background to understand Denis's complex past with its pot-pourri of exotic places, parents, the stage and his homosexuality. The elder Gielgud's sexual preferences were no secret within his family. Their father Frank was a London stockbroker, born into an immigrant family. Frank's mother had been a Shakespearean actress well known across the Russian Pale of Settlement and the family took its name from a Lithuanian village, Gielgaudskis. Lewis's mother Kate had even better stage credentials; with Dame Ellen Terry and Marion Terry as her great aunts she was an 'ex officio' member of the British theatrical aristocracy.[52]

Born in 1894 Lewis Gielgud epitomised that generation of young

---

[52] *Oxford Dictionary of National Biography 2004-7 'Sir (Arthur) John Gielgud' by Morley, S. and Sharp, R.*

men, perhaps rightly enshrined in folk memory as 'golden', so many of whom were to vault to their death over the sandbagged tops of Flanders trenches, nonchalantly waving their men on with a leather-bound 'swagger stick'. He had been a King's Scholar at Eton, thus from an early age part of an intellectual elite, and an Exhibitioner at Magdalen College, Oxford, finding his friends among philosophers and writers. He himself contributed serious verse to the University poetry journal (in later life he found time to translate Greek poems and write two novels). In 1914, as Denis and Emma were watching the German troops marching into Brussels, Lewis was commissioned into the King's Shropshire Light Infantry. Badly wounded at the Battle of Loos in 1915 he survived not least because his mother Kate came out to France to nurse him in the field hospital (more or less taking charge of it in the process).

Invalided out for a brief spell behind a War Office desk, Gielgud was soon transferred to Paris, working in the British Mission to the Armistice negotiations. He had spells on the staffs of Field Marshal Hague, Marshal Foch of France and the French Prime Minster Clemenceau. His experiences must have provided some fascinating and probably depressing insights into the minds of the men who between them had sent so many millions to their deaths. After the war, Lewis found himself grappling with its insoluble human consequences as a senior official of the International Red Cross. When war came again, he joined the Intelligence Corps, with the benefit of much bitter experience and with a fluent command of French, the language in which he interviewed Denis. Characteristically Denis found the interview rather like an audition and equally characteristically, felt he had not got the part.

He was wrong. Gielgud had seen something he liked, even though he or another officer noted delicately on Denis's personal file under the heading '*Other Interests*', 'Stage only, and all that that implies'.

Denis was en route to the Arcanum only provisionally, since he had first to be 'security cleared'. Nowadays those entering Government service for especially sensitive posts and high-level information access, are used to the rigorous process known as Developed Vetting, in which security officers take a seabed level trawl of several months through a candidate's private and family life, school background, travel history, internet habits, friends, health and financial affairs, interspersed with face to face interviews designed to discomfit the applicant into revealing his or her deepest secrets.

Back then it was dangerously simple. Denis's name was 'run across the cards' at MI5's Registry (a somewhat unusual cuckoo squatting in the magnificent baroque nest of Blenheim Palace to which it had been forced to move after the Germans bombed its temporary home in Wormwood Scrubs prison) to see if the hundreds of thousands of entries in its index held anything detrimental about him. A sheet of paper giving his background details and stamped 'Secret' was sent around to a Captain Strong at MI5, and returned a few days later with the laconic scribble 'NRA', or 'Nothing Recorded Against'. It is mildly intriguing for those who study these things to see that a carbon copy of the same request carries the notation 'C.X.', suggesting that SIS was also involved in the SOE clearance process, an involvement which would have given them a handy insight into SOE's recruits. Their answer was 'NT', or 'no trace'.

In October 1943 MI5's Maxwell Knight, best known for running penetration agents against the British Communist Party and diplomatic targets, was drawn into the investigation of a particularly flagrant case of loose talk, loose behaviour and betrayal by an F Section agent. He was warned that to rely on this 'negative vetting' approach was dangerous. Knight thought far more should be done to check SOE agents' backgrounds and to make a more rigorous assessment of their characters and psychology during training. He added, a touch unfairly, that SOE's concept of the criteria for an agent was 'in many respects basically wrong. Physical toughness, the spirit of adventure and the rolling-stone type are all assessed too highly while mental stability, genuine loyalty and patriotism are rated too low.'[53]

In Denis's case nothing was done, as far as the files show, to check with the Foreign Office, that the background to his employment was

[53] *Maxwell Knight, OBE, 1900-1968. Head of MI5's Section B5b, author and naturalist; see his 'Frogs, Toads and Newts in Britain' 1962*

appropriate. Nor were any questions asked about his time in Greece, his supposed marriage or indeed anything else.

To Denis, learning that he had been accepted must have been a surprise as great as hearing he was to play Hamlet at the Old Vic. To SOE at that point in the war he was a Godsend, albeit in an unlikely disguise. (One of the many cover names Denis was to use during his time with SOE, this one for work while in London, was Dieudonné or roughly translated, 'God's Gift'.) He was middle-aged, cranky, he had never been to school, let alone the sort of school where most of his interviewers had effortlessly absorbed cricket and the Classics, and the implications of his theatrical background had not gone unremarked. On the other hand he spoke fluent French (he remembers it was rather better than his English). He had the actor's gift for following a script and a director's orders, slipping with conviction as much as artifice out of the skin of his real identity into another's personality. The life of a homosexual in 1930s London also placed a premium on artifice and dissimulation. Seedy black-mailers, police provocateurs in public toilets and magistrates with Old Testament views meant that being caught breaking what was then the law was a traumatic nightmare that all too often meant social and professional ruin; conventional middle class professional life had no place for overt gays. Masking the real self, much as an agent has to do in hostile territory, was essential for survival.

Denis was determined, and he was patriotic. Asked to note his political views on one of the forms in his personal file he wrote 'British imperialist', a comment which resonated naturally enough then; today anyone making that sort of admission would be put under Special Branch surveillance under suspicion of adherence to some right-wing extremist group. In the box asking about religion, he wrote 'Church Of England', just about a safe choice even today when filling in official British forms, though not necessarily accurate in Denis's case, since in a brief aside in his autobiography he tells us that he was 'RC'. Outweighing all the possible negatives however, he was not only a French speaker but thanks to Lady Aberconway, he was that almost priceless resource, a trained wireless operator.

The core of SOE circuits in France was the organiser, the man or woman in charge supported by a courier, usually a woman, to carry messages and money around the circuit, and the wireless operator, nicknamed the 'pianist' who provided the vital link with London. Denis would surely not have been told that at that stage in the war an operator in hostile territory might expect to function for little more than six weeks before the Germans picked up his or her trail. This was the result of a combination of security lapses by SOE on the one hand, and the technical and penetrative skills of the German counter-intelligence services on the other. We shall look at this lethal cocktail later, but first we have to usher Denis into the heart of SOE.

SOE's mania for mystification was such that few beyond the most senior Government circles even knew its official name, though it had not prevented the kind of gossip overheard by Denis in the Portsmouth pub, and which had spurred him to make his approach. Under the anonymous cover of 'the Inter-Services Research Bureau', SOE occupied several buildings rather unglamorously sited on London's Baker Street, better known as the fictional lair of Sherlock Holmes and the corporate headquarters of the retailers Marks & Spencer; SOE's main office was at number 64. In the best traditions of the spy novel, encounters with its French agents were not in the office but in a third floor flat at Orchard Court, in nearby Portman Square, more often than not, because of the lack of space in the black tiled Art Deco bathroom.

We have already summarised SOE's origins and mission, with perhaps undeserved brevity. But its history and growth have been exhaustively researched, as have its never ending Whitehall conflicts, which resembled the internecine feuding of the families of medieval Florence and must have taken up a disproportionate and debilitating amount of its senior leadership's time and energy. Powerful ministers squabbled over 'turf' and demanded action (leading to the quip in SOE's early days, cited by M.R.D. Foot, that the innate caution of its senior cadre of City solicitors meant that the organisation was 'all May, and no Slaughter').

The Foreign Office was (often not without good reason) skittish about the immediate and post-war effects of some of SOE's political machinations in Europe. The Secret Intelligence Service (SIS) felt upstaged by SOE's creation, and was anxious to preserve its status and its monopoly in military and political intelligence. It played up to the full its genuine concerns that its clandestine efforts and agents in Europe would be jeopardised when SOE's noisier activities attracted German attention. Such scant evidence as exists in the public domain about SIS work in France suggests that they had a point. Its institutional mindset may also have played a part. A friend of the present author, who had reason to know, once remarked of SIS 'they trust nobody and despise nearly everybody'.[54]

There was friction too with the RAF, between SOE's pressure for aircraft to drop supplies and agents, and the RAF's conviction that bombing German industrial targets was a higher priority. SOE had to beat off robust Whitehall attempts to take it over or shut it down on at least two occasions: the first when SOE's Cairo HQ was seen to be overstepping its mandate by meddling in politics in Yugoslavia and Greece, the second when its Dutch operations were totally unravelled by the Germans in a sophisticated 'radio game' that SOE's security woefully failed to spot.

As Maxwell Knight's criticisms show, MI5 too had serious reservations about the way SOE selected its people, and debriefed them when they came back from the field, and were especially concerned about its radio security. The concern was well founded. Though SOE did not know, a key element in MI5's success in running double agents back against their Nazi masters was that it was reading the coded radio traffic of the German intelligence service. If they could do so, it was prudent to assume the Germans might be equally successful in reading SOE's transmissions.

There was even considerable disharmony within components of SOE itself. For instance the tricky demarcation line between its 'wholly owned' French Section and a separate unit, the RF Section, ran as a fractious joint venture with General de Gaulle's Free French administration in London, from separate offices in Dorset Square.

A linguist has claimed that the Japanese translation of 'joint venture' is 'same bed, different dreams', which from the history seems

[54] *Elliott, p. 216*

directly applicable to SOE's complex relations with the French, and vice versa. However at an operational level French agents yielded nothing in terms of bravery and sacrifice to those of F Section. A 1941 SOE memorandum by Sir Frank Nelson[55] makes the Baker Street attitude abundantly clear. It states, 'The ideal is to allow the Gestapo and the de Gaulle Staff to think we are cooperating one hundred per cent with each other – whereas in truth, whilst I should wish you to have the friendliest day to day relationship and liaison with the de Gaulle people, I should wish you at the same time to tell them nothing of our innermost and most confidential plans, and above all such bases as you may establish in France must be our bases and known only to us . . . the whole of our HQ organisation and field organisation would be entirely concealed from the French . . .'

The division fed de Gaulle's visceral distrust of all things Anglo-Saxon and he lost no opportunity to complain about being kept in the dark about SOE operations in France. When Churchill went to Algeria in November 1943, the Free French Commissioner for Foreign Affairs René Massigli (later a much admired Ambassador to London) tackled him on the subject and an urgent message demanded an explanation from Baker Street. Lord Selborne, who had succeeded Hugh Dalton as Minister for Economic Warfare and thus as the political 'master' of SOE fired back trenchantly that 'the Gaullist [intelligence] organisations are partisan in internal French politics and tend to bayonet those who will not bow the knee to the Cross of Lorraine'.[56]

Moreover, 'the security of the Gaullist organisations is lamentable. They have been repeatedly penetrated by the Germans and in spite of all SOE's protests insist on maintaining a centralised machinery in violation of the primary canons of secret service'. In the light of Professor Foot's analysis of the Germans' considerable counter-intelligence successes against SOE[57] under the tactful heading of *A Run of Errors 1943-1944*, Selborne's further comment might be seen as something of a fudge, if not downright parsimony

[55] *1883-1966, businessman, former MP, at the time CD, or Director of SOE, Mackenzie p. 230*
[56] *Roundell Cecil Palmer CH, PC, third Earl of Selborne, 1887-1971*
[57] *Foot p. 289 et seq*

with the truth. But as a man with other heavy responsibilities at his Ministry and no intelligence background he was surely only passing on a brief given to him by SOE. He told Churchill: 'SOE now has some seventy British officers in France each with his own circle of workers. This organisation has never been penetrated though individual cells have occasionally been scuppered.'

Selborne rounded off by rejecting the Gaullist claim that SOE's contacts 'are all Communists'; a major bone of contention was the Gaullist objection to the British supplying Communist Resistance elements, on the not unreasonable grounds that the latter were vying with de Gaulle for control of post-war France. Some might be Communists, Selborne conceded, but SOE's basic principle was to contact French officers 'who gather brave spirits around them' regardless of their politics.[58]

If SOE might be said to have played a rather robust game of three card brag, SIS approached its work with the finesse of a professional bridge player. They kept a careful eye on SOE, and contrary to SOE's posture, maintained close ties with Gaullist intelligence, cemented by its control over their supplies, sea landing and air drop resources, and wireless codes. Even more delicately it was on intimate terms with officers in the 'special services' of the rump Army and Air Force allowed to Vichy under the Armistice. It also had highly productive relationships with the French networks run by exile governments in London, notably but not exclusively, the Poles.

But happily we can bypass these Byzantine machinations and focus on Denis's work for SOE's French Section, though one more digression is relevant. In its earliest incarnation SOE also had responsibility for propaganda (whether 'white', i.e. identifiable sources putting out a clearly partisan line, or shading quickly to 'black'). Such propaganda included radio stations purporting to represent defeatist or anti-Nazi voices, underground newspapers, leaflets, sophisticated techniques for spreading subversive rumours, less sophisticated but sometimes more effective ones like bribing

[58] *See Selborne, Bibliography*

foreign newspaper proprietors and journalists and efforts to shape opinion in neutral countries.

After another bout of acrid Whitehall infighting, these initiatives were soon hived off into a separate organisation known as the Political Warfare Executive, or 'PWE'. Like SOE, PWE used a cover name in its dealings with the outside world, in its case the 'Political Intelligence Department' of the Foreign Office. It comes into our story because scrappy notes in the personal file indicate that when he was recruited, and for some time while in training, Denis was seen as a wireless operator who would support PWE agents in France. One file entry suggests that he was even considered as a potential PWE agent. This would explain why his first interview after Gielgud had approved him was with a six-man panel in Oxford, not a location usually associated with SOE.

In 1939, as part of the web of propaganda initiatives, the Foreign Office asked the Royal Institute of International Affairs to create the blandly named 'Foreign Research and Press Service', headed by the historian Arnold J. Toynbee, who had played a similar role in the First World War.[59] At the outbreak of the Second World War Toynbee and his staff moved out of a nervous London to the calm and 'dreaming spires' of Balliol College, Oxford, which we can assume is where Denis faced the selection board. Somewhere on the fuzzy interface between PWE, the Press Service, SOE and the BBC glided Dr Leslie Beck,[60] a don at Magdalen College, who had made the philosopher Descartes his academic specialisation and French politics his main interest for PWE.[61]

Denis tells us that he went through a weekend 'propaganda course' at PWE's grand HQ at Woburn Abbey, though he anonymises Beck as 'Dr So & So' and claims he never remembered anything he was taught. From his brief description the course was aimed more at techniques for spreading rumours and disinformation in the field, than propaganda in the strategic sense. The personal file includes a letter to Dr Beck from one of Denis's instructors, a

[59] *1819-1975*
[60] *1916-1978*
[61] *See paper by Tombs, E, in Bibliography*

Captain G.M. Forte, asking Beck for his ideas on the 'cover' Denis should use in France, noting that Denis was at an 'advanced stage of training' and developing some thoughts of his own on this. The letter gives yet another evaluation of Denis: 'His only failing . . . is a certain lack of confidence in himself and what one might almost call a timid nature. I do not however think that this is a serious weakness as I found that on exercises he has shown up very creditably in comparison with others of what one could call a much tougher type'. This is the last, or almost the last, we hear of the PWE notion, and we can return to Orchard Court and SOE's mainstream French Section.

Its proximity and strategic importance made France a key SOE target, and the French Section had more than its fair share of heroes and especially heroines whose bravery, and in too many cases cruel fate in German hands, have rightly been much written about and filmed. There is thus a natural tendency to see it as the personification of SOE and even to view its head, Maurice Buckmaster, as 'Mr SOE'. Indeed an English subtitle in Marcel Ophuls' film describes him as 'Former Head of the British Underground' as though he had been in charge of the London Tube.

Important though the Section and his accomplishments were, SOE was far larger than its French initiatives alone and made a major impact in many other war theatres. And in his role as Head of the French Section, based on a 1942 snapshot of the always fluid organisation chart,[62] Buckmaster was not a 'lone wolf'. He reported to Colonel D.J. Keswick, over whom sat Brigadier Mockler-Ferryman. Above the Brigadier was the Director of Operations and a prime mover of SOE, then Brigadier, later Major General Colin Gubbins,[63] who in his turn was answerable to SOE's then Chief, the merchant banker Sir Charles Hambro and alongside him the equivalent of a Corporate Board of Directors.

Over and above SOE sat its political master, first Hugh Dalton and later Selborne, who in turn answered to the towering, inquisitive, goading Churchill. The latter's appetite for 'raw'

[62] *Mackenzie p. 763*
[63] *Sir Colin MacVean Gubbins, GCMG, DSO, MC 1896-1976*

decrypts of German Enigma traffic (the Ultra Secret, as it came to be called) is well known. He also liked to be kept informed of SOE's adventures and received regular reports from Selborne both in narrative form and in tables (some of which are hard to follow) which listed arms dropped, sabotage operations mounted and resistance losses. Selborne knew his audience; the summary for the period from October to December 1942 begins with what reads like a flattering allusion to the Prime Minister's much-repeated mandate to SOE to 'set Europe ablaze'. Selborne wrote, 'The spirit of Resistance in Europe grows daily stronger and SOE continues to stoke the furnace.'[64] (Buckmaster nevertheless made clear in a letter to the author of a book on SOE in 1956 that he had been 'personally and solely responsible' for F Section.)[65]

---

[64] *Selborne, Bibliography*
[65] *VA papers*

7

An Unsentimental Education

In Marcel Ophuls' film, Maurice Buckmaster is seen striding out briskly through 1960's Chelsea, near his flat in Wellington Square, past the still drab shop fronts, lightened by the brief flash of a background miniskirt, lauding Denis's bravery in excellent French. He is dressed like Central Casting's vision of a British spy-master, in a well-tailored suit, glossily polished shoes, bowler hat at just the right angle, swinging a tightly furled umbrella with metronomic precision. Except that Buckmaster doesn't have a neatly folded copy of the *Times* under his arm, he is the living embodiment of 'Major Marmaduke Thompson', the stereotypical British officer created by the French humorist Pierre Daninos to try to explain the British to the French and vice versa.

His life and work deserve a far fuller and more personal account than space allows here. Born in 1910, the son of a brewery owner, he was unable to take up a Classics Exhibition at Magdalen College, Oxford (Lewis Gielgud's alma mater) when his father's business fell on hard times. After six years in a City merchant bank he moved to the Ford Motor Company, managing its French subsidiary in Paris for three years (which gave him a command of French, though it was too short by perhaps half a lifetime to allow him, or indeed any other foreigner, to comprehend the quiddities of France and the French) before moving to the more down to earth setting of its European Head Office in London.

When war came he was commissioned into the Intelligence Corps, and saw solid service with the Expeditionary Force in France before lining up under German gunfire to wait his turn as one of the last to leave in the evacuation from Dunkirk. After a spell in Dakar he joined SOE in 1941, his only focused preparation being short courses in military intelligence and photographic interpretation. He thus came to SOE without the instincts honed through years of canny clandestinity, manipulation, winning, buying and if need be, betraying confidences, the black arts which, along with genes hardwired with suspicion, SIS and MI5 would regard as the agent-runner's basic skills.

But he made up for it in sheer hard work. He had an ability to make and stick to decisions. He was loyal to his agents. He had an outward self-confidence that served to bolster those of his men who got to know him, which was not easy in the operational pell-mell of the SOE. In any event as he looked back on his career in 1958 Buckmaster was firmly of the view that his role and that of other senior officers at SOE headquarters 'was not that of spymasters but of active and belligerent planners of operations to be carried out in advance of the Allied landing [in Europe]'.[66] At first reading, a recent comment that 'Buckmaster's temperament inclined him more towards enthusiasm than prudence'[67] seems unkind, but it may in fact simply reflect Buckmaster's own view of his considerable responsibilities.

To Maurice Buckmaster all his geese, that variegated flock of agents, were swans, sometimes long after they were heard to cackle. He seems to have given them often exasperated but unflagging support, sometimes as in Denis's case, in the face of the negative judgments of others or despite random acts of folly. His declared policy that 'I tried to judge each man on his merits, but there was one thing we could never afford to do – give a man the benefit of any doubts,' was, apart from its unintentional chauvinism, far from invariably followed. Indeed he wrote later that he knew 'we were taking a bit of a risk with Rake' and that had he applied later in SOE's evolution, he might well have been rejected.[68] From Denis's standpoint Maurice Buckmaster might be seen as stepping in the shoes of Francis Joseph, the father he hardly knew. On the same lines Virginia Hall and even more Nancy Wake, with whom Denis was so

[66] *Buckmaster p. 43*
[67] *Dictionnaire, p. 381*
[68] *Buckmaster pp. 47, 66*

embroiled in danger, both women of considerable verve, may perhaps have filled part of the maternal void left by Emma.

Denis was not only gaining a surrogate father, and in a sense joining a new if decidedly odd family, he was about to go to school (albeit rather late in life), and to a succession of them at that. In September 1941, after a brief meeting with Maurice Buckmaster, Denis (now entered in SOE's books as '16411', the first of a string of cover names and aliases) took a Southern Railway train from Waterloo down to Guildford. It was there that a 30-cwt Army truck stood in the forecourt to take him and a group of 'new entrants' to Wanborough Manor. Two months later Japan would attack Pearl Harbour and bring the US into the war.

For now the talk was of the German siege of Leningrad and a new edict compelling the wearing of the Star of David by Jews over the age of six in all German held territory (in a cynical twist to this demeaning targeting, Jews had to hand over one precious clothes rationing coupon for each Star). Also in the news was a German submarine attack on the American destroyer USS *Greer*, an incident which helped accelerate US entry into the war. Whether Denis even noticed the match with his theatrical *nom d'emprunt* is an interesting but unfruitful speculation; in fact the ship was named after a distinguished nineteenth century American Admiral.

The Manor was one of the many British country houses from the Solent to Scotland snapped up as training schools by SOE after they had been emptied by a lethal combination of death duties, taxation, wartime evacuation and an acute shortage of domestic staff, conscripted or lured into munitions factories and war-boosted industries by the prospect of high wages. SOE's property portfolio was so extensive that jokers claimed its initials stood for 'The Stately 'Omes of England'. Guy Burgess who (according to Kim Philby) first conceived the idea of a training school for saboteurs during his spell in Section D of SIS a forerunner of SOE, suggested maliciously that 'Slop and Offal' were more appropriate.[69]

---

[69] *Though they included several 'Stockbroker Tudor' mansions tucked away on Lord Montagu's Beaulieu estate they were not all 'stately'. Among SOE's other trophy properties were a former roadhouse on the Barnet By-Pass, two factories in Watford, a garage in Birmingham and a display hall in the Natural History Museum*

When the Manor was entered in the Domesday Book centuries earlier, the scribes could not have imagined that one day the oxen, the corn, and the bent-backed peasants would give way to highly-strung men and women, learning the less rural arts and crafts of unarmed combat, weapons training, and the use of 'plastic explosive'. In addition, map reading, Morse Code and learning how to shake off surveillance were key skills to be mastered. The Manor's medieval Great Barn was now used to store guns and ammunition rather than grain.

Formally, the Manor was a 'Preliminary Training School'. Its main aim was to pick out those who really had 'the right stuff' to be SOE agents by watching how the 'students' performed under stress. Hardcore training came later. Informally, those who went through it dubbed it 'the Mad House'. Many of them arrived with little or no idea of the work for which they were being appraised, or indeed about SOE. There were many factors that contributed to an atmosphere of fantasy. There were real bangs, simulated butchery and strange obstacle courses confected by the instructors to test ingenuity under pressure. The instructors conducted rude awakenings in the middle of the night to haul students away for interrogations which even though simulated still created an air of menace and a taste of what the real thing would be like. They were also given lessons in how the French handled their knives and forks, and taught the legerdemain skills of 'brush contacts' to pass on messages. All of this accumulated in a fantasy atmosphere, especially for a generation fortunate enough to grow up without exposure to reality television.

Denis had a hard time. So did his instructors. His version first – a classic 'Grumpy Old Man' skit. He was training to be a Morse operator. None of the other black arts were relevant, so why should he be compelled to master them at the say-so of 'some young whippersnapper'. As for exercise, why should he risk rupturing himself on the parallel bars: he was fit enough anyway. Then came a bolt from the blue. He was summoned back to Orchard Court to be confronted with the accusation that he was taking drugs. 'Of course I do', he laughed at a shocked French Section inquisitor.

'Everybody knows it.' Ever since his nerves had been frayed by the *Lancastria* catastrophe he had taken a sleeping pill at night and a Benzedrine tablet in the morning to shake off the drowsy after-effects.

For those exposed to present day US television, sleeping pills hardly count as 'drugs' any more. Commercials that promote their use (with fluttering butterflies and the implied promise of easeful early-morning intercourse) are staples of the so-called 'prime time' evening newscasts. So too are treatments for erectile dysfunction ('Viva, Viva Viagra . . .' the macho 'close harmony' group croons in a recent but thankfully short-lived clip), diabetes, haemorrhoids, flatulence and bladder control ('Gotta go, gotta go, gotta go right now'). Even in the 1930s cocaine and morphine were in wide use among the international 'smart set'. So it comes as a surprise to see such a fuss made about Denis's mild habit, all the more since Benzedrine was part of an SOE field agent's staple kit, used to ward off fatigue.

But whoever made the judgment, it was certainly not Buckmaster. Denis's version is that he was told, 'we've decided you're not suitable for us'. He swept out in a huff, off to his London *pied à terre*, the Pastoria Hotel. Never one for spelling, he calls it 'Pastori's' (it became the fifty-eight roomed 'Radisson Edwardian Pastoria' in St Martin's Street just off Leicester Square, but the last name, like so many other links with the past, has recently been quietly dropped). He had a good dinner, telling us that the Pastoria always offered a remarkable menu, despite the exigencies of wartime. It was managed by a former Maitre d'Hotel at the fashionable Grosvenor House on Park Lane, whom Denis had got to know while he was performing in cabaret there.

During the meal, Denis decided that if they were 'going to treat me like an 18 year old' he was better off out of SOE. He knew of a part that would soon be available in a new musical comedy and would talk to his agent about it in the morning. He relaxed but before he had time to digest his dinner, let alone pop a sleeping tablet, there was a knock at the door – the Pastoria's security must have been rather lax – and a 'little man from SOE' appeared, asking

him plaintively to reconsider his decision to leave. With uncharac-
teristic restraint Denis pointed out that he had not left, he had been
fired. The 'little man' begged and pleaded. Wireless operators were
so badly needed. In the end Denis relented, and went back to
Wanborough, ending a little drama that might have been scripted in
a weak moment by the author of *Mercenary Mary*.

The personal file version is briefer and less dramatic. In the first
report from Wanborough Denis (at the time still earmarked for
work with PWE) was said to be 'very keen, particularly at Morse and
is doing very well at this subject'. Contrary to his recollected aversion
to the parallel bars, his instructors found him 'very fit for his age and
expresses a liking for exercise' though 'a trifle effeminate'. He was
'very humourous and has personality. Always bright and cheerful'.

The sleeping pill affair is touched on lightly in a file comment on
18 September that Denis had left the party two days earlier. He 'is
to some extent a drug addict. His chief trouble is insomnia . . . He
stopped taking the tablets after the first few days'. Nevertheless the
instructors stressed that he was a 'very generous man and most
popular with students and staff'. By 29 September Denis was back
in the fold and proving 'Most enthusiastic about Morse. Has cheered
up the party.' The personal file does not include Denis's dramatic
sequel, in which he claims that as he could not sleep well, he took to
drink in place of pills, quite a lot of it, a switch which was duly
reported back to Baker Street. Denis stormed into the office of
Wanborough's 'absolutely charming' and 'very good looking'
Commanding Officer, Roger de Wesselow of the Coldstream
Guards, to declare that it was either drugs or drink, 'take your
choice. Otherwise I go!' Though his memory of this exchange may
have a touch of *l'esprit d'escalier* he claims he never heard another
word on the subject.

Denis passed out of Wanborough successfully, despite himself,
and despite two reprimands for security lapses when he was heard
talking carelessly to outsiders about his training. In his critique of
SOE's security MI5's Maxwell Knight detected a tendency among
training officers 'few of whom can be regarded as professionals (as far
as my knowledge goes) to gloss over errors of security and behaviour

committed by their recruits for fear of bringing adverse criticism upon themselves'.

Denis moved briefly to bucolic Buckinghamshire where the village of Grendon Underwood, another SOE site to be found in the Domesday Book, was the main hub of the Executive's worldwide signals circuit; another station was at Poundon near Bicester. As Mackenzie remarks of Grendon[70] in an uncharacteristically lyrical trope 'the easiest way to impress an outsider with the scope and power of SOE in its prime was to shew [sic] him the main wireless stations . . . To the layman it looked as though there were a forest of wireless masts, acres of floor space, hundreds of girl operators and decoders; a sort of telephone exchange planted in a corner of agricultural England, an exchange which looked normal enough but which served some very curious subscribers.' (The masts and the girls are long gone, but Grendon has remained in the public domain as the site of Britain's largest high-security jail for serious criminals with psychiatric problems. There is also an 'open prison' nearby.)

Though any fuss escaped the personal file, Denis tells us that here too he played 'the odd man out'. He insists that he was there to improve his Morse. It was his view that Grendon's insistence that its students also learn how to service and repair the clumsy SOE wireless transceivers (which at the stage weighed a hefty 30 lb., though with later technical improvements the weight was gradually whittled down) was a waste of time. Denis did not even know how to mend an electric fuse and wasn't going to start now. He got his way.

Then it was time to get serious. At the end of September 1941 Denis reached Arisaig, on the remote north-west coast of Scotland, looking out over the islands of Eig, Rum and Muck and the larger mass of the Isle of Skye. Worn out rolling stock, and the strains of war, meant that the trip was still a far cry from the streamlined comforts of today's 'Deerstalker Express', which leaves London at 7.30 p.m. and reaches Fort William around 10 a.m.

Denis was not senior enough to have been allotted a sleeping berth. He would have been crammed three a side in a passenger

[70] *P. 736*

compartment, trying to get comfortable on the scratchy moquette upholstery, and probably arguing with his fellow passengers about the heating. As daylight faded, air in the compartments began to smell and taste of smoke and soot from the coal fire of the steam locomotive. Light from the blue lamps was too dim to allow passengers to read but gave just enough of an eerie glow to make for uneasy sleep as the train rattled north.

Outside the steamed up windows was the darkness of the official blackout, sliced from time to time by searchlight beams. The train would often stop in the middle of nowhere for no apparent reason, and then, buffers clanking, jolt back into motion. When it hissed to a halt at the many stations en route, it was impossible to tell where one was, even after wiping the condensation from the windows to peer outside, since most station signboards had been removed as a security precaution. A lurching walk to wait in line for the pungently overused toilet meant navigating corridors (now a forgotten feature of railway travel) crammed with servicemen and women, smoking, flirting, playing 'Pontoon' for pennies or simply slumped on their haversacks and kitbags trying to snatch a few moments of sleep, 'getting a quick kip' in service slang. Compared to the journeys that lay ahead of him, it was Pullman class luxury.

From Fort William an Army truck took Denis along the narrow road through the forested hills past Loch Eil and Loch Ailort. They journeyed through a barrier manned by sentries who guarded what had been declared a 'Prohibited Area,' to which only the uncurious, not to say dour, local crofters had ready access. This was less because of SOE's presence there than the Navy's concern about German spying or sabotage efforts against its berths and training waters. But the security cordon suited SOE too, allowing its students to rampage across the hills and paddle in and out of creeks and across the lochs, or blow up sections of railway track, without the benefit of spectators.

Denis joined a mixed group, about fifty strong all using pseudonyms and all speaking French using the '*tu*' form as a sign of their close camaraderie. They were there for four weeks. A month at Arisaig House today would be followed by a sizeable credit card bill; it is now a small luxury hotel. Its granite walls are softened by billowing banks of rhododendrons, and there is a plaque in the lobby that acts as the only memory of SOE's presence. It is hard for the guests sipping cocktails and nibbling salted almonds to conjure up the 'Terminator' skills which were at the heart of its SOE curriculum. These included silent killing, by knife, garrote, a strategically placed blow with the heel of the hand, or even a tightly gripped matchbox, how to strip, load and fire pistols and submachine guns, how to read maps, how to survive make-believe raiding forays over the wet hills. The only hostile elements nowadays are the almost invisible midges, which turn a summer evening stroll into a cruel and unusual punishment.

The main House was one of a group of ten former shooting lodges in the area used by SOE and other paramilitary groups. Legend had it that they had originally been acquired by Colin Gubbins in his brief pre-SOE role as chief of the 'Auxiliary Parties'; a clandestine service was hastily organised in the war's early days to offer guerilla resistance to a German invasion. The Scottish estates were to be the equivalent of Hitler's 'last redoubt' though manned by fighters in well-ventilated kilts rather than unsanitary Teutonic *lederhosen*. But the Parties were soon disbanded as a 'nice try' but a forlorn hope.

If the Arisaig trainees felt harried, their instructing officers were also under pressure. One of the early commanding officers, James Young, looked for two special skills. They had to have the capacity to down half a pint of whisky after dinner, and also to master the intricacies of the Eightsome reel. The sweaty combination must have led to as many bruises and bumps as hand to hand combat.

Denis tells us that though he kept up his Morse practice, for the rest 'it was almost a complete waste of time . . . I refused to do PT . . . I refused to have anything to do with explosives or to handle firearms . . .'. This led his supervisor to report, as Denis recalls, though there is no note on the personal file, that 'Rake is hopeless' and by his account to another appearance in front of the long-suffering Buckmaster, who sighed that Denis was 'making things awfully difficult'.[71] Denis reiterated that Morse was why he had been

---

[71] *This sequence underscores the danger of memoirs as sources; the 'hopeless' comment was first made by Buckmaster in 1958 and quite likely simply recycled by Denis ten years later because it fitted his image*

taken on, and Morse he would give them but he would have nothing to do with explosives or guns. He says he pointed out to Buckmaster that he was actually doing SOE a favour since he was so inept that if he so much as handled explosives there was bound to be a disaster. Denis concludes his account by telling us (though the personal file does not) that he was pulled out of Arisaig, spent some time in London wining and dining new recruits, and sent on two more wireless training courses.

The personal file version is again less negative and less coloured than Denis's account. In two brief weekly reports from Arisaig he gets good marks: 'The type of man who makes friends very quickly with anyone, as his pleasant manner and good humour cannot fail to please. His main preference is still for Morse' and a few days later '. . . has not shown a great deal of interest in the course. His chief concern is to get on with his Morse training. As fit and popular as ever'.

In the final report from Arisaig, which does not hint at any demarche or early termination, his performance and his dilemmas are spelled out in more nuanced detail. Under the heading 'Explosives and Demolition' for instance the report says that Denis 'dislikes explosives in principle but is quite ready to use them if he must'. And when it came to firearms, his trainers reported that far from refusing to handle them he had a 'fair knowledge of the weapons. Dislikes the noise of the Tommy gun.[72] Fair shot with .32 automatic', the report added, a skill which might have surprised or alarmed Denis's friends.

His instructing officer summed up with a phrase familiar to many parents and grandparents reading school reports, 'he has shown great eagerness to learn where the subject interested him, i.e. Morse. In other subjects he has listened attentively but I think with the thought at the back of his mind that he is not likely to need these subjects' in his role as a wireless operator. 'He has been invaluable as a peacemaker and has kept up the spirits of the whole party.'

The Arisaig Commanding Officer at the time Denis passed

[72] *The .45 calibre submachine gun, brainchild of US Army General John Thompson, manufactured by the Auto-Ordnance Corporation and much favoured by paramilitary units like SOE and the Commandos as well as the weapon of choice of Chicago gangsters*

through (whose signature is illegible but who does not seem to have been the reel-maven James Young) tapped a deeper vein. Denis, he wrote, on 6 October 1941, 'states that he has no fear of death and I believe him. He is in spite of his apparently lighthearted outlook, obviously serious about his job and should be a very good man working alone or with others . . .' Denis touches on the theme of courage when he speaks directly to us in French in *le Chagrin*: 'I think deep down what I wanted to do was to be able to display the same kind of courage as my friends who had become pilots and so on. Being a homosexual at that time one of my strongest fears was that I lacked the courage to do certain things.' He had earlier told Ophuls that 'I think in life one often takes into account what one has to lose. As far I was concerned I had nothing to lose. I had no relatives. I wasn't married – so what difference did it make?'

The French word he uses – '*parents*' can mean either 'parents' or 'relatives' – is an odd turn of phrase since at the time of his missions in France, Emma was very much alive, as was that barely visible sister.

Denis does not mention, nor does the personal file, any time spent down at the SOE enclave in Beaulieu, though he would find himself there later in his career. We next see him back on the train, to face the last and most fearsome training ordeal at the Parachute School at RAF Ringway, long since subsumed into Manchester Airport.

He reported to yet another sizeable house, this time near Knutsford in the Cheshire countryside, which would be his base for the Ringway course; SOE agents were billeted separately from more conventional warriors also going through parachute training. Here too his version and the personal file tell the same story, though the latter less histrionically. For Denis 'it was hell'. After six days of 'pretend' but still bone-shaking practice jumps from a high platform onto sandbags, he was wrapped into his flying suit and webbing parachute harness and found himself waddling to the aircraft 'with my legs apart like an old man with waterworks trouble'. Here we need to remind ourselves that he was no bulging-bicepped master of martial arts, but closer to Jim Wormold, the diffident vacuum cleaner salesman turned naïve SIS agent portrayed by Graham Greene as 'Our Man in Havana'.

Denis was a middle aged musical comedy actor, 5 feet 8 inches in his socks, for whom 'costume' meant straw hats, vividly striped blazers, and tap-dancing shoes, all topped off with Max Factor's theatrical makeup. Denim jump suits, cork-padded helmets and black smudges on the cheekbones to dull the sheen of the skin were not his idea of 'costume'. Whatever adventures he had been through in his life, nothing can have been quite as terrifying as the thought of leaping out into nothingness, relying on a single strap attached to the aircraft to jerk open the parachute as the jumper plummeted down, always assuming the parachute had been properly packed in the first place.

Richard Heslop, another SOE man of courage whom Denis was soon to encounter in the field, remembered being told by a straightfaced Ringway instructor: 'Remember, sir, if anything goes wrong and your 'chute doesn't open, let us know, quoting the official serial number stamped on the back of the harness, and we'll issue you with another one. If you can't remember the number, it doesn't matter – they're pretty decent about that sort of thing here.' It was several seconds before Heslop saw the joke, though his laughter was more hysterical than amused.

Denis did it despite all odds. He made four jumps, though he needed the not-so-gentle pressure of the instructor's knees in his back to get him through the jumping hatch. But when the last test came, he balked. It was a jump in darkness, this time not from an aircraft but from a wicker basket under a tethered gas-filled balloon, with only the instructor for company, hanging 600 feet up in the night sky over Ringway. Something about the black stillness, the absence of thrumming engine noise and the buffeting of an aircraft slipstream, paralysed Denis with fear and after several altercations an irritated ground crew winched the balloon, a cowed Denis and a vexed instructor back down. Even Heslop, to whom fear was only an infrequent visitor, remembers being 'petrified' by the balloon drop.

Again Denis does himself less than justice. Although the Ringway report in the personal file has a possible reference to the knee-pushing, it is otherwise laudatory: 'One cannot help admiring this man for his courage. Although he is getting on in years, he has taken part in strenuous PT to the best of his ability. Is fairly hesitant before leaving the plane, by no means hesitant to go up and do the jump. Fit. Has the respect of all at this school . . .' And of Maurice Buckmaster too, who must have decided with a shrug that Denis was too valuable to be rejected. After all SOE had other ways of infiltrating agents.[73]

In December 1941, Denis was commissioned as a Second Lieutenant on the Army's General List. Two more wireless refresher courses in early 1942 brought reprimands for loose talk. The plainclothes Field Security policemen SOE used or covert surveillance of its trainees heard Denis 'talking indiscreetly in English and French' and suspected he had even shown off by operating his wireless set in a friend's drawing room! The Commanding Officer of the Radio School at Thame Park (another Stately 'Ome, once a Cistercian Abbey, now again a private estate of some grandeur) wrote with weariness that he had 'tried to explain the absolute necessity of security mindedness . . . I am afraid he does not yet understand this'.

The reproof did not stand in the way of his promotion in April 1942 to the acting rank of Lieutenant. 'Beware Greeks bearing gifts', according to the old adage (one that Denis would have had particular reason to heed given his Athens experience) and the gift of a second 'pip' on his uniform shoulders should have been a warning that he was on the edge of the biggest adventure of all, the round-about journey into France to face the daily threat of capture, brutal interrogation and even death. Soon after the second promotion, Maurice Buckmaster told Denis he should get ready to leave at short notice, and that he should stay away from London until he was sent for again.

In that final countdown, agents spent time alone, brooding, staring vacantly at a cinema screen, enjoying several good meals or at

[73] They were all perilous, but less than in the First World War when agents went behind enemy lines in free-floating balloons, dumping ballast as they glided through the clouds, or were dropped from a Royal Flying Corps biplane relying on a newly developed parachute optimistically named the 'Guardian Angel'

the homes of parents or lovers pretending that they were going away on a routine service posting. Iconoclastic as ever, Denis waited for the call 'at the cottage of my old friend Douglas Byng'. He assumes either we know, or would not be interested to know, that Byng was a considerable stage personality. He began his career as a versatile actor in light comedies and revues, but developed something of a specialty as a female impersonator and pantomime 'Dame', with a repertoire that though risqué, was carefully pitched to avoid the censor's blue pencil.

Noël Coward once described Byng's night club act as 'the most refined vulgarity in London', although it is hard to see much refinement in the titles of such camp choruses, still available on record, as 'I'm Mummy, One of the Egyptian Queens', 'Hot Handed Hetty, the Vamp of the Jetty' or 'The Mayoress of Mould-on-the Puddle'. Today they evoke memories of that other music hall trouper Max Miller, 'the Cheeky Chappie', a pudgy purveyor of *double entendres,* melded with the glittery drag act of Danny la Rue. But Byng was much admired, and had a successful career spanning more than half a century.

It is interesting to recall that in 1938, four years before this farewell weekend, the infant BBC television service, soon to be shut down by the war, had presented a twenty minute solo sketch by Byng. It would be even more interesting to know quite what the SOE driver made of it all when he arrived at Byng's cottage to take Denis back to London for the ritual 'good luck, old chap, and bon voyage' meeting with Maurice Buckmaster and Colin Gubbins. We can only imagine the house party spilling and trilling out onto the terrace to wave Denis goodbye, the driver stoically staring straight ahead; it must have struck him as one of the more idiosyncratic adieux in SOE's annals.[74]

[74] *Douglas Byng, 1893–1988. His diaries and correspondence, now in the Theatre Collection of the Victoria and Albert Museum, make no mention of Denis*

8

Riviera Rendezvous

As Buckmaster told Denis, SOE had a choice of secret and dangerous ways to get agents into France. Some went in by parachute (not without injury and mishap, including an unintentional descent on to the roof of a police station, and another into the centre of a prisoner of war camp). Others were ferried, wet and seasick on high-speed Motor Gun Boats, smacking through the Channel waves under cover of darkness to rocky Brittany coves, the Captain peering for the pinpoint of torchlight from the shore that would signal they were in the right place. Many went in crammed behind the pilot in the tiny single-engined Lysander aircraft flown into French fields by brave pilots squinting to catch the flicker of the recognition signals and landing lights laid out by their reception committee.

Denis would take a more circuitous route – a flying boat from Poole harbour in Dorset to Gibraltar. It fulfilled its centuries old role as a vital British naval base dominating the entrance to the Mediterranean, but now it balanced at the tip of a Spain that while nominally neutral was politically much in sympathy with the Nazis. From there he faced a long and perilous sea journey to the Riviera.

But he cannot climb aboard the Short Sunderland flying boat without introducing another McGuffin. We have heard nothing about Emma for several years, nor will we for a long while. Writing of his childhood, Denis gave us the briefest glimpse of an unnamed sister, who had been sent off to England before Denis joined the Circus – a phrase with unwitting echoes of John le Carré. Now, changing trains at Bristol on his way to Poole he blandly tells us that he met his sister (still unnamed) 'whom I had not seen for some time'. He admits that if the encounter had happened in a novel, it would be 'just too much of a coincidence'. He adds two details: she was in the uniform of a pilot in the Air Transport Auxiliary, and she was married to a schoolmaster. (According to the personal file in which Denis names her as his next of kin his name was Aurelius Jones, a presumably coincidental reminder of the long vanished Margaret Morgan Jones.)

They chatted, they parted, and she vanishes from the story, bringing to film buffs' minds Celia Johnson and Trevor Howard in their farewell, so restrained, so British, in Noël Coward's 1946 film, *Brief Encounter*. Instead of a train puffing away in a billow of steam, our soundtrack is that of the roar of the Sunderland's four Bristol Pegasus engines as it lumbered at 16,000 feet over the Bay of Biscay to the sunshine of Gibraltar at just under 200 m.p.h., fortunately avoiding any German interceptors. There Denis was in for more waiting – endemic in service life and especially wearing with a risky mission ahead – in the care of Major Hugh Quennell, SOE's 'man in Gibraltar'.[75]

The British intelligence and security services were all in a high state of alert. MI5 worried about the critically important Naval Dockyard, which made Gibraltar a priority target for German and Italian espionage and sabotage forays relying heavily on the hundreds of Spanish workers who passed into and out of Gibraltar every day. On the other side of the coin, potential saboteurs and sympathetic Spaniards were grist for the mill of MI5's 'XX' or 'Double-Cross' deception operations, always keen to find men and women who could be 'played back'.

A monitoring station run by the Radio Security Service, (initially an adjunct of MI5 and later transferred to MI6) operated in deep cover. It scooped up German intelligence signals traffic to give the 'XX' masterminds in London an extraordinary insight into what their opponents in Berlin did or did not know about their 'turned' agents. SIS was busy running its own agents into France and North Africa, and its affiliates at MI9 had their hands full with the escape

---

[75] *Hugh Quennell, 1903-1955, solicitor. According to Guy Liddell— Diaries p. 222 – Quennell had to resign from SOE in February 1942 after a botched attempt to run a ship laden with explosives into Tangier. If so he did not sever his connections with the secret world; after the war he served on at least two boards of companies with intelligence connections*

lines out of Europe. SOE's 'half brother' PWE had also made considerable but eventually unsuccessful efforts to install a radio transmitter on the Rock for propaganda broadcasts to North Africa and Spain.

Denis spent an agreeable week in the Rock Hotel; SOE and Quennell were presumably unaware of MI5's bleak view that the Rock, along with the Reina Christina in Algeciras and another hotel in Tangier, were all 'in the hands of the Germans'.[76] Eventually Jacques de Guelis,[77] one of F Section's senior staff officers, flew in from London to give Denis his final briefing and to hand over a large bundle of francs (perhaps £15,000 in today's depreciated money) he was to carry in to give to SOE's main Riviera contact, along with some fresh coffee, unobtainable in the Unoccupied Zone.[78] De Guelis also handed over a Commando knife and the 'L' or lethal pill, a tiny rubber-coated ampoule of cyanide that all SOE agents could choose to take with them to bring capture and torture to a swift end if they felt they could no longer hold out.

If contrary to the entry in his personal file, Denis was indeed a Roman Catholic, as he implies in a passing comment in his memoirs, de Guelis might have reassured him as he had others that the Catholic hierarchy in England had issued a special dispensation permitting captured agents to commit suicide without it being regarded as a mortal sin.[79] Though modern Church doctrine does concede that the responsibility and gravity of suicide can be diminished in cases, for example, of suffering or torture, the notion of a special dispensation for SOE seems a little far-fetched.

Denis may well have felt what he really needed more than a suicide pill was a stiff drink. Almost as a parting aside de Guelis told him the last lap of his exodus would involve paddling himself ashore in a rubber dinghy, a novel and frightening prospect for a man who had never even rowed a boat. With nice understatement he recalls

[76] Liddell p. 204

[77] Jacques de V. Guelis, MBE, MC 1907-1945 remembered as a man of 'great charm, intelligence and courage'. Died after a car crash in Germany while reconnoitering intelligence targets toward the end of the Second World War

[78] And almost so in London. The coffee may well have come from Spain or Portugal

[79] Cowburn, p. 117

finding the idea 'very disconcerting' but it was too late to throw a tantrum.

Whether by some breeze of serendipity wafting along the corridors of Baker Street, or, less likely, as a result of thoughtful planning, Denis was going back to a beach he knew, at Juan les Pins, between Antibes and Cannes.

But instead of travelling in pre-war comfort on *Le Train Bleu* from the Gare de Lyon in Paris, he was a passenger on one of the most audacious and complex transport systems of the secret world, the Gibraltar flotilla. Its history has been fully told elsewhere,[80] but at the time the 'need to know' principle combined with Denis's innocent lack of curiosity about the wider aspects of the rum world in which he found himself, meant that he had no idea of its scale and real purpose. Its mission began as an urgent attempt to extract from France and North Africa the many thousands of Polish soldiers trapped or taken prisoner after the French collapse. Under the charismatic leadership of a Polish naval officer, Marian Kadulski, who like almost everyone else in this story used at least one other surname (in his case Krajewski), became part of a wider initiative. It involved submarines, two trawlers and several of the open-decked fishing smacks known as feluccas, which criss-crossed the Mediterranean between Gibraltar, the Riviera and the North African coast, changing paintwork and flags en route. It served not just the Polish government in exile, but also SOE, the prisoners of war escape organisation MI9, and SIS.[81]

Richards' tally[82] shows that between September 1940 and February 1943 no less than eighty-seven missions were undertaken from Gibraltar to the southern coasts of France and Spain, and to Tunisia. There were also many later operations from Corsica into Italy, and other adventures in the Adriatic. The Polish contribution to the Resistance and the critical role of Polish-led networks in

---

[80] *See Brooks Richards in Bibliography*

[81] A *smaller and separate enterprise, the 'Gibraltar Fishing Fleet' earned foreign currency for Whitehall's war chest by smuggling tobacco and other luxuries into Spain where they were sold for pesetas. Mackenzie, p. 236*

[82] P. *360 et seq.*

supplying SIS with a flow of vital military, naval and political intelligence, is another under-explored aspect of the Second World War. A history of the F2 network, long guarded by SIS but now in the National Archive makes the point that Poland, more so than most European nations, had a folk memory of 150 years of clandestine action against three occupying powers. Most of the younger groups of the Polish office corps had, in their college days, been involved in underground operations. Thus resisting the Nazis in France was second nature to those Poles who had been employed in French mines and factories or who had retreated there after their own country's collapse under the Blitzkrieg.

It is generally accepted that the first SOE officer parachuted in to France was Georges Bégué, on the night of 5/6 May 1941. By contrast the first Polish intelligence agent, Thadée Jekiel, codenamed Doktor, was dropped in as early as 6 September 1940. Over time F2 grew to some 2800 agents, many of them French. Their reports on U-boat, battleship and troop movements, industrial output, and on Vichy politics, sent back by radio and for a time on microfilm via the US Naval Attaché at Vichy, were copious and highly valued in London. Their history claims for instance that no German U-Boat left a French submarine pen without its departure being signalled to London. It is little wonder that SIS grew nervous at the possible reverberations of SOE's operations on German alertness.[83]

The voyage from Gibraltar to the Riviera and back was about 1600 miles. But these were not smooth and pleasurable round trips, with the passengers basking in deck chairs in the sun. Like the Aegean, always portrayed in tourist brochures as a stretch of calm azure water, but in reality prone to vicious squalls and storms, the Mediterranean can be unforgiving. The flotilla had to contend not just with spells of foul weather but also with diversions to avoid prying Spanish or German aircraft, and Vichy patrol boats. The open-decked feluccas made their own way, manned by a six or seven man Polish crew, while the agents and evaders covered most of the distance in the relative comfort of the trawlers and the submarine, sometimes as in

---

[83] *See 'Edwin', Bibliography*

Denis's case in sequence. The larger vessels then waited offshore over the horizon while the feluccas, commanded by Krajewski or his sidekick Buchowski did the 'heavy lifting'. They ran inshore by night under the noses of the Vichy gendarmes to land agents and pick up their wet and weary compatriots and ferry them back to the 'mother ship'. Even non-mariners can appreciate the seamanship of the Polish felucca captains, who navigated by the stars, and used memory and coastal landmarks to find quiet beaches or negotiate tiny creeks and river mouths. Out at sea they had to keep their tiny boat balanced on the waves alongside the trawler or submarine while the passengers scrambled aboard; an unexpected swell could splinter the wooden felucca against the larger vessel's steel hull.

Richards[84] gives us the text of Krajewski's detailed log for what he knew as Operation MIMOSA, and we can compare it with Denis's own memories. Understandably Denis and other agents saw the operations as centred on getting them 'in country', as today's spy jargon has it. It would be an overstatement to say that for the Poles who were risking their lives, putting British secret 'assets' ashore was a secondary consideration. But they must have felt these were Polish operations just as much as they were British, and that there was real psychological and patriotic importance in pulling their fellow countrymen out of enemy reach to fight again; they also exfiltrated F2 network couriers. The operation in which Denis was put ashore was just one element in a chain of voyages that had begun in the 'no-moon period' of April 1942 and had involved landing and lifting agents, Poles and politicians in and out of Port-Vau, Antibes and Miramar de Esterel.

When Denis's turn came in May, Krajewski was already en route out of Gibraltar in his Moroccan-built felucca *Seawolf,* steering by a wooden tiller. A single triangular sail and a small engine powered it. Krajewski coped with a malfunctioning compass whose bearings had to be validated by the stars. In his own account Denis does not mention names, whether of men or vessels, but referring back to the actual log,[85] we know that the first leg of his own voyage was on

---

[84] *Richards p. 116*
[85] *Richards p. 112 et seq*

the *Tarana*, a 200 ton diesel-engined trawler, built in Holland in 1932. In his book Denis springs another of his surprises, telling us when he climbed aboard he found he knew its captain as 'an ex-chorus boy from *Mercenary Mary*', and that they had 'terrific drinks all round . . . refreshing all kinds of very ancient memories'.

We know from the records that the *Tarana* was under the command of Lt E.B. Clarke, who was from the Navy's Volunteer Reserve, rather than a career officer. We know nothing of his life before the war but the Poles remembered him as 'a very pleasant and cheery fellow' and 'jolly', suggesting a personality at least ebullient, and quite plausibly theatrical. Clarke warned Denis on the first night out not to worry if he heard noises on deck. When Denis ventured up the next morning he found that the *Tarana* had been transformed. For the benefit of watching Spanish and German eyes it had left Gibraltar flying a British 'White Ensign', its hull black and its topsides a metallic grey. Now a green and red striped Portuguese flag snapped in the morning breeze, and the hull had become as brown as Mrs Assernacher's chocolate cake: swathes of artfully draped fishing nets concealed machine guns and lifeboats.

We know from Richards [p. 150] that Clarke and his British and Polish crew held the flotilla record (six hours) for this 'rebranding' which had to be done at the start of each trip and reversed on the run home. Both Clarke and Denis must have felt they had come a long way from the high-spirited hoofing of the *Mercenary Mary* chorus though high speed set changes between scenes were something they had both seen many times in that earlier, distant life. If either of them had donned striped trousers, a pom-pommed hat and a blue blouse to hoof it in a Gilbert & Sullivan chorus, they might have recalled the hearty refrain of the crew of HMS *Pinafore*:

> *'We sail the ocean blue,*
> *And our saucy ship's a beauty.*
> *We are sober men and true,*
> *And attentive to our duty'*

Denis, attentive but horribly seasick, remembers Clarke asking him how he had come to get involved in the 'ridiculous nonsense' of SOE.

'Well, you know . . . it's all rather like a musical comedy. That's why I thought it would be rather fun.'

'Hang on to that, old boy', Clarke advised 'I wouldn't be at all surprised if there were moments when you'll need all your sense of humour.'

The first moment was close at hand. After three days the *Tarana* hove too. Alongside was a submarine. Out of its conning tower and onto the *Tarana*, like a scene from the Sarassani Circus's First World War spectacular *Torpedo Los* played out as a mid-ocean reality show there clambered, one after the other, thirty-one unshaven, hungry Polish escapers. Then it was Denis's turn to make the reverse journey, scrambling inelegantly down the rope ladder to the submarine's slippery hull (reminding us of the Snakes and Ladders analogy we have used from time to time to illustrate his career), the hatch closing to seal him into its oily, claustrophobic embrace. The embrace that was less than welcoming since its Polish captain turned out to be a lugubrious depressive, who wondered aloud for the next thirty-six hours why he and his crew were risking their lives and the lives of their families, by playing a part in these clandestine operations. The depression was infectious. Denis sank into a state of gloom. He was supported only by his memories of a typically theatrical exchange with E.B. Clarke on the *Tarana* about the inevitable ups and downs of clandestine adventures: 'Oh, well, it must be alright in the third act, otherwise nobody would pay to come to see it.'

Then it was time for another precarious scramble down the rail on the submarine's hull, onto the open deck of *Seawolf*. She was now flying the French flag, and was under the care of Krajewski. He was far more cheerful than his submarine counterpart despite a tough trip out from Gibraltar, when his crew were throwing up, and his compass sent him badly off course. Denis spent thirty-six hours pitching and tossing towards the coast on the felucca's open deck, chewing uncooked bacon and rough bread, the toilet a precariously balanced bucket. Krajewski concedes in the log that it was hard to spot the agreed landing area in the darkness. Their runs into the shore were made more hazardous by the risk that *Seawolf* would be silhouetted against the bright lights of a battery of acetylene flares slung between a line of French fishing boats to lure their catch. (For those who believe that life imitates art, that 1942 image had been foreshadowed by Pablo Picasso in 1939, in a figurative and in the view of some critics, foreboding, style in his 'Night Fishing at Antibes', now in the Museum of Modern Art, New York.)

It is an interesting insight into Denis's strength of character that on the final run-in on 14 May 1942, the 41-year-old ex-chorus boy prevailed over the tough as nails Pole in a sharp argument about which beach was which. Krajewski initially claimed that it did not matter; he might as well land Denis at Cannes since it was not that far away from Juan Les Pins anyway.

One of the landmarks he was using as a cross bearing was the lighthouse at la Garoupe, above Lady Aberconway's splendid château. This was a trick of the mariner's trade that he may or may not have bothered to share with Denis, a mere landlubber. Denis persisted and the two men eventually parted on good terms. Denis's heart must have almost stopped as he half-rolled, half-fell off the felucca into a tiny rubber dinghy already loaded down with his suitcase, and his heavy wireless set. He had also been given a fishing rod to explain away, if challenged, what he was doing out on the sea close to midnight.

SOE did not seem to have envisaged that a man in a rubber dinghy carrying a full change of clothes, a black leather coat, a British wireless set obviously not made for listening to chamber music, a poison pill, a Commando knife and a large amount of cash might seem even to the most witless gendarme to have been after bigger fish than the local anchovies. Fortunately gendarmes were few on the ground. Short of money, its army restricted by the Armistice terms, short of police and short of fuel for boat patrols, Vichy did a far less efficient job than the Germans to the north in guarding the long and as yet undeveloped Mediterranean coastline. At that time it was still underdeveloped. Its woods, marshes and cliffs were punctuated by tiny bays, and the deep Provençal inlets were known as *calanques*. Even the resort beaches, though still busy by day, were only cursorily patrolled at night.

Men and women going into danger have often delivered themselves of rallying cries, some of them clichés, some memorable. As Denis paddled towards a beach that seemed never to come any closer, his remembered self-encouragement was in a class of its own: 'Pull yourself together, duckie. You'd never live with yourself again if you gave up now . . .'

He made it. Wet, terrified, and confused, as de Guelis, his Gibraltar briefing officer had given him the wrong contact address. But he made it.[86]

Before we follow Denis into Vichy France, there is another loose end – not the first and not the last. Telling this part of the story in his autobiography, Denis is consistent in his use of 'I', in other words it was his adventure, he was on his own. But Professor Foot[87] records that another agent landed from the same felucca; Krajewski's log[88] speaks of 'putting the agents ashore in the dinghy' and Richards's summary of the Polish missions[89] actually names the second agent as Charles Hayes. It is clear from Denis's post-mission debriefing by SOE that he and Hayes landed together. A typically laconic entry in Maurice Buckmaster's private diary seems to refer to a pre-mission meeting with Denis and 'Charles'.[90]

What can we make of this? Is it possible that though he and Hayes were on the same felucca, they went ashore in two separate forays, to meet up later? Given the loads they were carrying that would have

---

[86] *The same day the London press reported the arrival in Paris of a far more sinister visitor, whose presence in a way underscored why Denis and the men and women of SOE were risking their lives. Himmler's SS Deputy Reinhard Heydrich made a quick trip to the French capital to confer with Wehrmacht and Gestapo chiefs, and a group of fawning Vichy civil servants, among them, tellingly, Darquier de Pellepoix, Pétain's Commissioner for Jewish Affairs, to step up the response to the Resistance and to make sure the Vichy police were ready to play their key role in the roundup and deportation of Jews. For once Nemesis was agreeably swift. On 27 May Heydrich was ambushed in Prague by SOE-backed Czech resistance fighters and soon died of his injuries. The Germans took terrible revenge*

[87] *p. 197*

[88] *Richards p. 116*

[89] *ibid, p. 365*

[90] *V.C. Hayes MBE. On a later mission into France he was betrayed to the Gestapo. Captured, badly wounded, after a savage gun battle, he was executed in the Gross Rosen concentration camp. Foot, p. 280*

been the most prudent tactic, and seems the most plausible explanation. Beyond that we have to wonder whether Denis, who by the 1960s was not a well man, was so self-centred, so confused, that he just forgot? Was he even after so many years remembering some SOE discipline drummed into him so long ago that you should give away nothing more than you need to. The point is not central to our narrative nor on balance does it call Denis's overall veracity into question. We remind ourselves, 'old men forget'.

9

La Zone Nono

We have no idea whether Denis ever played Shakespearean roles; if he had, he might have recalled the opening scene of *The Tempest*. He had landed, wet and frightened, on a foreign shore where he would encounter mystery, a complex plot and the Vichy and German police as a monstrous collective Caliban.

France in the Second World War was rather larger than Prospero's island of magic. But it is a world which Anglo-Saxon commentators even at this distance in time need to address with circumspection. Even the headline terms, 'Armistice', 'Occupation', 'Resistance', 'Collaboration', 'Liberation' are freighted with uncountable shades of meaning, depending on whether the speaker or writer is English, French, Polish or Spanish – or indeed German. It is remarkable that more than sixty years since the end of the Second World War a French TV programme about the late President Mitterrand's ambiguous involvement with the Vichy administration provoked a sharp press exchange on the meaning of 'Resistance' and 'Collaboration', including an analysis of which of two authoritative French dictionaries, the *Petit Robert* and the *Petit Larousse,* offered the better definitions.[91]

The British mainland was not occupied, so there are no behaviour benchmarks; only the Channel Islands came under German rule, and there the harsh realities and human dilemmas of domination and survival were painfully felt. As the historian A.J.P. Taylor commented in the 1960s, 'It was perhaps fortunate that British patriotism was not put to the supreme test.'[92]

Had the Germans occupied Great Britain, *le Chagrin* could as

[91] *Le Monde, Langue Sauce Piquante, 29 April 2008*
[92] *Taylor, p. 493*

readily have been filmed in Coventry as Clermont Ferrand, and would have highlighted the same conflicts and contradictions. These headline subjects have been, continue to be, and will go on being extensively researched and disputed. Denis was not a scholar, so we need only sketch the broad picture he would have been given in his London briefing, what he might have read in the newspapers and what he saw and felt on the ground, leaving judgments to history. The Armistice, seen in much of the world outside France as a capitulation, left France split into two principal zones (with other subdivisions, and with Alsace Lorraine simply subsumed into Germany). The main Demarcation Line ran across the heart of the country like a clumsy surgery scar, from the Basque country behind Biarritz south of Bordeaux up to Vierzon, south-east to Moulins, north to Chalon sur Saône, east to Dole and south to Geneva. This essentially put northern France and the Atlantic coast, 24 million people, the bulk of French industry and its most fruitful farming country, under German control.

South of the line, the Unoccupied Zone (colloquially known as *La Zone Nono,* or *Non-Occupée),* was mostly rural, poor and sparsely populated outside the major industrial cities such as Clermont Ferrand and Lyons. Its 16 million people, including those on the Riviera, were coming to terms with the reality of life under the collaborationist, authoritarian and anti-Semitic Pétain adminis- tration. After brief stops in Bordeaux and Clermont Ferrand, Pétain and his motley crew of colleagues had come to rest in the spa town of Vichy, whose name would come to serve as shorthand for them and their times. It suited the Germans since it was far enough from Paris to ensure that the centre of real power would not be bothered too much by the politicians. It suited the politicians because Vichy's many Beaux Arts hotels, though chilly out of season, could accommodate the Ministers, the bureaucrats and their families and hangers-on. It was also close to Chateldon, the country estate of Pétain's self-made First Minister Pierre Laval, whose 'pork barrel' style of politics had seen to it that the town of Vichy had one of the most modern telecommunications hubs in France, with a global reach.

Pétain and his Ministers deluded themselves that Vichy's mineral springs would invigorate a new France, a reborn country based on what they proclaimed as the core French values of '*Travail, Famille, Patrie*' ('Work, family and the motherland'). They were a deluded and dangerous bunch. The cardinal delusion was to think that they had one iota of independence; they were a puppet government and nothing of moment happened without German approval. Hitler, Himmler, Goering and other Nazi satraps each had their own representatives at Vichy. A 'German Police Delegation' not only worked with Vichy on Jewish deportations, but also kept a close eye on Pétain himself, his visitors and his movements, and routinely received copies of his correspondence from a suborned French policeman in his entourage. They were disingenuous, convinced that collaboration actually meant a partnership, and was the only solution both pragmatically and in the longer term interests of France and Europe.

Hitler saw things differently. The French had lost: 'Today France is utterly finished', he exulted after the Armistice. They would no longer be taken seriously as partners and Vichy's role was to administer the country at minimal cost to Germany and supply whatever Berlin demanded by way of resources and manpower. Despite all this, Vichy indulged itself in the further delusion of believing that its role was not just to administer France in the hope that it could soon convert the Armistice into a favourable peace treaty, which would draw a line under the war. Vichy wanted to believe that its key role was to reform the country, to take it back to its roots in the soil and the Church.

In those early days a demoralised nation, which was broken in spirit and geography with more than a million of its husbands, fathers and sons still in German hands, drew much genuine comfort from the venerable Pétain. The hero of Verdun, he was a man who had floated serenely above the mire of Third Republic politics. His ice blue eyes, white walrus moustache and walking stick suggested that he was the father, or more appropriately the grandfather, and saviour of the people to whom he promised 'the gift of my person'. As reality sank in, and the risks inherent in feasting with panthers became ever clearer, the gift brought disillusion rather than deliverance from evil. His patriotic catchwords were soon adapted by cynics to *'Tracas, famine, patrouille'*, or, loosely translated, 'Hassle, hunger and Huns'.

The tawdry, ramshackle style of the regime, not to mention the Marshal's enviable libido, are neatly caught in a story he told one of his Ministers. Getting out of the lift on the wrong floor of the Hotel du Parc which served as his headquarters as well as his temporary home, he opened the first door he saw. He found himself in a bathroom where a pretty young secretary was tapping away briskly on a heavy typewriter precariously balanced on a rickety folding table. She was perched on the porcelain bidet, a scene which would have given a little frisson to any F Section agent who remembered the bathroom of the flat at Orchard Court. What was she typing, the Marshal wanted to know. 'The Constitution,' she told him. 'You've got your hands full', he twinkled back, a phrase she seems to have misheard, as she blushed and told him 'these pleated dresses are deceptive, I've actually lost quite a bit of weight since the Armistice'.

Recounting the story later, Pétain said he thought she was 'rather cute' and he decided to stay 'for a bit of fun'. Perhaps seeing all too clearly where this might end, she told him that if he went on flirting, he would get her into trouble with his wife. 'What a thought', I told her. "Her jealous? At her age?"[93]

Architecturally, climatically, gastronomically, and superficially, Juan les Pins was the same as when Denis had left in 1939; a fashionable casino, pine trees shading the beach, cafés and restaurants to whose owners and wealthier patrons 'rationing' and 'shortage' were from some foreign language, words that other people worried about. Psychologically, it was another world. Behind the sunny façade, and away from the greed and glitter of the promenades, it was a world of hunger and fear. To the cool eyes of the *New Yorker's* Janet Flanner's writing a few months later the Riviera was 'a large uniform plain of deterioration, in which no-one is starving, everyone is hungry and food is an obsession'. Perfumery,

[93] *J Benoist Méchin, cited by Buisson p. 121. The story of Pétain's controversial marriage to the divorcée Eugenie Hardon is a saga in itself. See e.g. Williams, Bibliography*

that staple south of France industry, had shut down. Fields that before the war had been an Impressionist patchwork blaze of scented colour, with bees buzzing indolently through the lavender, jasmine, mimosa, roses, and narcissi. Now they were now largely given over to desperately needed vegetables, and the vats and distillation plants found a new role in the manufacture of medicines.

Behind the blackout curtains of the Monte Carlo Casino, Flanner saw French black marketeers and holiday-ing Germans accompanied by 'an occasional [Vichy] collaborator let out for a run' playing roulette for 'thumping' stakes. But in the villages just a few kilometres away up in the hills the birth rate had suddenly dwindled, and those growing up were malnourished and riddled with rickets; even a mild infection could prove fatal. Most cats had been eaten, and dog food was as likely as not to have been confected from the cadavers of less fortunate animals.[94] The historian H.R. Kedward[95] has pointed out that while the south of the country had wine and fruit in abundance (because most of France's basic foods came from farms in the Occupied Zone) working men in Marseilles and Nice came closer to 'desperate hunger' than most communities in urban France.

Fear gnawed at the gut as sharply as hunger. The Unoccupied Zone had absorbed a sizeable number of Jews, many French, even more of other nationalities. It was a refuge, but not a safe haven, the last corner of a wheat field in which terrified rabbits huddle as the combine harvester bears down. German anti-Semitism was a cancer bred in the bone, and when the Nazis gave it free rein it took only a few years to turn from discrimination to murder. Some who have tried to understand Vichy have claimed that its own hostility and prejudice were intended to drive Jews out of French life, not to exterminate them, a distinction without much of a difference to those who were its targets.

But Vichy initiatives to seize Jewish businesses, and to throw Jews out of work by limiting their ability to work in the Civil Service or the professions, and to restrict Jewish children's access to education, were launched spontaneously, and without German pressure.

[94] *The* New Yorker, *9 November 1942*
[95] *Kedward, p. 7*

Indeed its very first Statute on Jews adopted a harsher definition than the Germans themselves of what elements of parentage constituted a Jew. Parisian Jews were restricted in where and when they could shop, and were banned from all but the last carriage of the Metro. It was to the French police, not the Germans, that Jews reported in trepidation to have their Indentity Cards stamped 'Juif'. The central role of Vichy officials and police in the round up and deportation of Paris Jews to die in the gas chambers is perhaps the foulest stain on a record of disgrace.

It is true that the Catholic hierarchy eventually raised its voice against the deportations, and that many individual Frenchmen and women risked their lives to help and shelter Jews in those dark times. And in a tiny but deeply moving gesture, a Paris priest is said to have pinned a yellow Star of David on the Christ Child in his Christmas crib. Nevertheless the judgment of Robert Paxton, the first major chronicler of the Pétain regime, that Vichy's measures against the Jews 'were of great help to the Germans when the more bestial programme of the Final Solution began' may be something of an understatement.

It did not take much imagination for those trying to put a brave face on things in *la Nono* to conclude that it was only a matter of time before German boots would be crunching on the Riviera pavements. The 120,000 to 130,000 Jews in the Unoccupied Zone (especially those who were not French or had only recently acquired citizenship) were already in terror of the knock on the door, the truck, and the train to an uncertain fate. Those with money scrambled for visas and exit routes to a world not that keen to take them in. Those without sat and shivered in the sun, 'doomed to live in perpetual fear' in the words of the *Times*.

Apprehension, much compounded by rumour, was not confined to the Jewish community. Anyone who wanted to retaliate (namely communists, trades unionists, displaced Polish soldiers, the handful of Gaullists) knew from German ferocity in the north just how terrible their vengeance was. Every act of assassination or sabotage was repaid in blood many times over by the execution of batch after batch of Frenchmen, many randomly selected, some fingered with the connivance of Vichy. Just a few days before Denis landed, the Germans had shot out of hand five 'Communists and Jews' after an attack on a Wehrmacht soldier in the Paris Metro, and warned that 'if the assailant is not discovered within eight days fifteen other Communists and Jews . . . will be shot. In addition 500 Communists and Jews will be sent to labour camps in the east.'

Vichy followed along, fighting its version of the war on 'terror' with special courts, no-nonsense judges, and even a tribunal that could order summary execution of 'terrorists' and those who helped them. Even so, in Lyons a few days after Denis landed, a crowd of 'students and workmen with a strong middle class element' surrounded the Salle Rameau concert hall to discourage anyone wanting to buy tickets for a concert by the Berlin Philharmonic. The performance should have begun at 8 p.m. but despite intervention by the police and many arrests could not get under way until 10.30 p.m.; the orchestra played just one piece and 'then silently dispersed'.

As the summer passed, British news reports gave further grim glimpses of French reality. In August the *Times* reported that Vichy had rounded up 4,600 stateless Jews who had been 'surrendered to the Gestapo for deportation' as well as interning some 20,000 Jews, mainly foreigners, in its own concentration camps. Vichy's racist actions were just a small-scale reflection of the roundups of stateless Jews in the Occupied Zone, 'pending early deportation'. This move was ordered by the Germans but carried out by the French police; the deportees were crammed into French cattle cars and clattered away in the night in filth and fear to the concentration camps. The German controlled newspaper *le Petit Parisien* declared that 'This measure is the first step towards the elimination of all French and foreign Jews from the French national community.' In September the Vichy police even snatched ten monks from the island community of Sainte Marguerite, the largest of the Lérins islands about half a mile off the Riviera, near Cannes[96] and charged them with 'Gaullist activities'.

But though attitudes were changing rapidly as German brutality,

---

[96] *Also the site of fortress prison, whose most famous tenant was 'The Man in the Iron Mask'*

racialism and the effects of its economic pillaging of France became daily more evident, even as 1942 unfolded, London could not take for granted that every Frenchman would welcome British agents with open arms, or declare themselves for de Gaulle. Even among actual and prospective members of the Resistance there were shades of difference and dividing lines that were far from clear even to their fellow countrymen, let alone to SOE agents, for whom French political, class and religious nuances had not been a theme in their training.

Some in the valley of ambiguity simply and understandably lived in terror of the pervasive power of an authoritarian state and its German puppet-masters. Though in a minor concession to French sensibility, the Armistice stipulated that there would be no uniformed German presence in *la Nono*, some of the anonymous 'officials' attached to the Armistice Commission and its economic teams were clearly men from the Gestapo, and the hotels and villas in Vichy itself were crawling with senior German police and intelligence officers.

Few heard de Gaulle's first bravura broadcast from London. Among those who did or who learned about it at second hand, the reaction was coloured by the myths and realities, which still seared the French collective memory. This was encapsulated in the cynical cliché that the British were always ready to fight to the last Frenchman. After all, Britain had abandoned French troops at Dunkirk, and British warships had sunk the French fleet at Mers el Kebir, in July 1940, when 1300 Frenchmen died.

On 25 September 1940 French aircraft bombed British installations at Gibraltar in retaliation.[97] Food shortages across France had been made worse by the British blockade of the Atlantic and Channel ports. Some believed Vichy's line that the war had been a product of 'Jewish capitalism'. De Gaulle's London power centre did not appeal across the board as the answer for France's future; and there were rival contenders to represent the true voice of France. Once unshackled from the conflict of loyalties inherent in the brief

[97] *Paxton p. 71*

Nazi-Soviet alliance, French Communists looked to Moscow not London, for a post-war power model.

In the French heartland, the Protestant minority, with folk memories of persecution and massacre, were perhaps quicker to understand what was happening than some rural communities whose village priests echoed the Roman Catholic hierarchy's initial support for the new 'French State'. And at the end of the day most French people were more preoccupied with survival than with resistance, with or without a capital R. One recent commentator[98] suggests that the tide did not turn until the autumn of 1943, when the dream of a German defeat began to take shape as a real possibility, and when Vichy's policies and behaviour had stripped away the last vestiges of its credibility.

When Denis first landed in France, SOE's main objectives in the Occupied Zone were to disrupt the ability of French industry and infrastructure to support the German economy and war machine. As time passed the targets were to become more military; in Bourne-Paterson's words: 'the railway line, the telephone cable and the canal . . . replaced the factory'.[99] In Vichy France, Baker Street's mandate was fuzzier, dictated by political considerations. There could be explosions if they were not too loud and could not be traced back; factories might catch fire as long as no British hand was seen holding the matches.

The contradictions and improbabilities facing SOE agents in this unhappy, wounded country are neatly caught by Denis's first contact in France, the gynaecologist Dr Levy, his wife, who bred Siamese cats, and their three pretty daughters. Dr Levy, originally 'talent-spotted' by the dashing de Guelis, took considerable personal risks as in effect an SOE 'reception committee', though the exchange of passwords devised for him and Denis seems rather out of place for a Riviera doctor's surgery.

'I wonder if you can tell me where I can get some good oysters?'

---

[98] *Dictionnaire, p. 799*

[99] *See Note on Sources and Bourne-Paterson's Report in Bibliography. Professor Foot's History and Maurice Buckmaster spell the Lt Colonel's name with one 't'. Mackenzie and Denis use two. Following Professor Foot is never a bad course*

'No, but I know where you can find excellent shrimp.'

It smacks more of SOE as refracted through the British TV comedy series *'Allo 'Allo.* He claimed to have Communist sympathies, which Denis and other SOE callers found sat oddly with the excellent black-market food to which they were treated. But he also[100] had the knack of appearing to support three or four mutually antagonistic political groups at the same time, and if a scathing comment of Bourne-Paterson's is correct, 'developed an inordinate greed for money'. Dr Levy was also in contact with one of his close neighbours, André Girard who ran the CARTE circuit, underscoring again the flabby security consciousness which prevailed in the south, no doubt because while the Gestapo hovered in the shadows, they were not omnipresent as they were in the Occupied Zone.[101]

SOE's main adversaries in the *Nono* were the Vichy gendarmerie and its counter-intelligence services. The CARTE circuit which Denis, luckily, had little to do with, was a 'delusion . . . and a snare' for SOE. This was not unlike the spell cast on the intelligence community in Washington in more recent times by a bevy of well-tailored and persuasive Iraqi exiles. Girard's pitch to SOE was that his circuit reached into the highest echelons of the Vichy military, and that if only it was nourished with money and weapons, it would rapidly multiply like a powerful bacterium from clusters of sabotage cells into guerilla groups and eventually a sizeable 'secret army'.

SOE, as it was bound to do, took the approach seriously. It is far from clear whether Girard really had this sort of reach but before it could be tested he was undone by his mania for record keeping. This led him to create a card index of actual and potential members, listing their personal information in meticulous detail. In November 1942 a courier carrying 200 of the cards to Paris fell asleep on the

[100] *P. 204*

[101] *We shall generally follow precedent by using the generic term 'Gestapo' though until late in the war SOE's main adversaries were the German Army's Abwehr, or counterintelligence organisation, and its bitter rival, Heinrich Himmler's SD or Sicherheitsdienst, which eventually absorbed its competitor. There were indeed Gestapo units in the main urban centres, and to those who fell into German hands, the distinctions were not obvious; indeed in Paris the task of physical torture was often subcontracted to collaborating French criminals. It was the criminals who perfected the interrogation technique known as la bagnoire, or immersion in icy water to the point of drowning, that others have so enthusiastically adapted for modern times*

train, his briefcase was deftly filched by an Abwehr agent and as Professor Foot records 'Carte's downfall was thereafter only a matter of time'.[102]

Denis was using a forged identity card purportedly issued in February 1942 in the name of 'Denis Joseph Rocher' (the transition from 'Rake' to 'Rock' and then to 'Rocher' as the French equivalent, must have made it easier to remember). Though he later remembered that it showed his profession as '*artiste de music hall*', the original describes him rather more mundanely as '*Acteur*',[103] and born in Paris in 1897. Since there is no evidence that he had ever been to the seat of the Pétain government, giving his address as '65 boulevard Gambetta, Vichy' (then an apartment building close to the main railway station) seems an unnecessary hostage to fortune. The handwriting on the card is very similar to Denis's own, rather than that of a town hall clerk, though that may simply reflect how those cards were prepared. It is mildly curious that he has signed the card beneath his photograph as 'Denis J. Rocher.' In at least one contemporary French view,[104] a Frenchman would have signed either with all three names, or as 'Denis Rocher'.

Luckily for Denis, neither the odd identity card, nor the insecurity and collapse of the CARTE circuit caused him any problems, but it would not be long before another agent's carelessness would put him under threat.

The Riviera was a transit station, and sleeping in a secret hideout in Dr Levy's wine cellar, and briefly in a camouflaged coal hole in a nearby villa soon palled. What modern writers of spy fiction call 'Tradecraft', and the Russian secret services '*konspiratsiya*', was either not taught too intensively at the SOE schools, or the lessons were soon forgotten under the beguiling Mediterranean sun. Denis decided to look up an old acquaintance, M. Miracca, the urbane manager of the Palm Beach Hotel and Casino on Pointe Croisette in Cannes, whom he says he had known before the war when Miracca was Head Waiter at London's Café Royal on Regent Street. The

---

[102] *p. 205*
[103] A *copy of which was kindly provided by the collector Ian Sayer*
[104] *Institute Francaise London, 2007*

Café was then a fashionable rendezvous not just for 'see and be seen' society evenings in the gilded *fin de siécle* main restaurant but also for regimental and institutional dinners in its red plush and gilt private rooms.

In July 1937 these included a gathering of 400 aproned Masons of the Provincial Grand Mark Lodge of Middlesex. Among them, like one of those minor characters who appear and reappear briefly in Anthony Powell's *A Dance to the Music of Time* sequence, was 'Mr Burnett-Brown'.

Denis mentions that Miracca had also worked at the Grosvenor House. He may have been politely skirting over, or may not have been aware of the less respectable events in the West End in 1926 and 1927. These led to a Detective Sergeant Goddard going to jail for taking payoffs from the proprietors of night clubs and 'disorderly houses' in exchange for turning a Nelsonian eye to breaches of the law, and tipping them off about imminent raids. One of those tipped off, according to press reports, was a 'Mr Miracca', part owner with one Ribuffi of a club called 'Uncles'. By the time the case came to trial, Miracca had gone to France and was unavailable as a witness.

In Cannes, fifteen years later Miracca offered to give Denis a room 'no questions asked', which strongly implies that Denis had at least hinted at the real reason he was in France. The Palm Beach was much in vogue for German officers in civilian clothes on triumphant and lustful leave from the north, flaunting their 'horizontal collaborator' girlfriends. It was perhaps a less than ideal base from which to operate a clandestine wireless set with its aerial slung out in the open along the roof, though others might argue it was perfect cover. (The Casino's *Directeur des Jeux*, René Casale was also an active SOE helper, though there is no indication that Miracca knew this.)

But Denis's destination was Lyons. In another demonstration of apparent obliviousness to security, at the end of May 1942 he and Hayes were waved off at Nice station by the Levys and their daughters, even though Levy claimed to be under close surveillance by the Vichy police.

10

Lyons and Tygers

After Denis and Hayes stepped apprehensively off the train at Lyons' Gare de Perrache, Hayes vanishes from our record, though not that of SOE[105]. Denis however was heading for challenges, which would make his sea journey and the night landing seem tame stuff. He had arrived in what was then France's second largest city, 300 miles south-west of Paris, where the rivers Rhone and Saône flow powerfully together.

Denis would have known from his pre-war years about Lyons' Roman origins, its reputation for fine food and its key role in the silk trade. He may have been briefed in very general terms by Jacques de Guelis on its importance as a hive of SOE activity, a focal point of the escape lines for downed RAF pilots and a focal point for Resistance groups of every stripe – Communists, Gaullists, Free Masons and Catholics.

The wartime overcrowding, the unchecked subletting of apartments and rooms, and the warren of interlinked passageways in the older part of the city made police surveillance a hard task. It was difficult to find people and even harder to trail them. Lyons had become a centre of clandestine newspaper publishing, much helped by an influx of radical journalists who had gravitated there from the Occupied Zone. *Combat, Le Franc Tireur* and *Liberation (Sud)* rolled off presses hidden in the ancient rabbit-warren of the Croix Rousse. The dangerous tasks of getting paper and ink, running the presses and especially distributing the material, without getting caught, were for many their first steps towards a deeper involvement with the Resistance.

---

[105] See above, p. 97

But as he walked across the bustling platform and up the steps Denis certainly knew that the tall, elegant woman standing at the top, holding a copy of the *Journal de Genève* as the prearranged recognition signal, was the SOE's Virginia Hall. She was the American-born 'housemother' to anxious secret agents and escapers, orchestrator of plots and plans, fixer of false papers, pay mistress, briber of Vichy police, and a virtual FedEx hub for the movement of wireless sets. All in all she was the centre of gravity of that entire clandestine world, much as all those years before, the tiny universe of Denis and the child acrobats at the Sarrasani Circus had revolved around Mrs Jarrett. Her life has been well chronicled by Judith L. Pearson.[106]

To fit her into Denis's story we need only sketch out here the highlights of her road through life, from a comfortable country house in Maryland, on the US Eastern seaboard, to Lyons. Educated in Europe, she had interesting years abroad in the US Foreign Service before hitting what today would be called a 'glass ceiling' which blocked further promotion. As Denis was scrambling out of Nantes when the Phoney War suddenly turned real, she was carrying wounded soldiers in a blood-splattered makeshift ambulance for a French medical service. She reached England, where her languages and her character, and her determination to play a part in the war even though her country was still neutral, were soon picked up on the SOE radar.

In early 1941 she was on her way to 'the Mad House' at Wanborough. She had two major assets over and above strength of character. One of course was her fluent French. But certainly more important for SOE was that as an American, if appropriate cover could be arranged, she could legitimately work on Vichy territory. As part of a complex interplay of foreign policy issues outside the scope of our story, even though the US was at war with Germany, Washington and Vichy were (for the moment) in a state of 'neutrality' and still had diplomatic ties. Through a family friend she was soon accredited as a correspondent for the *New York Post*, and the way was clear for her to travel openly to Lyons via Portugal and Spain.

---

[106] *See bibliography*

Set against these assets, Virginia Hall had one handicap, which others would have thought a major impediment to normal living let alone an energetic clandestine life, but which she had schooled herself to see as no more than a minor irritant. Below her left knee, her leg was artificial, a carefully sculpted leather-sheathed wooden calf and foot, linked by a precision engineered metal ankle joint. She had lost the lower limb after a shotgun accident in 1933. But the prosthesis, which she nicknamed 'Cuthbert' had not stopped her driving a makeshift ambulance over cobbled French country roads, nor from taking a full part in the tough exercises at Wanborough. Though she was, at least, excused the parachuting course.

Characteristically her first motherly move was to take the skittish Denis to relax in a small café. Here, for the first time in many months, he was able to get a cup of real coffee; by now 'coffee' usually meant a confection of roast barley, malt, lupin seeds and carob nuts. In conversation with him she would have been conscious of security and would have passed on information only on a 'need to know' basis. We do not know what she told him about the mood in Lyons.

We know from the memories of a British artist, Norman Lytton, that German demands had left the area woefully short of food; he saw housewives going to stand in queues at 4 a.m. only to come home hours later with baskets still empty. Bread was a mixture of bran and rye, and families were lucky if they saw a small piece of meat twice a week. But good meals were still to be had for those with money. And as we shall see later when we follow Denis to Paris, there were plenty of them. Some were traders and manufacturers profiting by selling to the German Armistice Commission, avid buyers of anything that could be used by the Nazi war machine. Others turned anything in short supply into stacks of cash via the thriving Black Market.

Some industrialists supported Marshal Pétain not simply because they were doing well out of lucrative government contracts, including trading with the Germans themselves, but because, as Lytton observed, they believed Vichy's authoritarian stance would help control the 'dangerous enthusiasm' of their Communist work-force. Lytton, who had been living peacefully in the city for some years (but who in early 1942 was just getting ready to leave), estimated that at best sixty per cent of the local people favoured the Allies. Of the forty per cent who backed Vichy, half were in his view positively anti-British and the other half simply 'fence-sitters'.

It is doubtful whether Virginia Hall would have given Denis a frank appraisal of the SOE setup in the region. In the words of the official historian,[107] it 'was never tidy and seemed to grow monthly more confused', mainly due to the personalities and turf wars of various circuit organisers. It would have scared him stiff and under the rules of the game, he needed to know only the bare minimum. Not long before Denis arrived a senior F section officer had made a risky visit to Lyons to try to impose order. His mission was followed up by the arrival (just before Denis appeared on the scene) of Victor Hazan, who was the Lancashire born, Casablanca-raised son of a cotton and shipping merchant. Hazan had been sent in with what the official history acknowledges as the 'titanic' task for someone of his age (he was then around 27) and mild-mannered personality, of resolving the organisational chaos by bullying or cajoling the squabbling circuit leaders into seeing sense.

Denis was soon hard at work. One of his first assignments was to back up Edward Zeff, operator for one of the larger circuits, who had arrived a month earlier and was already overloaded. Working his set six hours a day from a small suburban house, his timetable was fraught with the risk of detection, though natural caution and a good system of lookouts had, so far, kept him safe.[108] Denis also had to send and receive for Hazan, whom he knew only as *Gervais*. The latter's original mission was short-lived; he soon found himself shouted down or circumvented by those he sought to corral, much like a mild schoolmaster overwhelmed by an unruly classroom.

But Hazan's own SOE schooling was soon put to far more effective use in creating a pyramid of death and destruction. Over the final months of 1942 and into 1943 he trained almost one hundred Resistance fighters in the weapons and plastic explosive skills he had acquired in Scotland. Each in turn trained others,

---

[107] *P. 211*

[108] *Edward Zeff MBE, betrayed to the Germans on his way out of France. Survived the horrors of a concentration camp*

creating a pyramid of specialists in those black arts. His was a major contribution.[109]

Denis also operated briefly for Maurice Pertschuk, working under the name of *Eugene*, who had arrived in France in April and who at 20 years of age was one of the youngest SOE agents in France, remembered as 'delicate, highly strung, extremely intelligent'.[110] In distant echoes of that Balliol interview and the propaganda guru Dr Beck, Pertschuk was there primarily on behalf of PWE (his mission no doubt focused on the network of clandestine presses). Although he soon found sabotage a more productive approach to influencing public opinion, and was transferred to SOE.

Pertschuk has a part in the next act of Denis's painful odyssey. His background also brings up the point that F Section deployed a number of Jewish agents, women as well as men. They would have had no illusions about the murderous Nazi psychosis and Vichy's anti-Semitic slant, and Baker Street must have been even more aware of what lay at the black heart of the 'New Order' in Europe. They might even have known that in a technique that resembled mediaeval witch-finding, the Gestapo used 'physiognomists' (some of them White Russian casino croupiers steeped in alluvial Pogrom traditions). They hovered behind the police watchers in railway stations and at border checkpoints and claimed to be able to identify Jews by their facial features.

Thus to send in agents whose bloodline alone would add to their vulnerability seems to add an extra dimension of danger to an inherently perilous mission. It was presumably a dimension of risk carefully evaluated and explained to those who were selected and the decision left to them. Many brave men and women took it unflinchingly, not least because of their own incandescent hostility to everything the Nazis stood for. A similar if less painful point might be made about SOE's selection of Denis. A predilection for 'Looking for Love in All the Wrong Places', to borrow the words of the later 'Country & Western' song, did not fit well with a life in

---

[109] *VR Hazan MBE, 1915-2006, made it back to England in 1944 via the Pyrenees and Spain after the collapse of the* SPINDLE *circuit*
[110] *Bourne-Paterson p. 91*

which being careful and unobtrusive was a key to survival. As we shall see Denis's other wireless 'client' was Virginia Hall herself, his first assignment, as Judith Pearson relates, being a message requesting a replacement joint for 'Cuthbert'. The *va et vient* of agents and escapers through her apartment, and her contacts with US diplomats at the Lyons Consulate gave her many opportunities for sending written reports back to London, though both routes and indeed her role as the SOE centre of gravity, challenged orthodox security precepts, to put it at its most charitable. As Ben Cowburn, MC, a redoubtable and successful agent, wrote of the Hall household '. . . everybody brought their troubles to her and our HQ in London sent their troubles in the form of agents who were told to contact her to find [wireless] operators. She was so willing to help that when a needy visitor came she would give her ration cards away, wash clothing and make contacts for him.'[111] In an internal report cited by Bourne-Paterson, Cowburn was more direct, complaining to his SOE debriefers that one only had to sit long enough in her kitchen 'to see every British [circuit] organiser in France'.

For Denis, with one ear cocked for the signals and the other for the rap on the door that meant trouble, risk was everywhere, especially for the wireless operator. A Vichy official recalled being ordered to issue 200 false ID cards to be used in the Unoccupied Zone by undercover German intercept operators hunting clandestine transmissions. Though SOE and Resistance sets were the Germans' primary target, they also hunted for, but apparently failed to find, the sets operated by Reseau F2, which supplied SIS in London via the Polish Service in exile, with a steady stream of high-grade intelligence. Much of it was collated in and sent from Nice, but the 'Team 300' operation was in a class of its own, the other side of the coin. Hidden in a remote château near Uzés, twenty operators intercepted German and Italian military signals traffic, decoded it on 'state of the art' machines (it was Polish code breakers who first cracked the German Enigma machine) and sent 'hundreds' of messages back to London.[112] SIS were also beneficiaries of 'Source

[111] *Cowburn, p. 112*
[112] *Martres, p. 20 and 'Historique'*

Denis Rake as a young actor *(Author's collection)*

Denis Rake as matinée idol *(Author's collection)*

Denis Rake, RNVR
(Author's collection)

Denis Rake,
Lieutenant, RASC
*(Courtesy of
Constantine &
Buckley)*

Emma Luart

Nancy Wake's
forged identity card
*(Courtesy of Russell
Braddon)*

Virginia Hall
(Courtesy of Pearson)

Douglas Byng
(Courtesy of National Portrait Gallery)

The felucca *Seawolf* transferring agents to
SOE's clandestine trawler *Tarana (Source: Brooks Richards, unattributed)*

Maurice Buckmaster,
Head of SOE
French Section
(Author's collection)

Douglas Fairbanks, Jr
(Author's collection)

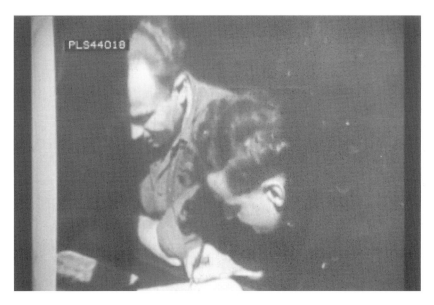

Denis Rake *left* coding one of the last messages of his war
(Courtesy of Russell Braddon)

Alex Schwatschko
(Courtesy of National Archives)

Denis Rake in 1972 *(Courtesy of BBC TV)*

K', a forerunner of the Cold War 'Berlin Tunnel' in which signals specialists of the Vichy Armistice Army tapped telephone lines carrying traffic between the German HQ in Paris and Berlin. It was rolled up by the German SD but not before it had gathered and passed on a valuable intelligence harvest.[113]

A wireless operator was also at risk when on the move. A woman courier could flutter and flirt her way through a police checkpoint, especially if her messages had been committed to memory rather than paper; even then, slips of rice paper pushed deep inside a half-smoked cigarette with a needle more than once provided Gestapo-proof concealment. With good quality identity documents and enough self-confidence, a circuit organiser could usually talk his way through unless the police had his details already. But the wireless operator, hefting his thirty-pound set in a brown suitcase, had little to offer by way of explanation if he had to open it for the police. (Though probably an apocryphal story has it that one flamboyant character in that predicament looked the policeman who had stopped him straight in the eye and declared *'Je suis un officier britannique. Voici mon poste de radio'*, only to be told *'Va t'en donc'*.)[114]

Even without the suitcase as a Mark of Cain, there was always the risk that something in one's papers did not seem quite right to the fish-eyed policeman, of making a simple mistake that betrayed you were not a local, like casually ordering a beer in a bar on a day everyone else knew was officially 'dry'.

Informers and busybodies were everywhere. Police checks in the streets and hotels were random but thorough; as Denis was to find out some rank and file *flics* might be prepared, or financially persuaded to look the other way, but no one could be sure. Lyons smelled more of fear, and sunflower-leaf cigarettes than of good cooking. But it was in the hour to hour operation of the wireless that the real danger lay. Leo Mark's dim view of SOE's wireless and code shortcomings, and its reluctance to face up to them, is essential reading for those who want to understand the details. As a result of Mark's prodding and initiative in London, procedures and security

---

[113] Dictionnaire p. 764
[114] *'I am a British officer. This is my wireless set.' 'Just hop it ...'* Foot p. 103

were improved. But at the time that Denis went into the field, one of the many things he did not know was just how exposed he was.

First he had to find a safe base from which to operate, a house or apartment on a higher floor where seventy-feet of aerial wire hung as a make-believe clothes line would not attract attention. Zeff had managed in one location, but commonsense suggested that switching sites was preferable. But that was just the start. At that time the operators were still tied to fixed schedules for communications with the listeners at Grendon Hall, and used a limited number of frequencies, for each of which a separate crystal had to be plugged into the set. Most of the messages were coded and decoded by the agents themselves, but they sometimes lost their codes, or were in a rush. So, Denis would have to work letter by letter to restructure their text using his personal code. His was diligently memorised lines of a poem by Victor Hugo, an unusual choice for a man with no formal education. Whoever did the coding also had to remember to include one or more prearranged deliberate mistakes known as 'checks', so that the girls at Grendon Hall and the desk officers in London could be sure that the message was genuine and not part of a German 'radio game'.

Professionals will rightly claim that this summary does scant justice to a complex skill set, especially since it all had to be done by the clock, under great strain, and using a code system in which one simple error in transposition, in adding or subtracting, could garble the entire message. It nevertheless encapsulates all the weaknesses in the system. Fixed schedules on a small number of frequencies made it all too easy for the German monitors, whether hidden in the *Nono* or bustling about more visibly in their detector vans in the Occupied Zone to listen out for transmissions.

All too often messages could be garbled by simple coding errors, sheer nerves on the operator's part, poor reception, or confusion over 'checks'. The standard procedure was for Grendon Hall to ask for these messages to be repeated in full, meaning that the operator had to stay on the air far too long, making it easier for hostile ears to locate the clandestine set by 'direction finding'. The Morse signals would be picked up by two fixed stations, or a pair of roaming plain vans, each some way apart; radar-like beams from their own receivers would intersect at, or close to, the transmission's source. If greater precision was needed, the local electricity could be switched off circuit by circuit, street by street, and house by house until the transmission suddenly broke off and the site was revealed.

Repetition of messages also gave the Germans multiple versions of the text for comparison. And codes based on reasonably familiar lines of poetry, hymns, or Shakespearean quotations meant that even without the computing skills of Britain's Bletchley Park, their skilled analysts could extract the plain language text all too easily. Even the system of 'checks' was ignored or overruled in those early days so that in France, as they did with even more fatal results in Holland, the Germans were able to capture some sets. They could 'play them back' to SOE to lure them into dropping arms or agents into the Gestapo's clutches. Also by monitoring the traffic for a while before they pounced the Germans could often learn to mimic an SOE operator's 'fist', the rhythm and speed of their fingers on the Morse key again deluding those on the receiving end at the 'Home Station' at Grendon Hall'.

Thus, like all operators, Denis lived on the edge. Although, as it turned out, despite a tricky brush with the Vichy police, what gave him away was ironically none of these 'occupational hazards'. He worked first from Virginia Hall's own apartment, then – briefly – from a room offered by the 'working girl' whose proposal of professional solace as well as shelter frightened him just as much as the prospect of a police raid.[115] Her place of business was on the ground floor. This was ideal for short-time visits but less so as the base for a short-wave wireless. Luckily Virginia soon found him (no doubt to all round relief) two locations, one an apartment in the suburbs, the other all the way over on the opposite side of the city, high on the hill of St Michel.

For someone as nervous as Denis, lugging the set across Lyons must have been a frightening ordeal. The heavy suitcase would have seemed scarcely less conspicuous had it had a built-in neon light

[115] See above, p. 116

flashing 'search me, search me'. Matters were made worse by the lack of transport. Velo-taxis, rickshaws built on the rear of a cycle frame and the rattling public tramcars were the only two options. There were hardly any conventional taxis left on the streets and anyone who wanted to hire one had first to get a permit from City Hall.

When a tram on which he was crossing town was stopped at a roadblock for a spot check by the police, Denis, who always travelled on the open rear platform as it offered a better chance of hopping off in case of trouble, decided to do just that, leaving his set behind. But his quick-witted manoeuvre was spiked by a well meaning old lady who called after him 'Monsieur, you've forgotten your case.' Denis stepped sheepishly back into the tramcar, where inevitably he was asked by a gendarme to open the case.

Manoeuvre number two, to pretend that he had lost the suitcase key, ended equally inevitably with a gruff order to accompany the gendarme to the police station. This was several streets away and this was France, Vichy or no Vichy, so a suggestion from Denis that the two of them stop at a bar en route was gratefully accepted. In the bar, taking an even deeper plunge into manoeuvre number three, Denis 'blagged' in fine Wanborough style, telling the gendarme he was an escaped French prisoner of war, without papers, that he was trying to scrape a living and that his case was stuffed with antiques. 'They're pretty valuable,' he murmured. 'I've got a customer for them and what I will make will keep me going for a long time. I've got some money with me. How much would it cost for you to disappear?' The short answer, after some ritual haggling, was 20,000 francs, then about £100. The gendarme was lucky; Denis was luckier still, since the gendarme could have taken the cash and still hauled him in. The scary close-call prompted the ingenious Virginia, whose contacts were extraordinary, to arrange for sets to be transported across the city in the municipal dustcarts, which solved that problem but which did not remove the next tripwire lying across Denis's path.

It was characteristic of Denis that for relaxation after a stressful day with half his mind tuned into London and half attuned for trouble, he reverted in the evenings to his cover as *Denis Rocher, Acteur*, appearing, as he relates, in 'restaurants and nightspots such as la Taverne Royale and la Cigogne'. In *le Chagrin* Denis makes no secret of the fact that his later nightclub acts in Paris were '*en travesti*', or 'in drag'. But in writing about Lyons he gives us no clue whether the night owls there were similarly entertained. Whatever he wore, billing himself as 'the Anglo-Belgian Tenor' might have been thought likely to arouse unwelcome curiosity, as well as, to modern ears, rather lacking crowd-pulling appeal. But even this was not what landed him in trouble.

Rather, it was a young man's lapse across a tea table, one of those fleeting but fatal slips that are so often the Achilles' heel of clandestine operations. Denis does not name the young man though he is identified in a post-war memorandum on the personal file, in unmistakably Buckmaster French, recommending Denis for the *Légion d'Honneur*. Like many agents on their first mission, the young man was rattled. Denis did his best to settle him in, blissfully unaware that his new colleague had an aunt who lived nearby. Slipping off on his own for the reassurance of a familiar face, a *tisane* and the nibble of a Proustian *Madeleine,* the young man blurted out to her why he had come to France, not realising she was a fervent Pétain supporter. His aunt did what she thought was her duty, and reported him to the police.

To keep himself out of trouble the agent gave them Denis's description, and as June began the hunt was on; he apparently had the *nous* not to betray Virginia Hall though her spider's web of contacts quickly registered that Denis was a target. Hall's first thought was that he should go back to England but Denis persuaded her, and she in turn persuaded Baker Street, that an operator was badly needed in Paris and he could be of more use there. He was unknown to the police in the capital, even if he was a familiar figure in certain arcane byways of the theatrical world. He was nevertheless penetrating the belly of the beast, entering the city where the Germans ruled, where counter-intelligence was sophisticated and pervasive and captured agents fell into the hands of the hard men of the Gestapo, not ambivalent or venal gendarmes. To get there he had to get himself across the Demarcation Line.

11

The Madame and the Pork Butcher

Like so much else in 1940s France, crossing the Line was a matter of whom you knew, whether you could afford it, and whether you would be betrayed.

Virginia Hall knew everybody, not just dustmen. One of her contacts, (named in Judith Pearson's biography as Germaine Guerin and in Denis's personal file as Germaine Dubois) was a Lyons 'Madame', whose circuit of working girls crafted a valuable patchwork quilt of gossip and intelligence out of random scraps of pillow talk. Germaine put him onto the 'pork butcher in the rue de la Barre' who ran a line crossing operation, tolerated by the Vichy police and the Germans in return for his agreement to 'shop' some of his clients from time to time. For French line-crossers, getting caught was a disagreeable adventure, ending with a fine and perhaps a few days in jail, before being pushed back into the Unoccupied Zone.

For an SOE agent with false papers who fell into German hands, the stakes were rather higher. The account of the journey in the personal file, later embellished by Denis in his book, suggests a Gallic version of a Wake's Week outing to Blackpool from some Lancashire mill town. The butcher ferried his passengers in a canvas-topped truck, powered like almost all French vehicles by a charcoal burner. He used it to carry carcasses from the market to his shop and hasty hose downs had not quite washed away the tang of dead meat.

Not that it deterred the customers, many of whom were regulars, black market traders, or ordinary folk with families on the other side of the Line, who treated the bouncy sixty mile trip north via Villefranche sur Saône and south of Mâcon to the crossing point at

Montceau le Mines like a jolly outing. They travelled with wicker baskets of picnics, food, wine and singsongs. They stopped for coffee at a farmhouse, then another break at a café for drinks where the party divided into small groups and waited for their guides. Over walls and fields, through woods, and up a final hill, on the far side of which, the guide told Denis, lay the Occupied Zone. Indeed it did, but when they saw the line of men in grey uniforms, the line-crossers realised that they had been 'sold' as briskly as a van-load of pork.

Like military police in any army, the German Feldgendarmerie were as unpopular with their own troops as they were with civilians. The brass chains round their necks, from which hung their silvered metal breastplates, embossed with an eagle and swastika, had earned them the nickname of '*Kettenhunde*' or 'Guard Dogs'. They were not as pathologically brutal as the SS, and those posted to the depths of the French countryside were by and large older men, not crack troops.

But to Denis, shivering with fear in the middle of a muddy meadow, a 'Hun with a gun' was a 'Hun with a gun', whatever his vintage. The last one he had seen was in Brussels in 1914. Now as he stumbled forward, the one clear thought in his head was that the Germans eventually sent line-crossers back where they had come from.

As he wanted to reach Paris, he needed to convince them that he had come from the capital, rather than Lyons, and was trying to get into the Unoccupied Zone, rather than out of it, to work at a Lyons brasserie his uncle and aunt had just recently bought. Why was he carrying a large roll of bank notes? This came, he ad-libbed, from selling a little café of his own in Nantes (a town he knew from pre-war days; we know he was also there during the Phoney War). But he had no possible explanation for the fact that in yet another inexplicable lapse of security, he was carrying four identity cards and a ration book, all ostensibly issued in Lyons by the Vichy authorities. His mind raced as he and a few other unlucky travellers were prodded at rifle point in a ragged line to the local schoolhouse, which doubled as the detention centre. He mimed a pressing stomach problem convincingly enough to persuade a guard to let him scuttle into the toilet, where hasty flushing, rounded off by the frenzied chewing of some troublesome remnants, disposed of the tell-tale papers.

After a brief stay in Montceau he was sent about thirty miles north-west to Chalon Sur Saône, where he now had to act out the 'legend' with all the professional conviction he deployed when standing in for the lead of *Mercenary Mary*. This time, though, the audience would be rather more hostile than a coach-load of middleclass mums having a day out in London for shopping, 'High Tea' at the Coventry Street Corner House, and a nice evening at the theatre. It was certainly smaller: only four uniformed German officers and a French inter-preter, the latter far more suspicious and unfriendly than the former. And his performance lasted the best part of a day.

The 'legend' was not pierced, despite Denis being led through a script booby-trapped with all the tricks and snares of which interrogators are so fond; some of that Wanborough training must have sunk in. He was crestfallen when he was photographed, finger-printed and told he would be taken under guard by train another fifty miles to the north-west, to Dijon, 'where they have experience'. He thought he had been singled out because of a chance remark by one of his fellow passengers, which blew a hole in his story by revealing where he had actually come from. In fact the Germans suspected he matched a physical description supplied by the neophyte agent in Lyons who had spoken so carelessly to his aunt.

Fortunately, Denis managed to avoid Dijon, where there was a base of a German counter-intelligence unit specialising, most effectively, in anti-Resistance operations.[116] The 'Black Market Blag' that had worked with the Lyons gendarme proved equally effective with his Feld-gendarmerie guard, who in exchange for Denis's entire bankroll bar a few notes, let him slide off the train at a rural halt south of the town.

Denis took a local train through the countryside to Paris, where he arrived without a wireless set, and without papers. He had just a few francs in his pocket and instructions from Virginia Hall, reminiscent of an Eric Ambler novel. He was to go to a bar on the rue du Faubourg-St-Honoré and look for a man 'with a Roman nose'.

[116] *Martres p. 47*

12

Paris by Night

He arrived by night in a city with many of the same human ambiguities, double standards and compromises of Lyons, all magnified beyond comprehension by the fact that this was not the *Nono*, but German territory, Gestapo country. Denis missed the planned première of *The Wizard of Oz* in Cannes but had doubtless seen it in London and when he got to Paris might well have shared the young Judy Garland's feeling 'we're not in Kansas anymore'.[117]

Much like the Riviera, the façade of Paris looked the same as he remembered it from the 1930s. It had escaped the bombing and shelling and the outdoor tables of the cafés were still crowded, though the grey-uniformed troops, and the Swastika flags and German direction signs which had sprouted around the city's heart, were an unpleasant reminder of reality. Behind the unblemished façade, the city shared with the rest of Occupied France 'much of the physical depression of a great sick-room and much of the mental stress of a great concentration camp', to cite a post-war PWE handbook.[118]

For most families the realities were food shortages, limited supplies of fuel for heating, and power cuts. Housewives in wooden-soled shoes queued for hours often to reach rows of empty shelves. Vegetables other than the despised swede and the Jerusalem artichoke were rationed. Real coffee and the traditional crusty 'baguette' were nothing more than memories. As they waited, they worried about the

---

[117] *The* Times' *anonymous cinema critic thought the Wizard's scenery and dresses were 'designed with no more taste than is commonly used in the decoration of a night-club' and, flashing his erudition in a style which would not go down well in a twenty-first century newspaper, remarked that only Hollywood could produce for a single scene 'an innumerable band of midgets which reduces to insignificance the collection of the Gonzagas or, if it comes to that, of Philip IV of Spain.'*

[118] *Ziman p. 6*

thousands of sons and husbands in German prisoner of war camps, and those who might be swept up to 'volunteer' for work in the Third Reich in exchange for some of the prisoners of war. Such an exchange was a Vichy 'pledge' honoured more in the breach than the observance. Rationed to three cigarettes a week, men carried bamboo canes with a pin at the end to pick up German cigarette butts tossed nonchalantly between the rails at the Metro stations.

Paris was quiet; most of the vehicles on the streets were German staff cars. Buses wheezed noisily along the boulevards, their passengers wheezing too as they breathed the charcoal fumes from the makeshift motor. In contrast the only noise from the ubiquitous velo-taxi was the driver's panting punctuated by the occasional ringing of his bell. Parisians mostly walked, cycled or took the crowded Metro, hoping that when they reached their station they would not run into an unsmiling gang of Vichy police or sinister Gestapo men. These men were made even more sinister by their leather trench coats, who loitered around the curve in the tiled corridor to make a snap check of identity cards.

The Metro was doing well: in December 1940 it was selling an average of well over 2 million tickets every day, and by May 1942, when Denis landed on the Riviera, this had risen to some 3.5 million.

Tired Parisians and slightly apprehensive German soldiers in transit, laden with their kit, jostled porters from the markets of les Halles. They were now deprived of their vans and forced to use the Metro to deliver wicker baskets of briny shellfish, and tubs of flowers whose scent blended strangely with the pervasive odours of soot, perspiration and sticky wool. Cinemas too saw their audiences rise sharply. They were warm, they offered a comfort blanket of illusion to shroud the harsh realities outside, and the darkness made them popular venues for romantic and more predatory encounters.

Bicycles were in great demand and towards the end of the Occupation were selling for almost the price of a pre-war car. Rubber was scarce so when punctured tyres were beyond patching they were filled with a string of wine bottle corks. At night the city was even quieter, and there were reports of owls hooting in the public gardens and even the chirp of crickets from the warm cellars of bakers' shops. It was quieter because the Germans enforced a strict curfew, at one point as early as 6 p.m. but later improved to 11 p.m. Some, especially foreign and French Jews, and Communists and Socialists who had sought sanctuary in the City of Light, lived in darkness and fear, hardly ever venturing out. Even ordinary citizens who fell into police hands a few minutes after the curfew might find themselves held as hostages and then shot in the spiral of Resistance attacks and German reprisals.

A widely believed story was that of a young Parisian husband whose wife was about to give birth to their first child. Disregarding the curfew he hurried off down the dark streets to fetch the local midwife, only to run into a French police patrol who locked him up, although with Gallic courtesy they sent a messenger around to alert the midwife. They told the father-to-be that he would have to stay in the cells until the curfew ended at dawn. Deep into the night, the phone shrilled. A German soldier had been killed and the Wehrmacht wanted hostages. The sleepy gendarmes said they had one to offer and a little later a canvas covered truck roared up and took the young man away with a bunch of other unfortunates to be shot in the woods outside the city. As he died at dawn, the baby was safely delivered.

Not everyone ran scared. But not everyone went hungry.

Cash was king. The imposition of a grotesquely artificial exchange rate gave the Germans francs to burn; it was almost Monopoly money. And a few fortunate French earned cash from the Black Market dealings (they were known from their principal stocks in trade as *les BOF*, or *beurre, oeufs, fromage* – *butter, eggs and cheese*) from lucrative business contracts with various parts of the Nazi war machine, the skim from clubs and pimping, profits from stealing Jewish assets at knockdown prices. It did not matter. In the short term, '*Pecunia non olet*' ('Money has no smell'), as the Roman Emperor Vespasian pronounced many centuries earlier. But having large amounts of cash at home was a risk in itself. And in the longer term, if the Allies won the war, anyone turning up to the bank with bundles of used notes in large denominations might find themselves with some awkward explaining to do.

Little wonder then that sales of châteaux were strong and that business at Paris's venerable Drouot auction house was booming, its salesrooms packed, as those whom the press scorned as 'cowards with cash', laundered francs into Fragonards and French furniture.[119] One major sale on 11 December 1942 brought in a record 47 million francs, a sum impossible to convert sensibly into today's values, but by any measure a very large amount of money, all the more for a city supposedly groaning under the yoke of an occupying army.

As a later French commentator wrote, borrowing from Voltaire, 'All was for the best in the best of all demi-mondes.' Or in the words of one of F Section's most experienced agents 'The calamity of occupation brings out the worst and the best. Like my brother agents I saw both. The worst was shameful. The best was fine, as fine as could be found anywhere'.[120]

Another sharp picture of the ambiguities of Parisian life at the time comes from a newspaper in Alsace, the territory annexed by Germany as part of its Armistice loot. The *Müllhauser Tageblatt* told its readers, 'Never has the contrast of dissoluteness and luxurious living, on the one hand, and famine and misery on the other, been as pronounced as it is now. Is it not symbolic that not only in China but also in Paris one finds coolies – naturally modern coolies? They carry in their bicycle trailers rich women returning from the market. A high French officer declared recently that 100,000 French people live better now than in peacetime, but the rest live worse than ever. Those who have money can obtain all they want. Forty per cent of all merchandise disappears onto the Black Market.'

There were, it pointed out, many restaurants in Paris where ration cards were redundant; bundles of cash would buy whatever the Black Market could offer. It added that an average meal in one of those places costs 300–400 francs a head, about the same amount as even the authorities recognised was the minimum that the average family needed to keep them fed for four days. That is, if the father was not one of the 1.5 million French prisoners of war, and still had a job. Even for those in work, post-Occupation inflation and wage freezes

[119] *Boterf p. 172*
[120] *Cowburn, Foreword*

had reduced real income by twenty-five per cent. It was not just the profiteers who lived well. 'Society', as Boterf observed, continued its rituals as if the war had never happened. There were bridge parties, cocktail evenings, openings, fashion shows, and receptions for visiting German film stars.

The old money crowd, the remittance men with parents or trust funds in Zurich or Uruguay, the 'Bright Young Things', and the literati found plenty of champagne to sip even though caviar was in short supply.

Real money bought not just real food. It also bought entrée to the nightclubs, which along with the theatres, music halls, opera and ballet, not to mention the racecourses and brothels, had all reopened with a swing just a few days after the Germans marched in. One can contrast the many contemporary photographs of nightclubs, bare breasted dancers, champagne bottles, jubilant Germans only too happy not to be at the Russian Front and their girlfriends only too happy to be somewhere warm, with the sad image of a cluster of elderly, shabby Parisians huddled around a pavement soup kitchen in front of a large billboard advertising almost as many shows as Broadway.

The extravaganza at the *Folies Bergère* and Susie Solidor's show at the Casino de Paris get prominent billing.[121] Though Shaw's *Pygmalion* would have no hidden message for a French audience, the German censor apparently saw nothing exceptional in the plots of *Macbeth* and *Richard III*, and their portrayal of tormented rulers. The former 'Magic City' theatre near Pont d'Alma was the centre for entertainment of a different and surprisingly modern kind. The Germans had requisitioned it as a TV studio from which grainy and flickering programmes were transmitted via the Eiffel Tower to hospitals in the region to entertain convalescent Wehrmacht soldiers. The three or four hundred wealthy Parisians who, accord-

---

[121] *Solidor provides one of a million examples of what was known in colloquial French as 'Système D', shorthand for 'Système Debrouille' or 'Système Demerde' (in English 'working the system'). Her last show ended well after the curfew, at 2 a.m. She lived outside Paris and had a private deal with a post office van driver who brought his truck to the back of the theatre after it closed and took her and her troupe home, lolling in safety on bags of mail*

ing to Boterf, could afford the expensive receivers, were also able to view from 10 a.m. to midnight a programme of 'revuettes,' news, interviews and even films.

An extra benefit for those who had the money for nightclubs, and probably also a few well-connected secret agents and refugees without papers, was that they stayed open all night, and were thus a safe haven after the curfew hour struck. One or two of them Denis was to know as a performer. Though some brothels such as *the Sphinx* and *le Chabanais* were reserved for Germans, the (many) others, distinguishable by a discreet sign announcing that 'The House is Open to French Gentlemen', offered the same nocturnal safe haven. (The brothel owners later complained that during the Occupation they lost a third of their customers and half their income. They still did well, and enjoyed material benefits in terms of curfew passes, extra rations for the working girls, permission to own cars, and generous fuel allowances.)

Piles of money could not quite block out the winds of war. June had seen Vichy badly rattled by RAF raids on Paris factories serving the German war machine, and news of the first of the crushing 1000 bomber raids on Germany's industrial heartland. It was perhaps in reaction to this change in the tide that Pierre Laval, Vichy's Premier, declared proudly that he 'ardently desired and confidently expected' a German victory, a statement he might have recalled rather ruefully when, after the Liberation he was propped up half-dead, to face a vengeful French firing squad.

Parisians might also have scoffed quietly at his confidence when, later the same month, a twin-engined Bristol Beaufighter of RAF Coastal Command (flying cheekily at rooftop height along the Champs d'Elysée in the middle of the day) dropped a large *Tricolour* flag over the Arc de Triomphe. It then strafed the German HQ in Place de la Concorde before roaring home at full throttle, unscathed. And even in the depths of despair, when Paris wanted to mark France's National Day, 14 July 1942 the menacing rumble of German tanks and armoured cars being deployed in the streets did not stop its people. They were careful to limit their groups to no more than six to circumvent the German ban on 'processions'. They came out on the street at around 5 p.m.; the men were sporting Tricolour ribbons, and the girls had red, white and blue flowers in their hats.

There is yet another perspective of Paris in those black times, this time through German eyes. It stands out for its portrait of a man and a life written in an 'I Am A Camera' style, the philosopher author floating above the mire of everyday concerns. It is to be found in the French translation of the Second World War journals of Ernst Jünger.[122] Now recognised as one of modern Germanys leading authors, Jünger was a man far too complex and full of contradictions to portray fully in a few lines; his Paris journals alone run to more than 1000 pages.

He was a loyal German, a proud soldier and an anti-Nazi. He had fought in the carnage of the First World War. He was a philosopher, a devout adherent to the Old Testament, a collector of antiquarian books, dangerously close to the Army plot to kill Hitler, and a man who risked arrest by saluting Jews forced to wear the Yellow Star. His life as a staff officer in the Wehrmacht headquarters in the Hotel Majestic meant that he dealt with the war at one remove, from behind a desk rather than in the mud of the trenches in which he had wallowed as a young man. He enjoyed good meals at le Tour d'Argent, Prunier and the Ritz and at private homes. At one of these his French hostess took pride in serving (among other delights) a paté of mushrooms, eggs and marrowbone jelly; a marked improvement on mashed swede and Jerusalem artichoke on which many Parisians subsisted. He truffle-hunted with a connoisseur's lascivious glee through the dusty shelves of Parisian booksellers, and rubbed shoulders and sharpened wits with French playwrights, artists, publishers, actors and actresses, between visits to art galleries and to Monet's garden at Giverny.

A random sample is unfair, but dinner at a brasserie in 1942, when the playwright Jean Cocteau shared his memories of a bedridden Marcel Proust, suggests Jünger's considerable ability to shield himself from reality with intellectual distractions. His

[122] *1895-1998*

concerns about the war were focused far away, on the dangers to his wife and son in the Allied fire bombing of Germany, though one of his better known pen-portraits, almost a pastiche of aestheticism, is of an early-evening British attack on Paris in May 1944, '. . . I was nursing a glass of Burgundy, in which a few strawberries floated. The city, its towers and domes reddened by the sunset, stretched out before me in all its powerful beauty, like a flower with its petals spread wide for a pollination which would prove fatal. It was pure theatre, a naked display of might underscored and sublimated by suffering . . .'[123]

Denis had no time for poetic flights of fancy. He was scurrying around in enemy held territory without papers. He could not get a hotel room let alone a decent meal, and even with his demonstrated skill at talking his way out of trouble, a police check would have been fatal. Denis's mission was to work as the 'pianist' for Ernest Wilkinson, also known as *Alexandre* or *Montfort*,[124] a 'pipe-smoking, slim, hawk-eyed' RAF officer in his forties. In one of those brief SOE biographies (which like a Chinese meal leaves the reader hungry for more) we learn that Wilkinson had been born in Missouri but spoke better French than English and had a French wife living in the Occupied Zone. Buckmaster described Wilkinson as '*un dur des durs*' ('as hard as they come').[125] He had recently parachuted in with Ben Cowburn, the 34-year-old oil engineer from Lancashire, and also married to a Frenchwoman, whose comments on the insecurity of Lyons we noted earlier. Cowburn himself had worked in France for several years before the war. He was now on the second of what would prove a highly effective run of four missions which rightly earned him an MC; along with George Millar's *Maquis* his memoirs of his exploits are among the 'the best of breed' for the genre.[126]

The story of what happened next comes with different glosses, but is essentially one of danger, amorous folly and sloppy tradecraft with nasty consequences. Denis told it in *le Chagrin* and in more detail in

---

[123] Jünger p. 708

[124] *'Mountford' in Denis's recollection and Mumford in the debriefing report. One source cites his Christian name as Edgar. His brother also served in SOE*

[125] *Foot p. 314*

[126] *See Bibliography*

his memoirs, and also gave a rambling account of it to his SOE debriefers in London, who rather surprisingly seem to have taken it at face value without questioning the obvious inconsistencies or pressing for fuller details. Some of it is reflected in the memoirs of others, including Maurice Buckmaster, whose account Denis later dismissed as 'strangely inaccurate'.

Denis tells us that, remembering carefree pre-war days, his first call was at 34, rue de la Colisée, in the 8th Arrondissement, a short walk from the Rond Point on the Champs d'Elysée, home of *le Boeuf Sur Le Toit*. To describe *le Boeuf* as a restaurant, a nightclub, or a bar understates its unique place in the capital's nightlife, though it was all three. This was its fifth base in Paris since it opened in 1922. It had built its reputation in the 1930s as a magnet, in Janet Flanner's words, for all 'the most brilliant figures of a brilliant epoch – the best known international painters, writers, poets, poseurs, actors and eccentrics'. Under a painting of a bull's eye painted one New Year's Eve by Francis Picabia (now in the Pompidou Museum) and the watchful gaze of the proprietor, Louis Moyses, its house pianist Clement Doucet 'read Rimbaud from a book propped on the music rack while whacking out early boogie woogie variations on Bach fugues . . .'. It was surviving nicely under the Germans (though the management insisted that they did not wear uniform), despite coming under attack in a Vichy newspaper, *le Franciste*, on the grounds that its monthly fuel allocation of 8 tons of coal was enough to supply countless private homes. 'The revellers are guaranteed a hot time,' the writer quipped, straining to make the point. He ignored the fact that under *Système D*, much of the precious fuel would have been quietly hauled away via the back door to be swapped for extra wine or choice cuts of meat.

Denis had been an appreciative and appreciated customer there in its pre-war days as the noisy, gossipy, 'see and be seen' Mecca of 'le Tout-Paris' and when he poked his head in (apprehensively, since these were different times) the barman recognised him at once. In special places like that, barmen do; it is as much a part of the job as a white jacket, a false smile and a juggler's touch with the cocktail shaker. 'O, put not your trust in princes', the Bible tells us, and as Denis had been reminded by his Attic idyll. Barmen are different. Denis took another plunge into insecurity and asked how he could get hold of new identity papers. Unperturbed, the barman told Denis that an important actor whom Denis knew well, named in the autobiography as 'Jacques Artel', was the man to see. As luck would have it he was appearing that evening at the *Comedie Française*, and if Denis strolled down the Champs d'Elysée, Jacques would certainly help.

While he was talking to the barman about 'Artel', the conversation was overheard by a gay Wehrmacht officer in civilian clothes who introduced himself ('was it accidental or did he hold onto my hand just a little longer than was necessary?'). He claimed to be a friend of 'Artel' and said he would drive Denis to the venerable home of the *Comedie Française* at the Palais Royale to see him.

In Denis's memory, the officer, 'Max Halder' (misspelled 'Hadler' in another account of Denis's life) was 'gentle' with 'sensitive hands' and a 'lovely sense of humour'. Denis goes on: 'Without realising what I was really feeling, I found myself thinking that this man and I could really become friends.' 'Artel', who declared Denis to be 'a real pet' and professed archly to being 'quite jealous', agreed to get the papers, and Denis agreed to spend the night with Max whose invitation had been uttered 'with an almost dreadful longing in his eyes'. It was, Denis says in *le Chagrin* 'a question of speed, as these things often are'.

Like 'Artel', 'Halder' is certainly a name invented by Denis. Though he tells us that Max was 'violently anti-Nazi', from an old (and by implication) Prussian family, there is no trace of any link with the German General of the same name, whom SOE incidentally claimed they had successfully denigrated in Berlin by planting false rumours that he had been plotting against Hitler. So who he really was we shall never know. Indeed as we shall see he may well have been a conflation of memories and personalities, even reflecting a flash or two of what we might call the 'Jünger type' of officer, the archetypical and rather rare 'Good German'.

We can get a little closer to 'Artel'. Important players at the *Comedie* become 'Sociétaires' or 'Full Members'. There is no 'Artel' on the list for that period, but from the chronology and Denis's comment that 'Artel' knew Emma Luart in Brussels, 'Jacques Artel' may well have been Jean Yonnel, one of France's most distinguished classical actors, who had also appeared at *la Monnaie* in Brussels. He was the 378th member, admitted to that distinguished group in 1929.

The *Comedie Française* was too French an icon for the Germans to put it under serious pressure, though its repertoire was closely watched and some scripts censored. Nor was it immune from vicious carping by the collaborationist press, which complained about its 'Jewification'. They had a singularly nasty vocabulary; another polemic on the Parisian music scene that spoke proudly of its having been 'de-Jewed'. Yonnel, born in Romania, also came under press fire for being Jewish, but worked without too much harassment throughout the Occupation. He was a man of imposing build and of considerable courage.

When the air raid warning sirens sounded during one performance Yonnel remarked to the skittish audience in a loud aside that he took a different view than some others about Allied bombing raids on France. And playing in Henri de Montherlant's *The Dead Queen*, lines such as 'Just kill, and the heavens will brighten' and 'The best and brightest of the kingdom are in jail' had younger members of the audience who caught the allusion to Resistance shootings of German soldiers, and the reprisals, stamping their feet and clapping, while two Wehrmacht officers stormed out in fury.[127]

Returning to Max, if a woman SOE agent had allowed herself a fling with a German officer, the criticism would be the same: it was dangerous and unprofessional, so much so that either then or later we might have expected it to get more scrutiny than it apparently did. Maurice Buckmaster referred to the episode, apparently without exciting any comment, when he wrote a memoir in 1958 and Denis tells the story twice, first in his autobiography, and again in *le Chagrin*. But the only possible reference to it in the personal file is a bland note by his interrogators that while he was in Paris 'he looked up a number of his stage friends', which, based on Denis's version, seems a masterpiece of succinct understatement.

[127] *Boterf, p. 65*

Denis continues the story. The morning after that first tryst, he left Max's rumpled bed to carry on with his mission, and look for the SOE officer 'with a Roman nose' for whom he was to work as operator. He can't have given a moment's thought (streetwise he was not) to whether he was being set up, in a male version of the 'honey trap'. Most of the Germans' considerable successes in penetrating SOE circuits, playing 'radio games' with London, to lure newly arriving agents and arms drops into their hands, were in the 1943-44 period[128] and do not need recounting here. But even during Denis's time in Paris, the German counter-intelligence apparatus was operating in high gear and he would have needed no reminder. He had been admonished about indiscretion more than once during his training, to the point that, to borrow a slogan from the British Home Front, 'Careless Talk Costs Lives'; we might well think – how much more so, careless love.[129]

But when he strolled along the rue du Faubourg-St-Honoré with an independent air the morning after their first meeting, Denis had put Max at the back of his mind and 'the man with the Roman nose' was his sole objective. By his account it was not until he had visited the bar for three or four days in a row, returning each evening to Max's flat in rue de Tilsit, a stone's throw from the Arc de Triomphe, that he spotted Wilkinson. This was due to a photograph Virginia Hall had given him, which he 'accidentally' dropped on the floor in front of him as a recognition signal. If its subject had known his picture had been in the hip pocket of Denis's trousers as they lay folded over a German officer's bedroom chair, he might have had arranged for him to be forcibly repatriated to London.

---

[128] *Foot pp. 289 et seq*

[129] *Denis was not the only SOE operator having an unusual time in Paris. His personal file notes that he remembered being told to steer clear of the confusingly named Dennis [sic], who was doing nicely 'running an enormous dress shop' in the capital and was not being a good boy'. He cannot have steered totally clear since characteristically, he could not resist adding that his near namesake was 'very tall [and] good – looking'*

13

'A Fine Romance . . .'

But without a radio, Denis was of no use to Wilkinson. A pianist needed a piano. Virginia Hall's attempt to send a set to Paris via a courier had not worked, and another attempt to get hold of one via a contact of 'Artel's' was also unsuccessful. So he and Wilkinson waited and fretted, though Cowburn was at least able to use Denis to send messages to London on another set about supply drops. Denis meanwhile prowled around the Paris suburb of Juvisy, just south of what is now Orly Airport, dressed in a borrowed set of railwayman's blue overalls, memorising the layout and security details of the nearby main railway lines to add to Cowburn's list of potential sabotage targets.

It was a frustrating period, with Max in the background. Though in *le Chagrin*, Denis describes the relationship through the golden glow of romantic hindsight, as lasting for several months, this cannot be correct, and the affair can have lasted no more than a few weeks at most. Buckmaster implies that in fact it was closer to a 'one night stand'. It was still an act of supreme folly, even more so since by Denis's account, for whatever period they were together, he and Max were not shy about being seen in public.

Denis says he appeared in drag – *'en travesti'* as he puts it more delicately in the film (presumably with an appreciative Max in the audience) at *le Grand Ecart* (under the same ownership as le *Boeuf*), *les Caves Caucasiennes* (whose staff probably included a liberal sprinkling of Russian NKVD and GRU tipsters) and *Chez Ma Tante*. The latter (literally 'At My Auntie's' but to French ears 'the Pawnshop', though 'Tante' itself is also pejorative slang for 'gay') was a favoured German haunt and may well be where Max and Denis were spotted by one of Max's brother officers who spoke to

Max 'very firmly' about the relationship. As Denis remembered the encounter, Max retorted in fine Rhett Butler style that 'I don't give a damn' and promised Denis that 'I will not be browbeaten into losing your friendship'. It would be fascinating but too much of a coincidence to think they were at le Boeuf when the Bouglione Circus put on a 'mini-show' called *One Clown Chases Another,* whose principal performer was a 'Marcel Dieudonné', one of Denis's early work names.

At some point in this muddled period, Denis says that Wilkinson found out that he was living with Max 'and he practically ordered me to leave. But I refused. He had been surly enough before but after this he never spoke to me unless it was absolutely necessary.'

Despite Max's defiance, it was Denis who broke things off, feeling as he says in *le Chagrin,* troubled that he was 'letting [Max] down in this double game business'. He had told Max that he was a Belgian cabaret artist and Denis was worried that if his real role and identity came to light, Max would be in great danger.

This was not just because Denis was a British agent. Though there were gays in the Wehrmacht and the Nazi Party, some at senior levels, homosexuality was officially deemed 'that Jewish pestilence'. In a speech to his senior officers in 1937, Heinrich Himmler vowed that homosexuals in the ranks of the SS 'will obviously be publicly degraded and handed over to the court. After the expiration of their court sentence they will by my regulation be taken into concentration camp and in the camp they will be shot while trying to escape.'[130]

Denis was also torn by the fact that though he had 'a deep affection' for Max, he could not forget that he was German and thus the enemy. He is blithely silent about the risk to which the liaison was exposing his SOE colleagues and their operations; had he been hauled in by the Gestapo, which was always possible, and broken, which is almost certain, he would have caused a security disaster of epic proportions. Many lives, French as well as British, methods, codes, the Mediterranean ferry system, the pivotal role of Lyons, London's organisation, and the identities of its senior

[130] *See Bibliography, Miller p. 169*

officers, all had been put at risk for a brief respite from loneliness and anxiety.

Denis seems oblivious to this, merely musing in his auto-biography, that had it not been for the war, he and Max might have stayed together for many years 'if not forever'. As it was, he could not bring himself to attempt any explanation, and 'so I went out one morning and never returned'.

His departure may have had a more mundane operational reason. Wilkinson was tired of waiting for a wireless. An agent without contact with London was an eyeless Samson in a Miltonian world, 'amid the blaze of noon, irrecoverably dark, total eclipse . . .'. The F Section mantra, 'when in doubt, go and ask Virginia', offered the hope of light. Denis and Wilkinson set out for Lyons, travelling via Toulouse in a high clandestine style in the circuit-breaker compart-ment of a locomotive, with the connivance of French Communist railroad men, a method pioneered by Cowburn. (In *le Chagrin* Denis comments that though it was perhaps impolitic to say so at the peak of the Cold War, the workers, most of them Communist, had been far more helpful to him and his SOE colleagues; 'they would give you the shirt off their back', he told the interviewer. In contrast the French bourgeoisie were far cagier; 'they had more to lose'.)

Denis makes light of the experience, though it was the stuff of movies or an Alan Furst novel. Clambering onto the footplate of the engine in the dusk, as it slowed on a bend near Juvisy was tough enough. Hiding in the claustrophobic metal locker with sparks crackling from loose leads and the ominous, bowel-loosening slowing of the train as it approached the Demarcation Line was infinitely worse. The noise from the train, its brakes hissing, wheels screeching, buffers clanking and endless door-slamming made for unbearable tension. With only a metal door between Denis and a concentration camp, the shouting of the German border guards and last minute doubts about the footplate crew – were they as staunch as they seemed? – created a level of fear that Denis could not have known before and must have stretched his nerves far beyond the contemplation of any instructor or psychiatrist at Wanborough.

But it worked. Ben Cowburn had reached Lyons separately and

was dozing on Virginia Hall's sofa when Wilkinson and Denis turned up, dishevelled but relieved, soon to be followed by Richard Heslop; can a 'safe house' ever have been so patently unsafe? Heslop, at various times in his SOE career 'Raymond Hamilton' and 'René Garrat' is best known in Resistance history as *Xavier*. He was the French born son of a British racehorse trainer and a French mother, a public school sporting hero who, before the war, had worked in Siam, Spain and Portugal, described in his personal file as 'a magnificent officer. He had all the great qualities: fearlessness, discipline, diplomacy, conscientiousness, self–sacrifice.'[131]

Virginia had found Denis a wireless set. Like a child with a new toy he records that it 'was a delight', much smaller and lighter, ten inches by seven inches by five, and thus easier to carry than the earlier model. But nonetheless unambiguously a clandestine wireless. If the attaché case was opened by unfriendly hands, the game was up.

Heslop, whose mission was to organise operations around Angers, in the Loire valley some 150 miles south-west of Paris, decided to join Wilkinson and Denis on their trip back across the line. They decided to head west first, taking the train about 220 miles across the heart of France to Limoges, from where they planned to get into the Occupied Zone using the same railway engine 'circuit-breaker' technique.

Wilkinson warned Heslop that Denis, who had spent four days in bed at Virginia Hall's apartment gnawed by diarrhoea, '. . . was in the theatrical business and he's a bit of a clown really, and as frightened as hell. He was caught crossing the Demarcation Line recently and put in jail, but managed to get out. His nerves are all to pieces but he's all I can get. We'll have to put up with him as best we can'. Heslop's first meeting with Denis confirmed that he was badly scared. 'But it takes real courage to admit you are scared and then carry on, especially after you have already had one taste of prison', he added generously.[132]

But here is the odd thing; there is not a word in these accounts about Max. He was Sherlock Holmes's 'dog that did not bark'. If

[131] Lt Col Richard R. Heslop, DSO 1907-1973, DNB Article 31226
[132] *Heslop p. 52*

Wilkinson knew, or even suspected, he would surely have told Heslop, and probably Virginia Hall too. Although F Section may have been accommodating to the foibles and indiscretions of its people, alarm bells would have clanged in London. The next phase of their respective missions would have been either aborted or put on hold until all the security implications had been analysed by putting Denis through some tough questioning. It is an intriguing thought that if MI5 had become involved they might well have been tempted to run Denis back against Max. Instead, a deafening silence. As we know from his memoirs Buckmaster had heard the story, though we do not know when he found out and from whom, (maybe from Denis himself), and even embroiders it by describing Max as an SS officer.

Denis tells us in *le Chagrin* that after the war SOE found out at his request that Max had been transferred to the Russian front and died there, an account that in itself raises several questions. SOE was swiftly dismembered when the war ended. If there was anyone left in Baker Street to ask, did they wonder why he wanted to know and how he came to have a German officer as a close friend? If they did make enquiries, whom did they ask? The German Army had ceased to exist, those of its records which had not been carted off to Moscow were blowing loose in the wind through the rubble of Berlin. How could one man's death be tracked through the snow among so many hundreds of thousands of uncounted and unburied corpses?

So was the Max story merely a figment of Denis's imagination? It is hard to say for sure; on balance there was something to it but at a minimum, he probably overstated the intensity and duration of the relationship. We remember Buckmaster's warning about Denis's tendency to over-dramatise. It is even possible, as we shall see later, that while he did indeed have a relationship in Paris, the character of Max was invented to cover up or blend with the identity of another man. But if there was an affair (no matter with whom) who knew, and what did they do about it? Was it covered up by F Section? After all, in the report cited earlier, Maxwell Knight of MI5 had commented on the 'very marked lack of cooperation between the French Section and [SOE's] security officers'.

But it strains credulity almost beyond limits to suggest that so many people could have been induced to stay silent and that beyond Denis's account, none of the files or memoirs other than Buckmaster's has a scrap of information on the matter. It becomes even harder to credit when we learn from Maxwell Knight's report that one SOE officer in France, whom he names only as 'Captain X', had some responsibility for overall security and maintained discreet contacts with the French police, a role in which he might have been expected to pick up some trace of such a dangerous association. And even if word did not reach SOE, there must have been SIS agents in Paris with their ears to the ground, all too ready to pass back juicy rumours about their rivals to the London gossip mill.

So what are we to make of Wilkinson's supposed fury when, apparently, he found out? Denis's account of his earlier history (from his time as a sergeant in France to his spell in Gibraltar waiting nervously for his first mission) makes it clear that he was hyper-sensitive to the feeling he was being ostracised or slighted; this will become even more apparent shortly. It is thus possible that some chance remark, some unintentional and irrelevant jibe by Wilkinson, chafing at the bit in Paris, may well have led Denis to leap in self-pity to the mistaken conclusion that his macho colleague knew the full story and was condemning him for it. There remains the hypothesis of transposed identity which we will come to as the story unfolds. Meanwhile we must move on. Real perils rather than surmise lie just ahead down the railway track.

When he and Heslop met on the Gare de Perrache platform the next morning Denis was still overwrought, hopping on and off the train 'like a fussy grandmother' as the minutes ticked by and there was no sign of Wilkinson. At the last moment he strolled up without a care in the world, and the train pulled away.

When they reached Limoges at 5 p.m., they did not know that the copper-roofed Gare des Bénédictins, built in 1929 in a mix of Art Deco and Second Empire styles, and crowned by a thirteen storey clock tower, was the florid signpost for the beginning of a long and dangerous journey. They were arrested the next morning, 15 August.

14

Dungeons and Dragons

There is no confusion about what happened. Why, is yet again a matter of debate. Denis, who was still unwell, took the last room left at the Hotel de France. The other two stayed elsewhere and after dinner together at the Café des Faisans, under the ice-blue eyes of the obligatory portrait of Marshal Pétain, they arranged to meet Denis at the hotel at 11 a.m. the next day. But he was not there. Heslop and Wilkinson then broke a cardinal rule of SOE tradecraft, which dictated that meetings should always have a fallback that evening or the next day; if the first pass did not succeed, you walked away. Instead they circled the block and came back, into the arms of five plainclothed policemen. Both thought, and Wilkinson (swayed perhaps by unvoiced memories of the Max affair) was absolutely convinced, that Denis had given them away, an impression fostered by the police, for whom encouraging thieves to fall out with each other was, and indeed is, standard practice. Even the more measured Heslop, who admitted that he too was, not surprisingly, scared, remembers being 'bloody furious' with Denis, 'always frightened, always twittering away like an anxious sparrow'.

He remembers Denis telling him afterwards that when the French police (who were actually on the hunt for foreign Jews) arrived at dawn to check the guests' papers, the sharp-eyed hotel manageress had informed them that Denis was acting oddly. This prompted them to come back at 8 a.m. and question him when he came down for the pseudo coffee and slice of bread that passed for breakfast. Being 'rather het up' Denis had calculated that if the game was up he would do better if he stayed with Wilkinson and Heslop and thus had let slip that he was meeting two friends at 11 a.m.

When he was debriefed in London later, Denis gave a slightly different version: the sharp young French police inspector found his story that he was looking for work implausible. He also thought his identity card a poor forgery ('you should have paid more and got a better one') and decided to take him away for questioning. As he was being led out, the manageress, who remembered the three men coming to the hotel together when they booked Denis's room, had called out 'Don't forget his two friends'. She had volunteered precise descriptions of them, down to the colour and patterns of their ties, which is why they had been so easy to spot on the street later.

Who knows who was really to blame? As always the truth lurks somewhere in the middle of the various accounts. It does not matter. Denis was ill, he was anxious and may have spoken carelessly. The three of them should not have been seen together, all the more since Wilkinson was carrying not only Denis's wireless set (he did not want to let it out of his sight) but also a pistol. He and Denis also had a large number of 1000 franc notes tucked away in body-hugging money belts. Even this might have been explained away in the *Nono*'s 'cash and carry' economy, except that the two sets of notes had consecutive serial numbers. They also lacked the double pin holes in the top left hand corner which would have substantiated them to anyone who knew how the system worked, as having passed through the hands of a French bank.

The cashier's standard practice was to pin large denomination notes together in tens when counting them. 'No pinholes' meant to a suspicious police eye that the notes must have come from the British or the Germans. (In fact SOE got them in Lisbon.) To cap it all, Denis and Wilkinson were carrying French identity cards ostensibly issued in different towns, but made out in the same handwriting.[133] Thus while Denis's agitation may well have given first the manageress and then the police a strong sense that all was not well, poor tradecraft and SOE carelessness escalated a problem into a disaster. (French readers of a certain age might be tempted to see in the story so far, and what follows, outlines of the colourful imagination of the creators of a long-running newspaper comic strip

[133] *Foot p. 197; a note by Buckmaster in the personal file says defensively that the cards were supplied by the US Consul in Lyons, not SOE, an echo of Brand Whitlock in Brussels in 1914*

les Pieds Nickelés ('the Lucky Sods') which first appeared in 1908. Its three heroes, Croqignol, Filochard and Ribouldingue (whose names it would take several unnecessary lines to try to convert from French slang into English) spend the First World War operating behind enemy lines in various disguises, regularly outwitting the clod-hopping and gullible 'Boche'. Over later years the three experience endless ups and downs, but always manage to get out of trouble by their mastery of our familiar friend '*Système D*'.

If Paris had its ambiguities between rich and poor, the police in Vichy France had their own painful conflicts of loyalty and self interest when it came to the Resistance and its British backers. Though Pétain stopped short of executing British 'spies' they might still be delivered into the hands of the Gestapo, and suffer unknowable consequences. More likely they would end in a Vichy concentration camp, of which the Marshal's regime had a wide and grim range, or a Napoleonic era jail. In an odd counterpoint[134] in July 1942 a French military tribunal in Clermont Ferrand sentenced to death three Frenchmen who had been working in the *Nono* as German agents.

When the Germans swept into the *Nono* a few months later they demanded that the trio be handed over, only to be told they had been shipped to jails in North Africa and could not now be traced. In April 1944 a dog clawed up the remains of three fox-chewed corpses from a shallow grave near the village of La Font de l'Arbre. Papers left on the bodies revealed that they were the missing German agents. A French police investigation, surprisingly thorough given all the circumstances, found the three had been pulled out of jail and shot by a group of French army officers and NCOs, but when the Germans retreated in the autumn, the case fizzled out.

In the summer of 1942 the more shrewd Vichy police officials, who watched the weathervane of war, had to weigh up keeping in with the Germans, anticipating the day the Wehrmacht would sweep away the line and grab control of the whole country, against the advantages of taking out 'reinsurance' with the Allies if, or when,

---

[134] *Martres p. 37*

they launched the much anticipated 'Second Front' by landing in Europe. In a typewritten note to Buckmaster on Denis's personal file, dated 21 September 1942, Virginia Hall outlines this sweaty dilemma in her own breezy style. She writes of *Pompey*, who was evidently a top officer in the Lyons Political Police, and an unnamed colleague, both of whom were concerned with 'information dealing with England'.

Both cooperated with her when it suited them. 'They are very much on the fence waiting to see which way to jump. They feel that should the British land, the French will go to their aid – that is, the official [Vichy] army – if they think it to their advantage and that there is ninety per cent chance of winning, otherwise they would let the British drop like hot-cakes and try to get a reward from the Boche for meritorious behaviour.' The inevitable complexity of her dealings did not escape the London security witch hunters; in an intemperate and apparently unsent 1944 file note about 'damn fools' who raised doubts about his agents, Buckmaster mentions that 'Miss Hall was accused for months of being a double agent in Lyons, and as far as I know no action was taken by security against her'.[135]

We need to understand this background of dangerous ambivalence, with its echoes of Claude Rains's deft balancing act in *Casablanca*[136] to make sense of the strange story of how Heslop, Wilkinson and Denis ended up in one of the grimmest jails in France.

Commissaire Guth of the Limoges Political Police, who was in charge of their case, was an Alsatian in his mid thirties with no love for the Germans who had annexed his homeland; other Alsatians took a different view and some were collaborating eagerly with the Gestapo in Vichy. He had already earned one black mark for poor security in January 1942 when an SOE agent, who had deliberately made himself unwell so as to get transferred from the same jail to Limoges Hospital, escaped from there with bursting stitches 'while the policeman at his bedside dozed' and made his way back home

---

[135] *Murphy p. 126*
[136] *Actually being completed at the time by director Michael Curtiz. Also starring Humphrey Bogart and Ingrid Bergman; it was released in January 1943. Modern eyes have claimed to discern a distinct homosexual undertone in the attitude of Rains's cynical Vichy police captain to the tough and mysterious Bogart*

through Spain.[137] Guth allowed his officers to give the three a professional though non-violent grilling. Confronted with Wilkinson's pistol, the telltale banknotes and the fake identity cards, the three could not maintain any semblance of real cover, though Heslop shifted his ground only to the point of pretending to reveal that he was a downed RAF pilot seeking to get home.

Once Guth had satisfied himself that they were British, and not a German 'plant' he relaxed, though as events unfolded none of the three seemed to have wondered whether he might be playing a double game. Denis was certainly convinced that he was genuine in his desire to help the Allies. He seems not to have turned a hair when Guth invited him home for lunch, arranging to pick up on the way the wireless set which Wilkinson had left under a pile of luggage in the hotel and which the police had not found.

Denis's first account after his return to England tells us that all three went to lunch with Guth, though he later wrote as if he had been the only guest, much perhaps as he blanked Hayes out of his version of his landing in France. But whether or not they were there, Wilkinson and Heslop (who had given their 'parole' that they would not escape) were allowed to wander virtually unescorted along the tree lined banks of the River Vienne and across over its ancient stone bridges.

Denis was still receiving 'the silent treatment' from Wilkinson, and Heslop remembers that 'he took to his bed and became quieter and quieter . . . nothing could bring a smile to his face. I think the thought that he had betrayed his friends worked on Rake's conscience . . . one day he was so ill he was taken to hospital.'

'It was a relief really as although I did not think he would volunteer information, he was unreliable under stress' a big risk since Heslop and Wilkinson were soon busy cooking up various, but in the event abortive, escape plans. Their cover stories survived a tough but non-violent interrogation by a visiting Gestapo team; Guth explained with a shrug that they were not supposed to operate on Vichy territory but they were in civilian clothes and anyway what

---

[137] *It is almost superfluous to say by now that Virginia Hall made the escape line arrangements*

could he do? It is quite possible that Guth too sensed Denis's vulnerability, and had him shifted to hospital to avoid German pressure.

What happened next is open to two interpretations. Either Guth decided that the Englishmen should be sent even further away from the Gestapo's reach, or someone in the Vichy hierarchy decided it was politic to show the Germans the gendarmes were indeed toeing the party line as defined back in Berlin a few months earlier by Heinrich Müeller of the Gestapo. He had authorised what he called 'sharpened interrogation' (a term with some twenty-first century resonance) for those who had 'plans hostile to the state', including starvation, sleep deprivation, exhaustion exercises, regular beating and confinement in blacked-out cells. Many of these techniques were in use, and had been long before Müeller encouraged them, at the prison in Castres in south-west France about one hundred miles north of Perpignan and fifty miles east of Toulouse, to which Heslop and Wilkinson were soon on their way, in shackles. Denis would follow, but only after a diversion which yet again highlights the shifting sands on which the various players were trying to find a footing.

News of the arrest reached Virginia Hall in Lyons in an unsigned note dropped through the letterbox of 'the consulate', presumably that of the United States. Never one to hang around, she took the next train to Limoges but the Maison des Prisonniers there denied any knowledge of the three men. She fell back on her source *Pompey* who undertook to find out what was happening; in a clear reference to the escape in January he told her that 'it would probably be impossible to arrange the same thing as before'.

There then followed a flurry of activity, which again might be taken at one level as an attempt at entrapment or penetration, but at another as one more indication of the dangers of those shifting sands. Maybe it was both. The next report came to Maurice Pertschuk, *Eugene*, the PWE agent, of whom we lost sight a few pages ago. He reported to Virginia that he had received a telegram from a policeman in Limoges asking him to tell *Marie* (Virginia) that *Justin* (Denis) was seriously ill in hospital and that she should come immediately. A quick check with *Pompey* confirmed Denis was in hospital but not badly ill, and that Heslop and Wilkinson had been taken to Castres.

A few days later Pertschuk received another wire from Limoges, asking for 5000 francs and saying that *Justin*, i.e. Denis, would be in Lyons on 4 September. Denis's explanation for this is that Guth told him while he was in hospital that he too would have to go to Castres. But Guth also informed him that if he gave his parole he would be allowed to stop in Lyons to pass on to 'the British Secret Service' that Guth, the two policeman who would accompany Denis and, Guth thought, many of their colleagues, were prepared 'to work for the Allies'.[138]

With more caution than many in this story displayed, Virginia Hall records that she did not meet Denis but instead sent a 'cutout' to whom he told a 'rather wild and woolly story' (probably a version of Guth's proposal). The cutout reported that Denis was 'quite ill with dysentery and an abscess in the face, and is generally shot to pieces'. Given what he had been through, this was hardly a surprise. There was worse to come.

In his autobiography Denis remembers that Virginia Hall told him to get back to England while he could, and that an aircraft was leaving that night. He said he refused, since he had given his parole.

Her version is that he told the cutout he was confident that if he went to Castres, the police colleagues of Guth who were with him could arrange for all three of them, himself, Heslop, and Wilkinson, to escape together, so he might as well go.

On 19 September, the two policemen, Inspectors Imar and Lescia, called at Virginia Hall's apartment, having sent Pertschuk's housekeeper Madame Maguy ahead as a messenger. How they convinced her and through her, Virginia Hall, of their bona fides is part of the story worth telling only because of the further insights it gives into that twilight world through which the police and their supposed opponents were stumbling, neither side fully trusting, but each seeking some advantage, political or financial, in the dangerous game. Imar and Lescia first called at Pertschuk's lodgings. Pertschuk

---

[138] I*t was around this point that Guth took away Denis's money and in the words of the SOE debriefers, quoting Denis, 'retained under seal his watch, his ring and his son's photograph'*

and Madame Maguy were out but his landlady, 'a good egg' in Virgina Hall's inimitable words, had just seen off two 'genuine' Vichy police who were looking for Pertschuk. Madame Maguy came back and the two 'good cops' helped her wind up an aerial wire the Vichy men had not spotted, and pack up a wireless set, which they guarded while she went off to see Virginia Hall to arrange for them to call.

She had faced a difficult decision about whether or not it was a setup. She was reassured, it was 'proof of their mettle', when they told her they had Denis's wireless safely hidden, which she could have at any time, and had kept all the forged identity papers out of hostile or German sight. Not only that, but they had made sure – Guth also told Denis this – that the notes of the various interrogations had been written in a way as to suggest that there was nothing against the three men except that they were British escapers, rather than SOE agents. She told them she would back a plan to escape from Castres but, as she advised London in her note, she felt 'my time is about up'. Vichy had her address and had probably left her alone 'because I reckon they don't exactly want to disturb an American at the moment'. She asked Buckmaster to arrange a passage out for her in October.

Pertschuk was also rattled. She reported she had given him a new identity card and ration coupons and that he would probably soon move to Toulouse 'with a heavy heart'.[139] When the PRUNUS circuit was penetrated and blown by the Germans, in large part due to operational carelessness he 'treated his captors with the dignity and spirit of a free man far beyond his years – he was not yet twenty two'. He died in Buchenwald.[140] As if this was not enough to juggle, Virginia reported that she was separately trying to find a home for Brian Stonehouse, *Celestin,* a young Vogue fashion artist newly parachuted in as a wireless operator who had nowhere to stay and 'has been dragged around from pillar to post'.

---

[139] *An accurate premonition on the part of this brave but unlucky agent*
[140] *Foot p. 275*

15

'Come, let's away to Prison'

Denis's heart must have been even heavier when it was his turn to be handcuffed and have his legs shackled, and to clamber awkwardly onto a bus in Limoges to make the 150 mile long journey via Brive-la-Gaillarde and Montauban to Castres. Typically, his main memory of the journey was that the guard who escorted him was 'quite good looking . . . and had a great sense of humour too'.

Castres was horrible. Its thirty foot stone walls blocked out any humour, daylight or humanity. It was a place designed to crush the spirit with silence and emaciate the body through a near starvation diet. Guth had lugubriously described it to Denis as 'the worst prison in France'. This was quite an accolade since 'hunger, lice and vermin' were endemic in all Vichy era jails.[141] Not much has changed; if he were to revisit any major French jail today, Denis would find the overcrowding, scurrying rats and omnipresent lice unpleasantly familiar. In 2006 the suicide rate was 22.8 per 10,000 prisoners compared to 9.0 in Germany and 13.2 in Britain.

Officially it was the solitary confinement wing of the prison complex of Saint Sulpice la Pointe. Saint Sulpice was a cluster of twenty barrack huts and to confuse anyone who might enquire, Castres was often referred to simply as 'Caserne 21'. According to a letter on Denis's personal file, Andrieux, the Chief Warder of Castres, had spent many years as head jailer on the prison ship *Martinique*. Until 1938 she ferried even less fortunate prisoners of the Third Republic across the Atlantic to Devil's Island off the coast of French Guiana, a job description evoking an aspect of French history best forgotten.

[141] *Dictionnaire p. 782*

When Denis arrived in the latter part of September, he struck Heslop and Wilkinson, who had been there for a couple of weeks, as looking a lot better after his hospital stay. He was put into their cell at first, with Wilkinson still adamantly refusing to speak to him, though for all three most of their spell in Castres was spent in solitary confinement, a regime which combined with a diet of bread and watery soup ground down even the tough Heslop. One French prisoner put the daily ration at twelve ounces of bread, known in jailhouse slang as '*brutal*' and soup with a few scraps of cabbage leaf and gristle; prisoners with cash could buy an apple from the warders every three weeks.

The days were long, and the nights longer. When one of the blue uniformed warders, the '*bignolons*' (remembered by the same prisoner as a bunch of 'drunks and thieves') blew a whistle, the prisoners had to climb into their bunks, and were not allowed to get up until the whistle blew again in the morning. But proper sleep was almost impossible; every two hours a warder shuffling along the landing in felt slippers, would flick on the ceiling light in the cell from outside, and slide open the squeaking iron spyhole cover to take a look at the prisoner. If the sleepless unfortunate had pulled the rough sheet over his head to try to shut out the light, the warder would bang open the door and scream at him.

The daytime discipline was no better. Locked in their cells all day except for a twenty minute spell of exercise and a weekly trudge through the hallways to the barber for a coldwater shave with a blunt razor, the prisoners were not allowed to lie on the bed, and if they sat on the wooden stool, they had to face the door. They were forbidden to read or write, a rule which Denis did not grasp at first and which earned him a tooth-breaking backhander from Andrieux. He also had his foot smashed when a French interrogator crunched down on it with his boot heel when he found Denis less than cooperative. Wilkinson too came in for regular beatings from Andrieux.[142]

---

[142] *His capture in Paris in 1944 and his death in a concentration camp meant he could not fulfil the vow he took then to come back after the war and shoot Andrieux dead; Heslop made the journey himself but Andrieux was not to be found. Andrieux did not have things all his own way; a tantalisingly brief French report says that on 17 September 1943 'foreigners' jailed in Castres took control of the jail for a short and no doubt brutally terminated spell*

But in the middle of it all there was one final reverberation of the escape plot. Imar and another policeman, probably Lescia, came to the jail to see Wilkinson and told him that they could organise false papers for an escape and men to act as 'guards', but they would need a car and fuel and for that they needed money. Thinking fast, Wilkinson decided that if they could produce false identity papers and authorisations, they could just as easily forge papers to get their hands on a car. The story did not ring true. He turned them down. His instinct was right to an extent since, though he was not to know, they had already had cash from Pertschuk. But a brief note on Heslop's personal file says that Imar's help 'had been discovered by the Germans', raising the question of what game was actually being played and what price Imar may have paid for his involvement.

As for Denis, he had enough problems sleeping without Andrieux's version of Gallic hospitality, and as he told his debriefers he became so troubled by insomnia that he took to beating his head on the cell wall to try to knock himself out. Even Andrieux was worried and sent in a doctor, who was not in the Castres mould and who treated Denis with kindness. He even spoke of trying to arrange a transfer for him to a prison with better conditions, and he slipped under his cell door scraps of paper with news from the BBC.

On 7 November 1942, there was a transfer, but not the one anticipated by the good doctor. Denis, Heslop and Wilkinson were brought separately to the prison office, where for a moment they didn't recognise one another. 'My God, what have they done to you,' Heslop remembers Wilkinson muttering. 'Not only to me, but to all of us,' Heslop replied. They were so weak he wrote later that if all the warders had suddenly dropped dead they still could not have taken a single step towards freedom.

They were told they were going to a camp at Chambaran in the Isère, about 250 miles north-east of Castres. It was for prisoners of war and on no account were they to tell anyone they were anything but captured servicemen. It was another day-long haul by train and coach across France via Toulouse and Lyons, but however gruelling and even though they were under guard, just seeing the outside world again must have been sheer joy after the gloom of Castres.

Wilkinson dented any feeling of relief on Denis's part by continuing to ignore him completely.

Joy too, of a physical kind, at Chambaran, where after months of deprivation the trio could share in the food parcels sent out for prisoners of war. It is a sign of those times that Heslop especially remembered his delight in tasting marmalade, corned beef and sugar. But the joy was short-lived. In the world outside the barbed wire the war, and France, were about to take a new tack. The Allies were on the brink of their landings in North Africa, Operation Torch, while back in Berlin Hitler and his generals were fine-tuning Operation Anton, the takeover of the *Nono*. Back in Lyons Virginia Hall, SOE's 'Mother Courage' was methodically unravelling her connections and getting ready to make the dangerous trek up and over the Pyrenees into Spain. As Denis would find out, at the best of times and in the best of weather it was a debilitating, gruelling slog for the fittest of men, and all the more so for a woman with a wooden leg.

The 'Torch' landings began on 8 November. 'Anton' was un-rolled two days' later and the first German troops crossed the demarcation line unopposed at 7 a.m. on 11 November, a date fraught with leaden symbolism as the anniversary of the First World War Armistice. It would take some while before the whole zone was securely in German hands but the window of opportunity for escape was closing. The Chambaran commandant Captain Boucher told the trio that he knew who they really were, that the Germans were on their way 'and they've already given orders that you should be shot'. Happily he had decided that they and several others who were at risk would be freed before that happened. He could give them rail vouchers, which would take them as far as Marseilles. After that they were on their own.

Denis, Heslop and Wilkinson would get out of trouble here too, but only for a while. First, there was a frigid parting of the ways. When they were clear of Chambaran, Wilkinson told Heslop that as they moved across France to find a route to safety there would be no place for Denis. 'That man is unreliable. Anyway, he may crack up and we can't afford passengers on this trip.' This was more or less the version Denis gave in his debriefing, though in his autobiography he remembers Wilkinson giving him a far more hurtful two word message to the same effect.

Yet again Denis found himself in hostile territory, a long way from home and saddled now with two new companions, British sergeants, who had been captured at Dunkirk and who were at special risk since they had allegedly killed a German soldier while trying to escape. Neither spoke a word of French. Denis tried to contact Virginia Hall in Lyons, only to find she had left.[143]

The trio then headed for the ancient city of Perpignan (close to the Spanish border) and an ideal jumping off point for escapers. They reached it via a 'safe house' in Grenoble, and the Marseilles apartment of two young sisters, one a sculptress, the other a painter, with whom the two sergeants struck up a warm overnight relationship, leaving Denis who wrote, 'feeling rather *de trop*'. In his initial account of what happened, though it was not elaborated in his debriefing, Denis says that while in Marseilles he contacted RENÉ and PAT who did escaped prisoners' work. This is certainly a reference to the escape line created by Ian Garrow and then built on by Albert Guérisse, a Belgian medical officer, under the pseudonym of 'Lt Commander Patrick O'Leary RN',[144] coincidentally with help from Nancy Wake. But as Denis remembered it, most of PAT's people 'had been arrested and they could not help'. A month later the PAT line was infiltrated either by a French traitor, 'Roger the Legionnaire' or a renegade British Sergeant Harold Cole, and Guérisse himself was arrested in March 1943.[145]

(Nevertheless there are signs that PAT did provide at least some background help, through a Frenchman named Nardain and 'a one –eyed Belgian known to the organisation as Jean', (a description entirely in keeping with SOE's popular image). And a later MI9 escape circuit message on Denis's personal file, sent over SIS channels states that he was 'evacuated by O'Leary'.)

The first Wehrmacht tanks crunched along Marseilles' once

---

[143] *Foot p. 222*
[144] *1911-1989. GC. KBE, survived Natzweiler and Dachau. Later head of the Belgian Army's Medical Service*
[145] *Foot p. 156; Wake p 81: Nancy Wake herself escaped arrest by the skin of her teeth.*

grand Canebière from the city centre to the Old Port on 12 November and we know from Denis's debriefing that by the time he reached Perpignan there were German tanks and trucks in the city, but as in the rest of the Unoccupied Zone it took time to tighten the noose; the first SS detachments did not reach Marseilles until early December.[146]

As at other points in the odyssey we need to remind ourselves that Denis was 'running' or rather 'limping on empty', painfully dragging the foot his interrogator had trampled on in Castres. He was a frazzled actor, his stomach a molten mess, dejected at being shunned by his macho peers because they thought he had 'shopped' them. He was a man one short step ahead of the Gestapo, a man who could not remember when he last soaked in a hot bath, a fastidious man plagued by fleas and lice. But he was determined to push on. 'I had had enough of prisons, beatings, companions who believed I had betrayed them, and running and hiding, to last a lifetime,' he wrote nearly twenty-five years later.

The French who helped on this last lap were also at risk. They were not heading back to England but would have to stay behind and convince paranoid SS men where their loyalties lay. This was especially true of Commandant Feti, head of the Perpignan Gendarmerie, a First World War veteran with Maquis links who sheltered Denis and the sergeants and found them the *passeur*, the guide who was to lead them over the Pyrenees. The guide was cut from the same shoddy cloth as the Lyons pork butcher. First, money up front, which luckily the two sergeants had, hidden in an aspirin tube, skimmed from running a canteen in one or other of their prisoner of war camps. Then a strange journey on a single-track railway up the first slopes of the foothills, to a village where they joined a mixed bag of other escapers. Among them were young Frenchmen seeking to avoid forced labour in Germany and exiled Spaniards who had been lying low in France since the Civil War.

---

[146] *Lyons became a major administrative centre for the Germans. An early arrival was Klaus Barbie, newly appointed local head of the SS, anxious to begin the hunt for Jews, resisters and also Virgina Hall from his new office at the Hotel Terminus. 'I would give anything to get my hands on that redheaded Canadian bitch,' he is alleged to have said, unaware of her real nationality or that she had already escaped*

We are now in the first week of December, and even in the foothills it was cold. As they climbed higher, they would be trudging through snow, perversely a relief for Denis since the cold numbed the pain of his damaged foot. Telling them they would soon reach Spain, just beyond the hill ahead, the *passeur*, in the finest traditions of his trade, announced that this was as far as he went, and loped away down the icy mule track. 'Soon' turned out to be another day and a half of breathless and increasingly painful stumbling. The intensity of the pain, the fatigue, and the anxiety are almost impossible to describe in the abstract.

In 2007 a group of young women from the Princess Royal's Volunteer Corps, successor to the First Aid Nursing Yeomanry or FANY, the unit to which most of SOE's women agents were nominally attached, decided to follow in the footsteps of Anne-Marie Walters. In 1944 as a 22-year-old courier for the WHEELWRIGHT circuit, she had crossed the mountains into Spain wearing a tweed skirt and gym shoes three sizes too large. Even with the benefit of eighteen months' training, without the risk of falling into hostile hands, well equipped with waterproof clothing, food, maps and a compass, and escorted by experienced guides, the 2007 group found it a tough three days of climbing and foot-slogging. And their trek was in the sun and crispness of autumn, not the dangerous depths of winter.

When after two days and three nights Denis finally staggered into Spain he found himself trapped on a slow-moving conveyor belt which was supposed to end in repatriation to Britain but which was jolted and diverted by petty bureaucracy, high politics and again, British security concerns. Several months of worry lay ahead behind bars and barbed wire. As the tide of war ebbed and flowed, Spain's shrewd Fascist leader General Franco remained 'neutral', sometimes more so, sometimes less. One consequence, other than the gratification of some of his colleagues who received generous bounty from British secret 'slush' funds to help them decide where their interests lay,[147] was that Spain had to strike a delicate balance in the way it handled the 'tired and huddled masses' who scrambled out of the

---

[147] *Some $20 million, by Professor Foot's account*

mountains day after day. It did not want to offend Britain, for instance, by holding escaped POWs for too long. Equally it was advisable not to provoke German anger by releasing too many British or Polish POWs to rejoin the RAF and get back in the fight. And Spain was a backward police state, without the administrative machinery to cope with these new categories of 'refugee'. Fortunately the Civil War had left it one useful legacy in the form of the large concentration camp at Miranda de Ebro, where the Franco regime had locked away and brutalised thousands of its opponents. It had been built roughly in the middle of the triangle formed by Bilbao, Pamplona and Burgos, on ground which had soaked up blood not just from the Civil War but in the early nineteenth century from the bodies of countless thousands of Spanish, Portuguese and French soldiers in the campaign to push Napoleon out of Spain.

Denis was arrested by the Spanish police and taken to Gerona where the British Consul who visited the jail refused to give him the blanket and cigarettes provided for British POWs on the grounds that 'SOE is not regarded as Army'. From there he travelled the 300 miles or so by cattle truck and train to Miranda. Some British prisoners complained of the camp's 'obscene brutality' and it was certainly filthy and overcrowded; when Denis was there it held 4000 men, four times more than it had been designed for, with two metres of floor space allocated to every seven men.

Writing twenty-five years later, Denis says of his time in *Baraca No.6* that 'I didn't find Miranda any hardship . . . . [it was] not only bearable but a place of happy experiences.' Indeed, though the inmates had to queue for hours to get water, they were given wine ('very bad' he later told SOE) once a week and were able to buy or barter food from Spanish Communist prisoners whose wives were allowed to flock around the gates and hand over bundles of provisions. Denis later boasted to SOE that he had actually put on weight. But a more likely reason for his mention of 'happy experiences' is the start of another sentimental friendship, described in *Rake's Progress* but ignored completely in the otherwise detailed account of this period in the debriefing report.

Here again Denis blurs the facts. He identifies his new friend as

Alex Shokolovsky, the 26 or 27-year-old son of a French mother and a Hungarian father. As research in the SOE files shows, (though there is no hint of this in Denis's own personal file) he was actually Alexandre Schwatschko, born in Cluj, in Transylvania, to a Russian or Ukrainian father and a Hungarian mother. When he and Denis met in Spain he was a dashing 20-year-old playboy who had served in the French Air Force.

More puzzlingly, Denis writes of their meeting in the chilly bustle of the Miranda prison yard as their first encounter, another Max-evoking *coup de foudre.* 'It was as if we both knew from the very instant we both looked at one another that we had to be friends . . . he was one of the most handsome men I have ever seen . . . a tremendous sense of humour . . . among the most intelligent men I have ever known,' he gushed. But was it really their first meeting? As we shall see the files suggest otherwise.

Late in December Alex left Miranda, under the impression that he was being transferred directly to England. Denis had a lonely Christmas, but in a letter he wrote to his friend Geoffrey Wincott in London on 28 December,[148] he tried hard to be cheerful.

Addressing Wincott as 'Dear old fellow' Denis tells him that it was 'only a very short time ago that I was lucky in escaping and reaching here. I arrived with a broken jaw and broken ankle but my foot [is] getting on OK and is to be out of plaster soon.

'Please try and find my pal Richard Ellis for me and tell him I am OK and that I may be back in our dear old country in a few months' time . . . I so hope you are well and that no unhappiness has come your way. I personally have had some really amazing adventures but I hope my name will appear [on] the bills of the theatres once more and that you won't have forgotten me. Please believe my thoughts to be with you and Richard very often. I have been seriously ill but am OK.

Yours,

Denis'

Wincott too was an actor. He played in Shakespeare at the Old Vic and those who have reached senior citizenship may remember

---

[148] *Courtesy Ian Sayer Collection*

him as Eeyore in the BBC's long running radio adaptations of *Winnie the Pooh*.

But he had unwittingly made his biggest mark on a worldwide audience as a relief announcer on the Empire Service of the BBC in those pre-war days when newsreaders wore dinner jackets, though nobody could see them, and clipped Oxbridge accents were *de rigueur*. Signing off one evening to the British Dominions of palm and pine, Wincott intoned the Mother Country's ritual *nunc dimittis*: 'Good night to you all – wherever you may be – goodnight from London.' But he was annoyed at some hitch by his studio engineers and gave vent to his feelings. 'The bloody fools. Christ. The bloody fools', he snapped, not realising his microphone was still on and that his parting shot was heard across the Empire, from bewildered sheep farmers in Australia, to bemused bankers in Hong Kong.

Denis's letter also puts into context memoranda exchanged between SIS, MI5 and SOE on his personal file which point a critical finger at Sub-Lieutenant Richard Ellis of the Royal Naval Reserve. He had given, perhaps in an Officers' Wardroom, and unaware that one of his listeners worked for SIS, what seems to have been a significantly overblown account of the French exploits of his friend 'Rake' on behalf of a 'Commando Secret Service'. He had added that Rake was now in Miranda. The memoranda suggest Denis should be spoken to about this when he returns, but though Ellis was rapped over the knuckles there is no trace of any further action.

The letter to Wincott passed through both Spanish and British censorship unscathed, but Denis would not be Denis if he did not toss us yet another puzzle. In the box identifying the sender Denis gives his name as 'Captain D.J. Greer', the stage name which he claims he used throughout his time in Spain. Though this was the name by which Wincott and his stage friends knew him, it may well have been some SOE security procedure, intended to alert them via a 'watch list' in the MI12 section at the London Censorship headquarters in Holborn that this was an SOE letter.[149]

[149] *We know from Richard Heslop's personal file, which has a three word reference to Denis's sister's address which the 'weeders' missed, that SOE were sensitive about correspondence relating to any of their agents who*

Just a few days' later Denis was on the move, to Jaraba, a small spa town in the hills between Madrid and Saragossa, which had been commandeered for internees.[150] There he found himself comfortably billeted and well-fed in one of its four large hotels, and had the even greater pleasure of seeing Alex, whom the merry-go-round of fate had temporarily dumped there too. Though its clientèle was now a motley crew of foreigners, rather than the Spanish bourgeoisie relieving their digestion with glasses of sulphur-smelling mineral water or easing rheumatic joints in the natural springs nestled in the sandstone rocks, Jaraba's life went on. The baths and restaurants were open, bars served tapas and sherry and, like Paris, the brothels were doing a steady trade. The story would have made an art house film.

One scene in particular might have been from *Death in Venice* remade by Pedro Almodovar. Denis, in the von Aschenbach role, tells us that Alex and others 'sometimes' visited a brothel in the narrow Calle Cauid, and he would tag along, 'not because I went to the brothels, but because it was such a very pleasant little place'. He remembered sitting at a café table one evening, sipping wine and listening to the singer, 'a somewhat raucous woman shouting her head off', and waiting wistfully for Alex to re-emerge. It 'rather upset me but he meant so much to me that I could even overlook it. After all, he wasn't really being unfaithful', he concludes generously.

By then not only Denis but even the Spanish authorities were concerned that he seems to have been left in limbo, and that no effort was being made to get him home. A visit by the British Military Attaché from Madrid brought the explanation: London was worried that the 'real' Rake had been caught and executed in

might have been imprisoned, whether by the French, the Spanish or the Germans. Those trapped in Spain were permitted to write home, but their letters often prompted their family and friends to get in touch with the War Office, in search of more news. SOE told the War Office Casualty Branch that any enquiries from SOE relatives were to be sent to the implausibly named Mr Ebenezer Potter at MI5's address in Curzon Street. MI5 would forward it to an SOE cover address in Northumberland Avenue, where a decision would be made on what to say. This would not include any avowal of an SOE connection or even that the person sought was in jail, since SOE thought that might in some way impair their chance of a negotiated release. The War Office were also told that if they heard from their own sources that an SOE agent was a prisoner, they should tell SOE but not the family

[150] *Though in his own initial statement Denis names 'Jaraba', when his debriefers went through it with him and wrote their own version they referred to it as 'Herrar' and three lines later as 'Herrera', probably as a consequence of someone's mishearing or mispronunciation of the Spanish letter 'J'*

Toulouse and that the man in Jaraba was an imposter sent to infiltrate the escape lines all the way back to London. To verify who he was, the attaché needed some personal fact that only the real Denis would know. A photograph would not do since the Germans would have been smart enough to send in someone with a close resemblance to Denis. Denis's claimed response – telling him the story of the Greek Prince and suggesting that it be checked in Greek newspaper archives which were then (but sadly no longer) held in the British Museum – does not exactly resonate with the ring of plausibility. It seems more likely that if Denis did try to reassure the attaché, he would have referred him directly to King George, who was closely in touch with Whitehall and SOE or to the Marquess, who had vouched for him when he joined SOE. There is no reflection of this episode on the personal file, though that does not make it untrue.

We know that SIS's MI9 offshoot had tracked him into Spain as Rake. And the flurry of exchanges on the personal file about Richard Ellis shows that SOE were well aware that he was in Miranda. Eventually the wheels turned, and via Madrid, Gibraltar and Lisbon, he carried a new passport in the name of 'Denis Joseph Greer, Civil Servant', reinforcing the suggestions that his stage name was being used as SOE camouflage.

Denis returned to Orchard Court in May 1943, to a nod of recognition by the janitor, Mr Park, a detailed debriefing, a reunion with Alex, and a nervous breakdown. This was a watershed. All he had to do was tell his story. After that, had he decided he had had enough, that in the jargon of the time, 'he had done his bit', that it was time to take an office job, go back to the stage, or to running a hotel in Queens Gate, no one could have blamed him. He could not even have blamed himself. Instead he carried on, not without diversions, towards an even more dangerous mission.

16

Nancy With The Laughing Face

On 19 May 1943 London enjoyed a warm day. The sunbathers in Hyde Park were distracted only by an anniversary march past of the elderly and infirm Home Guard, putting their best feet forward even though, in the words of the poet W.H. Auden describing a similar parade, 'some have gout and some have goitres, most of them have Bright's Disease. Uric acid has made them flaccid . . .'. London theatres continued to offer productions to suit every taste and provide a distraction from the war, from a Noël Coward season, through an adaptation of Grahame Greene's *Brighton Rock*, starring Richard Attenborough, to the 163rd edition of the *Windmill Revue*, with its nubile nudes posing pertly behind strategically-placed plumes under the hot-eyed gaze of the heavy-breathing men in the audience.

The mackintosh-clad voyeurs might have been forgiven for temporarily forgetting the mainstream of the war, where the balance of advantage continued to shift in the Allies' favour. The US Air Force had just smashed German submarine pens at Lorient, and destroyed over 120 Luftwaffe fighters on the ground in the Low Countries. In the Ruhr, floodwaters unleashed by the RAF's destruction of the Eder and Möhne dams with Barnes Wallis's 'bouncing bombs' were lapping at towns sixty miles downstream; literally marking a turn in the tide of war. It was too early to tell whether Allied bombing, especially of munitions plants, would seriously hamper Germany's war efforts, but as Winston Churchill remarked, there was no harm in finding out.

It was warmer still in the room, maybe at Orchard Court or perhaps at SOE's Security Section offices in Bayswater, where Denis was being debriefed, just five days after his return. He had first dictated his own version of events, and was now taken through it by two unnamed officers on the opposite side of a green baize covered table.

Their account, over nine pages of closely typed foolscap, refers to the fact that Heslop and Wilkinson believed Denis had been the cause of their arrest, and that they had parted company with him because they felt 'he was a danger to them'. But the context makes it clear that Denis had volunteered this, and there is no indication that the point was pursued further.

Denis wrote in his memoirs that he detected some suspicion on the questioners' part but when he repeated that it was the beady-eyed manageress who had first told the police there were two other men, and who described what they were wearing, they took a half hour break, and came back saying they had checked the point and were now satisfied. If so, quite what led them to this conclusion is unclear.

Richard Heslop would not return to London for another month, so his version of events, if it was different, had not yet been told. But there is nothing on his personal file to suggest that he blamed Denis: a series of radio talks he gave for the BBC in 1945, the scripts of which were vetted by SOE, is likewise free of any hint of criticism. It is curious that Denis seemed far more troubled by this part of the story. It was, after all, neither the first nor the last time a rattled field agent would slip up under pressure. In contrast he does not seem to have had the slightest concern that he would be quizzed about Max, potentially far thinner ice, or indeed his relationship with Alex.

Denis's debriefing reads as though it was conducted by policemen without too much knowledge of SOE and uncharacteristically incurious minds. There are many points on which one might have expected some close probing or follow-up, not least the Ellis indiscretion and the worry that the 'Rake' who turned up in Spain might have been a German plant. At a less critical level, in one of the forms Denis filled up when he joined SOE and which his interrogators would presumably have had in front of them, he notes that he spoke French and English at level A, i.e. fluently, but German only at level C. Yet he told his questioners that when he was being interrogated by German officers after trying to cross the Demarcation Line, he understood what they said to each other 'having been a prisoner of war in Germany all through the last war,' a Walter Mitty assertion his age alone would have called into question.

It was on the draft of this report that Buckmaster had noted Denis's predilection for dramatic effect. He also bridled at the opening line, which stated that Denis had been sent into France to work as an operator 'for Dr Beck of PWE'. This should be deleted: 'Rake was working for F Section'.

Overall an unkind reader might conclude that the questioning, though detailed, was rather pro-forma evidence for the file that Denis had been fully interrogated. As we have noted it was a laudable guiding principle in F Section and indeed throughout SOE that their agents should be given the benefit of any doubt. Had the Security Section run the interrogation, or consulted the cynics at MI5 they might have taken a harder line.

Even though the debriefing had closed a painful chapter, the pent-up pressures were too great for Denis to bear – most people, even those who take pride in their macho toughness, would have gone to pieces much earlier on in the story. He took to wandering around the West End asking bewildered passers by for the time and loudly disputing what he was told.

We might wonder why the Security Section was not on 'red alert'. Not only was Denis clearly on the verge of a nervous breakdown, but Alex, last seen in Jaraba, had eventually made it to London, and was soon to be attracting unnecessary attention to himself. Like all such undocumented and potentially 'planted' or otherwise dubious arrivals, he was being 'screened' by MI5 at the 'London Reception Centre' once the Royal Victoria Patriotic Asylum, a Gothic pile looming improbably over the muddy scruffiness of Wandsworth Common.[151]

Denis tells us that Alex had managed to send him a telegram telling him where he was, in a staccato style evoking Sebastian Flyte in *Brideshead Revisited* – 'Help. Am Imprisoned. Alex.' Denis introduced Alex to Maurice Buckmaster, who after several meetings took him into SOE under the name of 'Shaw'. (In another literary

---

[151] *Built in the late 1850s for the orphaned children of Crimean War veterans, and serving in the First World War as a military hospital complete with its own railway station, it has now been converted into flats, small workshops, design studios and at last visit, a French restaurant*

echo, 'Aircraftsman Shaw' was Lawrence of Arabia's alias when he joined the RAF to escape publicity.)

The first clue that Denis was not telling the full story about Alex is in the SOE French Section Roll of Honour,[152] which does not list a 'Shokolovsky' but does include a 'Lieutenant Schwatschko (General List)' with a note that he 'served as A. Shaw'.

Tracking from there to Alex Schwatschko's personal file, opens up a new and dramatic story. He meant a great deal to Denis but quite how and where they met needs to be disentangled. We cannot begin to explain the relationship and Denis's infatuation unless we bring Alex himself into focus. That is not hard. He leaps like a ballet dancer off the flimsy carbon copies and fading typescript of the file as a character larger than life, a conclusion borne out by the file photograph which for older generations evokes memories of Errol Flynn or Ronald Colman, and for today's readers hints at Johnny Depp getting ready for another piratical role. Byronic even.

A dispassionate SOE interviewer thought him 'Essentially a man of action, with a love of daring and adventure and may become bored if the work [in the field] is not exciting. Inclined to be vain and over confident. Assumes dominance by force of personality and impetuous through fearlessness. Motivated by immense hatred [of Germans] . . .' These are characteristics often attributed to Poles, but though the name Denis invented for Alex has a Polish ring, his family home was Cluj, in Transylvania, now part of Romania but when he was born in 1919, on territory that was part of the crumbling remains of the Tsarist Empire. Reading the story he recounted to his British interviewers is like opening a new novel by Alan Furst. Those questioning him accepted it at face value. Although, one commented that Alex's assertion that he 'had been intimately acquainted with German officers at St Nazaire belongs in the same category of boasts as his declaration that he was a friend of [General, Commander of the British Expeditionary Force] Gort and Churchill'.

With Europe at war, and much of his family past related to an area almost impenetrable even in peacetime, Alex's account of his life

---

[152] *Courtesy of the Special Forces Charitable Trust*

could hardly be checked for accuracy. Though it is surprising that the personal file gives no indication that any of his comments were run past Denis. Nor is Denis's personal file cross-referenced to Alex's. SOE's need for French speakers with a penchant for living on the edge meant that the admissions bar was still not being set as high as MI5 might have liked it. His name was duly 'run across their files' but since he had never had any connection with the UK it is only to be expected that no adverse trace was found.

His story was that he came from 'a wealthy and somewhat cosmopolitan family, and lived all his life in easy circumstances'. His father's family had been important landowners in the Ukraine but had lost everything in the Revolution. His father himself had been taken prisoner by Bela Kun's Communists in the short lived Hungarian Revolution of 1919 and had then fought with the White Russian Army vainly trying to beat the Bolsheviks. He had fled to France with Alex in 1922, leaving Alex's mother Yala behind. He had a successful career with a French industrial group and remarried.

The adolescent Alex had spent a great deal of time on the ski slopes but had applied himself just enough to earn an engineering diploma. At the start of the Second World War he had enlisted in the French Air Force and been sent to flight school, only to be swiftly demobilised when the axe-blow of the Armistice fell. He returned to a life of 'comparative ease', moving with what seems remarkable facility between the two zones to ski and stay with friends. That several of the latter (a Public Prosecutor, one of his retired colleagues, and an opera singer named Monsieur Forgue) were men, might suggest to the unkind eye that Alex might have hovered between playboy and toy boy, but there is no evidence of that. Indeed he told SOE that along the way he had fathered an illegitimate son.

The first surprise in his account is that in Alex's version, he and Denis had first met not in the Miranda yard but before the war on the Riviera. Given their respective lifestyles this is not implausible. But the mystery gets deeper. Alex claimed that they had also seen each other in Paris, while Denis was there on his first mission. He even remembered that they had met at a brasserie, he thought La

Coupole in Montparnasse. Denis had hinted that he was there on 'some clandestine activity for the British'. Alex, eager for action, had asked how he too could become involved, 'but Rake apparently was unable to offer him any assistance,' the file notes laconically.

Let us go back for a moment to the Max story. Many of its inherent improbabilities would be resolved if in fact we concede that the Paris affair really did happen, but see Max as a fiction, perhaps even one designed to promote book sales. If Denis's real lover was Alex, there would have been less of a potential hue and cry about security risks, and Wilkinson's brooding disapproval might have been sparked not by the fact that Denis was mixed up with a German officer but simply that he was involved with another man. A relationship between two agents in the field might well in itself have offended his sense of security, as well as propriety. The conjecture is legitimate but otiose; it is at moments like these that a researcher wishes for a Ouija board.

In any event, Alex had soon made his own arrangements to cross into Spain. He reached Miranda, saw Denis again and had put out his first feelers to SOE via the British Consul in San Sebastian. Other than to check out via SIS two other contacts Alex had reportedly made in Paris, the screeners concluded he was 'clean' and he began his SOE training using at one point the homely British cover name 'Donald Cunningham'. 'Rather selfish and not too intelligent', one officer noted, while another observed that he was 'rather reticent about his past and not liked by others'. Despite that, he was to prove his worth in the field.

Around this time the chronology is unclear. Although Alex was using an SOE 'safe house' in Earls Court, he and Denis were also together at the Pastoria. Denis was wandering the street like the Ancient Mariner, stopping 'one in three' and Alex promenading Signora Pastoria's poodle through Piccadilly underground station, using the 'Up' escalator to go down and not surprisingly, more than once attracting the attention of the hovering Military Police patrols. They would phone the hotel and Denis would have to 'go down and fetch him and smooth things over'. Alex also found time to meet a girl from East Sheen, whom he identifies in his personal file as his 'fiancée'. Denis does not mention this, but had he known, his reaction might have been the same philosophical comment he made about Alex's visit to the Spanish bordello: it 'rather upset me but he meant so much to me that I could even overlook it. After all, he wasn't really being unfaithful.'

It is hardly surprising that a psychiatrist diagnosed that Denis was suffering from mental exhaustion and recommended rest. SOE sent him off to the 'Rehabilitation Centre' at Buchanan Castle, outside the village of Drymen, near Loch Lomond.

At first sight that seems a long way to ship a man who, in between his jail spells, had travelled the length and breadth of France and Spain under trying conditions.

But SOE may have been playing a crafty game by seeking to get him as far away from London as possible. MI5 files show that for good reasons the Security Service was acutely suspicious of the risk that the Germans might infiltrate SOE, and SIS, by allowing agents who had been involved in 'blown' circuits in Europe and who might even have been the reason for their collapse, to 'escape' back to Britain to serve as spies. For an agent even to have been in German or Vichy hands (let alone, if we accept Denis's version, a German bed), raised a 'red flag' for SOE's Security Section in Bayswater and the MI5 counter-intelligence mavens in St James's Street. Perhaps under pressure he or she had given up more information than they should, or had even been 'turned'. In July 1943 MI5 prompted SOE to rule that any agent who had been 'in enemy hands' was to be segregated until the security aspects of his or her experiences had been investigated. It is possible that in sending Denis to Scotland Maurice Buckmaster calculated that there was no harm in putting a few hundred miles between Denis and potential inquisitors.[153]

The essential conflict was between an SOE hierarchy, which as we have surmised in Denis's case, was always inclined out of personal and institutional loyalty to give its agents the benefit of any doubt. A skittish MI5, conscious of its 'defence of the Realm' mandate, tended to regard anyone about whom doubts had been raised as

[153] *See paper by Major G.A. Wethered attached to Knight Report and SOE Security Section files KV/4 201*

'guilty until proven innocent', a high hurdle to clear in the middle of a war. [See. e.g. Murphy p. 97.]

Denis's temporary shelter from the potential icy blast of interrogation had been built for the Duke of Montrose in the 1850s with a high Victorian efflorescence of towers and battlements. Buchanan Castle's most remarkable 'patient' had been Hitler's Deputy Rudolf Hess, briefly incarcerated there after he flew to Scotland in May 1941 on his weird notion of a 'peace mission'. Seven weeks there brought Denis back to mental health; surgeons also inserted a silver plate in his injured foot. (He did better than the Castle, which was later allowed to fall to pieces because of some curious provision of UK tax law, and is now a ruin.)

When he got back to London, Denis was disappointed when Maurice Buckmaster told him that rather than returning to the field, he would have a spell as a 'Conducting Officer'. He reassured Denis that this was not a consequence of the contretemps with Wilkinson and Heslop, but simply because he had 'done his bit'.

The Conducting Officer was a central figure in the lives of all new entrants to SOE at the first stage of their indoctrination. They were bemused by the *Mad Hatter's Tea Party* world of Wanborough. During this time SOE was using every professional instinct, initiative test and psychological measurement, including the ink blot test, devised by Hermann Rohrschach in 1921, to assess personality traits from the subject's verbal associations with the blotted images on a series of ten cards. The Conducting Officer, who had to be mentor, father confessor, cheerleader, head prefect, class sneak (helped by the anonymous men of the Field Security Police unobtrusively attached to each group), and coolly calculating assessor, went through every phase of training with his charges. Sonya D'Artois, then Butt, who aged nineteen was one of the French Section's youngest volunteers, and who in May 1944 would parachute into France as *Blanche* to join the HEADMASTER circuit,[154] was one of Denis's charges and remembers him as 'the life and soul of the party, always laughing. He knew everyone and when we were

---

[154] *Now Mme Sonya 'Toni' D'Artois, MBE*

in London, he knew all the places to go.' The 'places' by Denis's account included 'the White Room', 'the Music Room' and 'other drinking clubs which were springing up like mushrooms around London at this time'.

Laughter was a quality much in evidence in another of Denis's charges Nancy Wake, a close friend of Sonya D'Artois, of whom the History[155] comments that 'her irrepressible, infectious high spirits were a joy to everyone who worked with her'. The subject of two biographies, she wrote her own story in 1985 and it is characteristic that 'laugh' or 'laughter' crop up times almost without number.

Born in New Zealand in 1912 and raised in Australia, she took a boat to New York and then Liverpool when she was 20-years-old, worked as a freelance journalist in the unhappy Europe of the 1930s, married Henri Fiocca, a wealthy French businessman. Had the war not interrupted her life, she might have lived in sunny comfort on the Riviera.

It is surprising that she and Denis had never met; Nancy and her husband were part of the Juan les Pins and Cannes 'set' and shared with Denis a good friend in the urbane M. Miracca of the Palm Beach at Cannes. The two of them could just as easily have run across each other when Denis was scrambling out of France and Nancy, with Henri Fiocca's unwavering support was working with the PAT escape line. They didn't, and reading both their memories of SOE, they seem never even to have discussed their respective parallel tracks over the Pyrenees. Nancy writes only that she knew that Denis had been 'in the field'. Neither knew that they would soon find themselves thrown together in an unlikely but intimate embrace of danger under German gun sights.

Denis had been a 'difficult' student. So too in her different way was Nancy; she was brash, no respecter of persons or institutions, and could out-drink many of her hard-bitten male colleagues. She personified the Australian instinct for 'cutting down the tall poppies', and like Denis came perilously close to being thrown out. When she was presented with the ink blot test she told the

---

[155] *Foot p. 365*

psychiatrist, a New Zealander, that he should be doing something useful rather than wasting his time and hers. And her attitude to one of SOE's senior officers and ace recruiters, Selwyn Jepson, cannot have helped.[156] He was, she remembered years later, a 'creep', who was 'so sarcastic that I decided he either had an ulcer or was constipated'.[157]

Somewhere in SOE, maybe simply in Buckmaster's office, better sense prevailed, as it had when Denis had problems. Her dislike for being told what to do was probably also coloured by the fact that she had 'been there, done that'. She knew danger, undercover work and the German threat first hand from her work on the PAT line. She knew about escape. When PAT began to collapse she too succeeded after several miscues in scrambling over the foothills and snowy peaks of the Pyrenees to Spain, and then England. Henry Fiocca stayed behind in Marseilles, sadly.

True to form, Denis's experience as a Conducting Officer was as idiosyncratic as his spell as a student. It was in this position that he accompanied his charges to their advanced training in the sylvan seclusion of the Beaulieu Estate. Here the snugly British names of the houses SOE had commandeered (The Vineyard, The Rings, The House in the Woods, and the like) were in marked contrast to the cutting-edge curriculum. This covered a multitude of subjects, depending on the role which prospective agents were intended to play. It included survival, commando training, lock picking, field craft and disguise. There was also a segment on the rudiments of political warfare, the basic elements of which had originally been compiled and, briefly, taught, by the double agent Kim Philby, perhaps to the mild amusement of his Russian handlers, though the NKVD were not renowned for their sense of humour.

At a higher level potential circuit organisers were taught the literally vital importance of living with 'the greatest discretion', and avoiding being 'conspicuous'; which was not counsel Denis had

[156] *1899-1989. A prolific author and screenwriter. His many credits include a neat illustration of the changing meaning of words. Going Gay was a 1933 film romance about a girl making her way in the world of Viennese operetta*
[157] *Wake pp 104-5*

heeded when he first went to France. They learned the people skills
of building a circuit by discreet approaches and, interestingly, in the
light of the 'set Europe ablaze' admonition, they were advised to
avoid 'random acts of sabotage which are merely inclined to upset
the local inhabitants and do no damage to the German war effort'.
Despite MI5's deep scepticism about SOE in the field, Tommy 'Tar'
Robertson, prime mover of the Double XX system, and a man not
easily impressed, commented after going through a training course
for SOE circuit organisers at Beaulieu that he 'came away with the
feeling that I had learned a great deal more about counter-espionage
methods than during the time [since the early 1930s] that I have
been with MI5'. However, given MI5's fragile and fractious
relationship with SOE, and Robertson's deft touch, this may have
been an exercise in fence-mending flattery. But he again warned that
radio traffic was 'exceedingly dangerous' and needed to be kept to a
bare minimum.[158]

One of the first groups Denis shepherded, one trainee broke a leg,
one shattered an arm and a third, a Frenchwoman, was stabbed
through the hand with a Sykes-Fairbairn fighting knife in an unarmed
combat session. She demanded compensation for the loss of her
prospective career as a dental surgeon. Other accounts tell of him
having minor spats with trainees, and he himself concedes he ran into
serious trouble when he refused to 'pass out' a group of French
Canadians. He argued that while they were brave and resourceful,
their accented French, and their total lack of knowledge of France,
made them unsuitable for the field. Senior Canadian officers protested
and yet again Buckmaster had to intervene. Denis was overruled,
though commonsense suggests he may have had a valid point.

It is not so surprising that he was moved on to lecture at another
SOE stately home. Milton Ernest Hall, a rather dour exercise in
Victorian Gothic, a few miles north of Bedford, was where teams
were being trained for the so-called 'Jedburgh' operations in
Occupied Europe. The 'Jeds'' mission was to provide sharp-end
support and liaison for the SOE and Resistance circuits on the

[158] *See Robertson, Bibliography*

ground after the Allied landings on D-Day. Each three or four man team would include officers from SOE, from the newly established US Office of Strategic Services, the forerunner of CIA, and a representative of the country into which they were to be dropped.

Denis's job was to talk to them about 'being an agent in the field', a role in which with his usual self-deprecation he says he 'felt rather a fraud'. He did not have to feel that way for long because after two weeks Maurice Buckmaster asked him to go back to France, this time as operator for the FREELANCE circuit. Its leader, or 'organiser' was to be John Farmer and its courier none other than Denis's exuberant pupil, Nancy Wake, who was to be parachuted in as *Madame Andrée* though to the French she was to be known as *Helene*. Farmer, with the work name of *Hubert* was a young Regular Army officer who had been in training at Milton Ernest but was moving back into the SOE mainstream.[159]

The D-Day landings were just two months away. The early years had been a time of underground work, recruiting, planning, training, sabotaging, as well as false dawns and false hopes. Many men and women of SOE and many in the Resistance had risked and often lost their lives. Now came the real trial of strength, arming and mobilising the Resistance to do whatever it could by ambush, attack, destruction of railways, roads, bridges and telephone circuits, to harass and maul and divert the Germans from all sides as the Allies pushed down from Normandy. Undercover agents would become more like guerilla leaders.

That Nancy and John Farmer were briefed (Denis does not seem to have been included) by an officer who would go on to be a future translator of Proust and much other important French writing, and literary editor of the *Observer*, catches the essence of SOE's eclectic talent pool. Notes made by Vera Atkins, Buckmaster's right-hand woman in F Section and devoted keeper of the SOE flame for so many post-war years, for a 1956 television programme[160] name him

[159] *John Hind Farmer MC, though Denis and the History both name Farmer, writing in 1985 Nancy simply calls him Hubert, perhaps because he later joined SIS, who at the time she was writing would still have been reflexively reluctant to see his name in print. For his later career see e.g. Dorril, pp 629-30*
[160] *Part of an ATV series on the women agents of SOE. The notes are annotated and probably typed by Vera Atkins and bear all the hallmarks of being drawn from SOE files, not then open to the public. VA Papers op.cit*

only as 'Mr Kilmartin'. But he was surely Terence Kilmartin, who had been on at least one SOE operation in France with the *Observer*'s future editor David Astor.[161]

At Kilmartin's memorial service in 1991 his friend and *Observer* colleague Clive James remembered that 'on the surface you were a keeper of secrets . . . a pillar of the cultural Establishment. Underneath you were an Irish hell-raiser, the kind of rapscallion you fondly characterised as 'the desperate chancer' the only London literary editor of modern times to have done time in a French jail.'[162]

Had he been around to share his perspectives with us today, Kilmartin might have seen distant Proustian undertones in Denis's story. This was the opaque, elusive and allusive life of a homosexual narrator in which aristocrats, Royalty and an important actor shimmer in the background, and characters like Alex, Miracca and Burnett-Brown come and go, some reappearing in *le Chagrin*.

And in the next chapter of the convoluted tale, the developments in France of which Kilmartin could give FREELANCE only a hazy vision, were to be played out in bloody battles which are part of French Resistance history and in which Denis and the FREELANCE team would put their lives on the line.

All Kilmartin knew, or told them he knew, was that hidden away in the rocky vastness of the Massif Central, a plateau of extinct volcanoes, rivers, deep gorges, tiny inbred villages, and rushing rivers, a Resistance leader known as *Colonel Gaspard* was in command of several groups of several thousand Maquis. They were hard pressed: they had no arms, no money and little food, and no contact with London.

It would be FREELANCE's task to assess the real strength and leadership of *Gaspard*'s guerillas, determine what they needed to make them an effective fighting force, to identify dropping zones and orchestrate with London the *'parachutage'* of arms, men and money. As 'organiser', Farmer was responsible for liaison with the Resistance, helping them to plan attacks and to develop and coordinate their strategy. Hard, almost Herculean tasks, calling for deft diplomacy and 'tough love'.

[161] Daily Telegraph, *obituary of David Astor, December 2001*
[162] *See Clive James in Bibliography*

Though much progress had been made in bringing the leadership together, there was still no single cohesive Resistance; some looked to de Gaulle in London, some followed the Communist Party diktats that emanated from Moscow, yet others like the Spanish Red refugees, had ideas all of their own.

All their leaders were men of ambition, even arrogance, and all were disinclined to take orders, especially from foreigners. However, SOE had the trump card of being able to call for guns, money and clothes from the hostile skies, like Shakespeare's 'spirits from the vasty deep' and to get the call answered with heavy black containers swinging out of the night sky on parachutes dropped by the RAF. Nancy Wake would be the courier, a job description she rapidly outgrew. The circuit's wireless operator, Denis, would follow in a few days.

Denis being Denis, things would not happen in quite the way they were intended.

But meanwhile Kilmartin told the team 'I think you will find it interesting but extremely hard work and no doubt you will come in for a good deal of active fighting.'[163]

Gaspard was the *nom de guerre* of Emil Coulaudon,[164] the strong-willed and physically compelling Resistance leader whom we have already spotted doing much of the talking in *le Chagrin*. Born in Clermont Ferrand, and taken prisoner in 1940, he escaped and returned to his home town to become deeply engaged with one of its principal pillars of the Resistance, the 'Combat' movement. The Germans viewed Clermont as perhaps the most dangerous Resistance centre in the southern half of France. The underground drew much of its strength from the workers in the huge Michelin tyre plant, outgrowth of a family business that had begun as a maker of children's bouncy balls, and other major factories such as the Aulnat aircraft engine works. Remaining aloof but with the hallmark resolution of the Resistance were the clandestine intellectuals:

---

[163] *These are his words recycled by Vera Atkins for a television script. They lack the rhythm of his rendition of Proust*

[164] *1907-1977, Légion d'Honneur, Croix de Guerre, and other decorations. Commemorated also by a street named after him in Clermont Ferrand*

teachers and students at the Blaise Pascal Lycée, the local university and the University of Strasbourg, which had been transferred to Clermont at the outbreak of war.

Clermont and the countryside around were littered with bent and blasted testimonials to the sabotage work of Coulaudon and his teams: a steel mill, a German radio station, a liquid oxygen plant, a row of 150 electricity pylons, a derailed Wehrmacht troop train, and several thousand tyres destroyed by fire at Michelin. The Michelin plant itself became a target of an RAF raid when the controlling family turned down an SOE 'offer' that if they allowed a Resistance saboteur to damage vital elements the factory itself would not be bombed. SOE had more success with this 'iron hand in velvet glove' approach to M. Sire, a Director of Peugeot, one of whose plants was turning out tank turrets for the Wehrmacht. A recent disastrous RAF raid had missed the factory but killed many civilians living nearby. The Peugeot family, already Allied-leaning, and anxious to avoid another bombing, readily agreed.

Coulaudon had moved swiftly up through the Resistance hierarchy and by the time FREELANCE was due to arrive he was head of the FFI (the Forces Françaises de l'Intèrieur) for the Cantal, Allier, Haute-Loire and Puy de Dôme. That London did not know more about him is in this case testimony to French security (so derided in SOE headquarters) and a lack of raw intelligence in Baker Street. But after the war *Gaspard*'s qualities were clear in Buckmaster's mind. He 'inspired confidence, affection, even love, in his people . . . a really wonderful man', though at the same time he was 'hungry – hungry for glory, hungry for everything'.

John Farmer had been briefed that he would be put in touch with the elusive *Gaspard* by *Hector*, another brave and brilliant SOE leader. *Hector*, whose real name was Maurice Southgate, was running the STATIONER circuit, whose tentacles reached across much of central France. That did not happen, as we shall see.[165]

Like so much else, what prompted Baker Street to send in the

---

[165] *Maurice Southgate DSO, recruited into SOE from the RAF when he was 29-years-old. Born in France and a furniture designer by profession he shared with Denis the experience of having lived through the* Lancastria *sinking*

FREELANCE mission was a mix of military needs and French Resistance politics. A short while before, Southgate had reported to London, on a meeting with Coulaudon describing the proud Frenchman as having approached him 'on bended knees' for arms and materiel, 'the French supply services having broken down'. Coulaudon had appealed to Southgate to put him in touch with London and FREELANCE had been organised in response. [Bourne-Paterson p. 80]

But just before Southgate's meeting, Freddy Cardozo of the Gaullist RF Section of SOE had had a separate but similar exchange with Coulaudon. Whether this had prompted Coulaudon to conclude that the French system had indeed failed and that he had better work with Southgate, we cannot know. It must certainly have bewildered him since, due no doubt more to the confused situation on the ground than the dysfunctional relationship between F Section and the Gaullists, when Coulaudon mentioned FREELANCE, Cardozo told him he knew nothing of any imminent British mission and warned him that it should be treated with suspicion. But in the end Cardozo and Farmer did manage to meet and agree to cooperate.[166]

Justifiable pride on both sides of the Channel makes this issue of cooperation a tangled one. The French and British perspectives can differ sharply. Was the Resistance a French affair, a key period in French history and the lives of so many French people, to which Britain and later the US made an essential contribution? Or, was it, as sometimes appears from some of the London-written literature, essentially an F Section triumph? The facts can be used to support either view.

For example the first parachute landing in the Clermont area was by two Free French agents in 1941. The number of supply drops did indeed reach a peak in 1944 when FREELANCE got into full swing. But according to research by the Montluçon historian Andre Touret, up to the end of 1943 the Allier Département alone had already received seventy-three drops, mostly handled by Frenchmen

[166] *Foot p. 385*

on separate French dropping zones. FREELANCE used fruits as dropping zone names. The French sites are an interesting mix of military history (Cambronne, Chanzy, Sarrail – evoking memories of the First World War Greece – and Wrangel), science and gun-making (Monge) and tributes to the Allies (Wavell, Eisenhower). Given the strong presence of Spanish Communist exiles in the Resistance, the choice of 'Franco' strikes an odd note, but may well have been a now obscure joke.[167]

Mackenzie's history[168] underscores the point. Up to 11 May 1944, arms drops by the Gaullist RF Section exceeded those of F Section by some margin, e.g. 45,354 Stens against F Section's 30,936, 17,576 pistols against 10,385 and 10,251 rifles compared to 6,694. Irrespective of their sponsorship, however, these were of course British arms carried on RAF or US aircraft. But as they droned through the sky, on the night of 29 April 1944, Nancy Wake and John Farmer would have been focused on the dangers ahead, not on some post-war 'league table'.

They flew from RAF Tempsford, just off the A1 trunk road a few miles south of St Neots in a US Air Force Liberator No. 42-40987Z. It belonged to the 406th Squadron and had an eight man crew. They knew they would drop somewhere near Montluçon; whether Baker Street knew or not, it was the target of special attention by German counter-intelligence as 'a communications hub, a working class town, turbulent and openly hostile'. In fact they came to earth some twenty miles to the north-west on the edge of the village of Cosne d'Allier. Nancy remembered she was severely airsick on the way, perhaps due to turbulence but quite likely because her farewell party at a Park Lane club the night before, had ended boisterously at 4 a.m.

The story of FREELANCE and the battle of Mont Mouchet is part of Denis's narrative and has also been told by Nancy Wake and her biographers. Later French historians have also explored it in some depth. The most straightforward source is the unpublished after-action report written by John Farmer, now in the National

[167] *Touret p. 234*
[168] F*oot p. 602*

Archives.[169] First of all it is the freshest, written only a few months after the events. Second it is the account of a professional soldier, not written with the encouragement of a biographer or publisher keen to draw out the most colourful strands. But the personal memories of Denis and Nancy Wake have to be woven in, and post-war French research also serves to round out the story. Indeed because so much of what happened next was told and retold by Nancy and Denis, John Farmer as the man in charge of FREELANCE has been rather pushed into the background. In her TV notes Vera Atkins tells the producer a touch dismissively that 'as Nancy soon became established as *Chef de Parachutage* there will be no need to emphasise the part he played'.

This is hardly fair. From what we know about the rough and complicated 'politics' involved in dealing with the various Maquis groups, in advocating tactics for, and in the middle of, several battles without seeming to impose them on a series of quarrelsome leaders, in orchestrating sabotage and generally making sure that London's strategic objectives were always kept to the forefront, it must have been a hard task. Writing of organisers in general, Bourne-Paterson remarks that they 'acquitted themselves with almost ambassadorial distinction'.

After the years of waiting, false dawns, sabotage, killings and reprisals, France was getting ready for the big battle. The divisions in the Resistance leadership (all of whom wanted to kill Germans and wipe them off French soil, but who disagreed about nearly everything else from the value of what their rivals were doing to the future direction of the country) were still much in evidence. But they did not stand in the way of a secret council of war on 2 May 1944, when John Farmer and Nancy Wake were still getting their bearings; it appears that they were unaware of it at the time.

Leaders of most but, typically, not all the Auvergnat Resistance groups met in the isolated hamlet of Paulhaguet, about fifty miles south of Clermont Ferrand. The issue in the smoke and rhetoric-filled farmhouse was whether the Resistance should carry on as small, agile bands of Maquisards or whether, with the Allied invasion imminent, it should concentrate its forces into large 'armed

[169] *See Bibliography*

redoubts' in mountain country. Most argued that the need to get the various groups and factions together under strong leadership was becoming urgent.

As more and more young men took to the hills to escape forced labour in Germany, the Resistance risked becoming undisciplined and uncoordinated, and less and less able to defend itself against a focused German onslaught. Some warned, presciently, that concentrating so many men on a handful of sites would offer the Germans tempting targets.

The exiled Spanish Communists and Anarchists, who had fled Franco's revenge after the Civil War (and who made an important but to date unsung contribution to the French Resistance) knew from bitter experience that lightly armed guerillas, however densely massed, could not hope to defeat modern armies in direct combat. Others argued that without strong support from the many Regular Army officers who had joined the Resistance, but who were not represented at the meeting, these large concentrations would lack the necessary professional leadership.

In the end the consensus was to group the Maquis of the Auvergne on three local sites: the 3000 feet Mont Mouchet, the hills and gorges above the la Truyère river, and the high steep slopes of le Lioran.

They evidently took not the slightest notice of a broadcast by Marshal Pétain a few days earlier when he had ranted that 'incited by foreign propaganda, thousands of [your] sons have taken part in activities which have created in France an atmosphere potent with disaster . . . It is in your interests to maintain a correct and loyal attitude towards the occupation troops. Otherwise I know of no other way more likely to bring upon you and the people the most terrible reprisals.' He rounded off, to an audience which had probably mentally and literally largely tuned out, that 'When the present tragedy is over and, thanks to the German defence of the European continent, our civilisation is saved from all danger of Bolshevism, then the hour will come when France will find and maintain her rightful place again.'[170]

---

[170] *The* Times *29 April 1944*

On 29 April, the night FREELANCE dropped in, the drone of Allied bombers flying sortie after sortie across France, bombing Luftwaffe airfields and railway lines, would have made the Marshal's peroration seem even more hollow.

Numbers were not a problem; guns and ammunition were. That was why FREELANCE had been sent in. Farmer landed spot on the target lights, with Nancy some 300 yards away. 'She was eventually found by a search party, revolver in hand, ready to shoot', he wrote afterwards. Two days later Southgate came to see them in Cosne d'Allier, catching Nancy having a head to toe wash in a tin basin in her bedroom, the pistol by her side, and gave Farmer 'some very useful hints'.

Also he almost inadvertently blew the whole operation. He took Farmer into Montluçon to give him a firsthand glimpse of everyday life in Occupied France. When they got there, Southgate decided he had too much work to do and left Farmer and a Maquisard to wander about on their own while he went off to his 'safe house'. The Beaulieu trainers drummed into their pupils that there was no such thing as excessive caution in the field; one tiny slip and they could be caught. So it was here. Momentarily distracted as he approached the house, and failing to check whether the prearranged safety signals (probably the positioning of shutters or flowerpots) showed all was clear, Southgate stepped straight into a German ambush.

With Southgate in Nazi hands defying every brutal attempt to make him talk,[171] Farmer had to cast about carefully until he found someone who knew someone else who knew where Coulaudon might be. After a three day cross country drive in a car stolen by the Maquis from the Gestapo in Montluçon, he and Nancy Wake crunched across the gravelled courtyard of the dilapidated Château de Chamblard near St Flour that Coulaudon had commandeered as his headquarters. They waited a week for him to appear. Farmer was disconcerted to find him less than welcoming, even though along with a list of military targets for *Gaspard*'s Maquis, Farmer handed over 2 million francs (money value comparisons are always tricky,

---

[171] *He withstood intense Gestapo interrogation without giving anything away, and survived Buchenwald too*

but perhaps 300,000 Euros today). But this was the man who just a short while ago had been 'on bended knees' asking for London's help. What had changed?

While some of the wariness was probably attributable to Cardozos's warning and Southgate's arrest it seems equally likely that Coulaudon's cool welcome was entirely pragmatic. They were of no use to him until Denis turned up and could make contact with London. Meanwhile, he urged that they should move over to Chaudes-Aigues, a suggestion which they felt was simply to get them out of his way, but which may again have been practical, since the village would be vital in what, after the Council of War he foresaw as the inevitable battle for Mont Mouchet.

So Denis was essential to the plot of this real-life drama. There were no stand-ins waiting in the wings. But at this key moment he had been waylaid by another band of strolling players, a part of the story for which we have to leave Farmer's account for a few pages and return to Denis's mixed-up memories.

17

On a Wing and a Prayer

Before he went back in the field, to climb what would prove to be a rickety and perilous ladder, Denis had to brush up on the new call signs, scheduling and coding techniques which had been introduced thanks in large part to Leo Marks, to improve SOE security.

When his time came to leave for France, Denis's version of Nancy's nightclub celebrations was a dinner at the Pastoria, made even more cheerful by the news from Baker Street that when he landed in France, Alex would be in charge of the reception party and would arrange for him to join up with Nancy and John Farmer. Alex had been sent in to join the SHIPWRIGHT circuit, which operated between Châteauroux and Vichy and was one of the two networks effectively and adroitly spun out of the collapsed STATIONER after Southgate's capture. [172]

Denis's fragile, silver-plated foot meant, no doubt to his great relief, that he could not be dropped by parachute. Instead he would be flown into France on a Lysander, the single-engined Westland Aircraft monoplane, painted matt black, which was the workhorse and the Trojan horse of SOE and SIS agent landings and exfiltration, not least because it needed little more than the length of a football field to land and take off.

The intrepid pilots of the RAF Special Duties Squadron had none of today's navigation aids; they relied on map reading, compass bearings, landmarks such as rivers, lakes and large towns to get

---

[172] SHIPWRIGHT's dashing organiser R.A.L.P. Maingard de Laville-des-Offrans DSO CBE, 1924-1986, an aristocrat from Mauritius, had parachuted into France in 1943 as STATIONER's wireless operator. Southgate's courier Pearl Witherington, later Cornioley, [1914-2008] went on to lead the WRESTLER circuit with great bravery and panache, for which she was awarded a military MBE and later CBE. See for instance Daily Telegraph obituary of 26 February 2008. Maingard's own story and the networks remarkable achievements have been eloquently told by Paul McCue; see Bibliography

to their destination, and an alert landing party to guide them down to the ground. Mostly the ground parties used flares or car headlights though some later missions benefited from early versions of the electronic beacon or even primitive ground to air walkie-talkies. Though Professor Foot's account[173] says at one point that Denis flew back with Virginia Hall, who had trained as a radio operator when SOE refused to take her and 'Cuthbert' back as a courier, its Appendix and Denis's reminiscences confirm that in fact his fellow passenger was a man, inimitably described by Denis as a 'sinister looking North African, slightly hunch-backed', whose Conducting Officer he had been, and whom he disliked.

Denis remembers the high anxiety of the journey exposed to the hostile heavens under the Lysander's perspex canopy, like 'flying in an electric light bulb,' all the more when German anti-aircraft fire began to flicker and bang in their direction as they crossed the French coast. 'I was petrified the whole time.' Three hours later, the recognition signals flashed in the darkness below, the Lysander swooped and bumped to a stop, its Bristol Mercury engine still running. Denis and his companion threw out their bags and scrambled down the steps fixed to the port side of the fuselage. They were greeted with a hug by an ebullient Alex and his reception party. Presumably for reasons of security, while Denis knew Alex would be there, Alex had not been told who was on the aircraft that night. In three minutes the Lysander's pilot pulled out the boost control override, gave the engine full throttle and it growled away into the night.[174]

Denis landed close to where his FREELANCE partners had dropped on the outskirts of the industrial town of Montluçon. He was well aware that they needed him badly. Until he reached them they had no way of contacting London. But he had no idea that they had moved to Chaudes-Aigues and it would take precious time – (at

[173] *p. 372 & p. 467*
[174] *If another example was needed of the vagaries of memory Maurice Buckmaster's addendum to Denis's obituary in the* Times, *a slightly amended version of what he had said in le Chagrin claims that his protégé's first message to London after this landing in France was typical of his courage: 'Landed in tree in midst of enemy troops. Waited hidden till they left in morning and joined* FREELANCE.*' More likely Buckmaster has misremembered another episode, but there were so many landings – comic, tragic, straightforward – that more than thirty years after the event he may be excused*

least a week) – before they did finally make contact. Denis pinned the blame for delay on Alex, who wanted to use Denis to back up his own operator, to show him off to SHIPWRIGHT's local contacts to demonstrate that London had not forgotten them, and so Denis claimed, to keep his friend out of the way of real fighting for as long possible. 'I think it's absolutely shocking that London has sent you. You're too old for these new conditions and, after all, you have done your share.'

Denis was not quite out of harm's way. A couple of nights with a small Maquis group ended in a skirmish with the Germans, and Denis moved from one supposedly safe house to another. Alex, code-named *Olive*, whose base was in Châteauroux, said he was trying to find where FREELANCE were. Alex's own approach to security was bold, even flamboyant. He had found himself a black Citroën, (the vehicle of choice of the Gestapo and Vichy police), a Milice uniform and a German pass. While the combination may have made him less liable to 'stop and search' surprises, and helped him roll through roadblocks, it was hardly the 'merging into the background' that SOE instructors urged on their trainees. It also seems out of keeping with the 'unostentatious efficiency' which was a hallmark of SHIPWRIGHT's organiser Maingard,[175] and Alex's relatively junior role as the circuit's 'Lysander expert'.[176]

Alex eventually declared that he had found out where FREELANCE was based and after what Denis recalls as a two day interlude of 'drowsy fantasy', good food and swimming in the riverside village of les Sept Chemins, a Resistance driver took Denis from Montluçon to Chaudes-Aigues. It was then a tiring and dangerous trip requiring an overnight stop. (It is now a matter of three hours on the Autoroute, though thankfully today, there is no need to bob and weave down country roads and farm tracks to avoid Feldgendarmerie checkpoints.)

Denis, now using the name *Roland*, found Nancy as she sat in the chilly early sunshine on a cemetery wall outside the hamlet of Lieutadès, up in the hills beyond Chaudes-Aigues.

Their cheery greetings opened our story and we know too that she

---

[175] *Foot p. 381*
[176] *Bourne-Paterson p. 82*

was under no illusions about where Denis had been. He in turn was well aware that his failure to make contact had caused her and Farmer needless worry and 'in true DenDen fashion he gave us a cock and bull story, which neither of us believed'. Farmer's account is more succinct, but not inconsistent with the embroidered version. He writes simply that Denis was delayed because of the disruption that followed Southgate's arrest.

Nancy and John Farmer were both fond of him but knew he could be 'completely unreliable'. And his homosexuality was no secret. 'Indeed it was always the first thing he mentioned, especially to women, who often found him too attractive for his liking.'[177]

They knew the real reason he had failed to show up but if they made a fuss, he might well go back to Alex in a huff. Now they had their operator, they could not afford to lose him. An operator in the hand, even one as temperamental as Denis, was worth two adrift somewhere in the bush with a boyfriend. So in the best British tradition, the incident was discreetly put to one side and life moved on. Denis radioed London on Farmer's instructions that FREELANCE was in touch with *Gaspard*, that his organisation had immense value as a fighting force, was situated in strategic centres in the Le Puy, St Flour, Aurillac region but had absolutely no stores and was in dire need of arms.[178]

John Farmer may have reflected from time to time about his unusual team – the forceful Nancy and Denis, nervous and temperamental. Denis adored and admired her, and she was fond of him, though with the exasperation and amused, often strained, intolerance of an elder sister always having to watch out for a scapegrace younger brother. The relationship has overtones of the theatrical prima donna who has come to rely on the cheery support of her slightly mad stage dresser, whose readiness to share gossip and a giggle, outweighs his habit of nipping at the gin bottle and making sheep's eyes at the lads in the chorus. Denis and Nancy had actually taken on a rather grander theatrical mantle. His nickname for her was 'Gertie', which in the context of a couple whose brightest years had

---

[177] *Wake p. 117, see also his 'coming out' to Virginia Hall, Pearson p. 130*
[178] *Bourne-Paterson p. 131*

been the 1930s suggests they had jokingly adopted the persona of the glittering stage duo of Noël Coward and Gertrude Lawrence. Coward's suavely single-minded homosexuality might have seemed tailor-made as a role model for Denis, not least because Coward too was widely alleged to have had a long-running affair with a Royal Prince, while Nancy shared Lawrence's charisma and ability to shine as a comedienne.[179]

For Denis and Nancy, banter was the way they kept up their spirits in a time of increasing stress and danger. As Denis wrote: 'Underneath, it was deadly serious, but in my experience of life, if you can laugh at something, no matter if it is quite ridiculous, it never seems quite so bad.' Nancy quickly stepped up from the role of courier to shoulder the heavy responsibilities of selecting safe dropping zones, sorting out the Maquis supply priorities, being on site when the planes droned overhead, and making sure the loads were safely dealt with. Her parallel role as Farmer's 'paymistress', handing out cash from her bag, the supply regularly topped up from London also boosted her stature, (in line with the Golden Rule that 'he who has the gold, makes the rules'), but from time to time put her at risk of being robbed or even killed. This was not a training exercise and some of the Maquis were not knights in shining armour. The money was used to buy food and fuel, to bribe police, prison officials and clerks, and importantly to allow Maquis families to keep body and soul together while the breadwinners were away killing Germans.

The stress was physical as much as mental. In one week Nancy, Farmer and Denis spent six consecutive nights in a series of lonely fields orchestrating RAF parachute drops of arms and supplies. As we have noted each SOE dropping zone, or DZ, carefully scouted by Nancy, had the name of a fruit – 'Peach', 'Raspberry', 'Strawberry'

---

[179] *Sir Noël Pierce Coward, 1899-1973, actor, composer, playwright, cabaret artist. Gertrude Lawrence, 1898-1952, actress and musical performer, original star of* The King and I. *She and Coward are especially remembered for their bravura performance in his sophisticated 1930 comedy* Private Lives. *When Gertrude Lawrence married the American theatre owner Richard Aldrich, Coward's congratulatory telegram was one Denis and Nancy would have enjoyed:*
'Dear Mrs. A.,
Hooray, Hooray, At last you are deflowered
On this and every day
I love you, Noël Coward.'

etc. and a number. Denis would code and tap out the request to London and give the phrase he would expect from the BBC's nightly series of obscure and whimsical 'Personal Messages' to indicate that the drop was on its way. 'Require arms for 100 rpt 100 men. Can receive up to 30 containers in DZ Plum 74. BBC message '*Tout ce qui brille, n'est pas or*'. [All that glitters is not gold].

By that stage they had probably moved on from using words in their personal poems as keys for coding and decoding, and were enciphering from 'one time pads', tiny silk sheets of randomly generated digits, produced in only two copies. The operator had one pad, the matching one was in Grendon. Once used, each line of numbers was – or was supposed to be – clipped off and burned. Before that, coding had been based upon personal poems selected by the agent or devised by SOE's mischievous, brilliant code guru Leo Marks.

We do not know whether Denis was still using the Victor Hugo verse. Nancy's poem, a confection of her own, was remembered by Marks as 'pornographic', and by her as 'unsavoury' but judging from the text quoted by Peter Fitzsimons, by today's standards it is no more than schoolroom ribaldry:

> '*She stood right there*
> *In the moonlight fair,*
> *And the moon shone on her nightie.*
> *It lit right on the nipple of her tit*
> *Oh, Jesus Christ Almighty.*' [180]

It is easy to forget just how hard Denis had to work, no matter how tired or sick he might have been. Before he started to transmit he had to make sure his wireless battery was topped up with distilled water and fully charged. If not, he would have to commandeer a bicycle, prop it up with the rear wheel off the ground, run a belt from the hub to a generator and get one of the Maquisards to pedal away until the batteries were charged. The aerial needed to be stretched over a roof or a nearby tree. Checking first to see he was following the agreed

---

[180] *Fitzsimons p. 187; Marks p. 590*

schedule, he would set about coding the message. This was hard enough in the relative peace of a training school in the English countryside, and calling for every ounce of concentration when gunfire could be heard in the distance, Maquisards were arguing volubly nearby, mosquitoes attacked like miniature dive bombers and, quite likely, toothache or a stomach bug added to the distractions. Sending needed a steady, unsweaty hand, and receiving called for laser-like focus. Listening today to practice Morse messages, which sound like staccato, random telephone dialing tones, it is almost impossible even with a crib sheet at hand, to distinguish dots from dashes, let alone one letter from another. To do so in the field, when as well as all the other diversions, the transmissions were often interrupted or blurred by static, was a remarkable skill.

When the BBC message came through, the team set out into the pitch-black countryside. They laid the flares to mark the dropping zone, and crouched in the bushes, one ear cocked for the approaching aircraft, the other for the sudden roar of engines and blaze of searchlight beams that would signal a German ambush. Once the parachutes were found, (which was not always easy in the bushes and clumps of trees), their containers had to be unloaded. Just one drop of twelve containers – and there were often more – would bring the Maquis 6 Bren guns, plus 1000 rounds of ammunition per gun and spare parts, 36 rifles with 150 rounds per gun, 27 Stens each with 300 rounds and spare magazines, 5 pistols with 50 rounds each, 40 Mills grenades, 12 Gammon grenades with fuse and tape, field dressings, and an extra 6600 rounds of 9mm and 3168 of Carton rifle ammunition.[181]

They were hauled away in bicycle trailers, farm carts, butchers vans, even the town ambulance, to be degreased and hidden in wine cellars, woodpiles and hiding places in the rocky hills; filmed in *le Chagrin* a local Resistant waves at the nearby woods and laughs that there are probably one or two arms caches that have lain forgotten there since the war ended.

The bulky containers had to be hidden too: up in church bell

---

[181] *Foot p. 475*

towers or down in one of the deep, dark lakes which filled the ancient volcanic craters, in the shafts of abandoned coal mines or in crumbling crypts in the local cemetery. Even the parachutes had to vanish. Sometimes they were buried. Beaulieu taught its agents to do this with such consummate care that a parachute could be hidden without a trace under the smooth grass of a newly mown lawn. More often they were spirited away so that their precious silk could be cut and sewn into equally precious underwear.

Then it was back to a farmhouse or a barn to snatch as much sleep as they could before the next day's work began, often with discussions with the Resistance, that could so easily turn into sensitive and awkward negotiations about who got what. Bourne-Paterson [p. 131] records that in June, July and August alone, there were sixteen air drops, bringing in a total of 282 containers and over 200 'packages', a remarkable haul considering the flying distance and the fact that the summer nights were so short.

Through it all Denis was tireless. He was fighting a kind of war and felt he should wear 'a kind of uniform: a khaki shirt and a cut down pair of Nancy's slacks'. Nancy's sartorial foible was that however the day had gone, and whatever lay ahead, she would always sleep in one of her satin nightdresses.

Operators were still the linchpin of any SOE circuit, so Denis's next detour is not in principle surprising. The unhappy end result is the same in his version and in Nancy's account, though they differ on its timing. Farmer does not even mention it. Put briefly, Denis says that in the last few days of May, Alex Shaw's operator was seized by the Germans. Alex sent a courier to Nancy asking if he could 'borrow' Denis, to which she agreed 'very reluctantly'. Denis was driven fifty miles or so to Alex's base at Châteauroux, from where he was to signal London to arrange a drop for SHIPWRIGHT on 6 June. On their way to where the SHIPWRIGHT radio was cached, he and Alex stopped for a quick bathe in a lake. 'We came out of the water, lay naked in the tall grasses and let the sun dry us and our love submerge us', as Denis put it in tones reminiscent of Elinor Glyn.[182]

---

[182] *1864-1943, novelist, pioneer of heavy-breathing romantic fiction targeted at women readers*

Picking up three Maquisards, one of whom knew the back-roads and so took the wheel, they drove on. In Denis's version they ran into a German patrol, who let them pass, but seemed suspicious. Soon afterwards, as they bumped along a country road past the iron gates of a large château, there was a burst of machinegun fire; the Germans had presumably checked the vehicle details and cut across to intercept them. The Citroën roared away at full speed out of range, but Alex had been hit and was dead. After trying in vain to dig a hole deep enough for a grave on the stony roadside, the others hid his body in the bushes and went on. Maquisards came from Montluçon to collect the corpse, which was cremated and interred in the town under the inscription 'Here lies a brave man who died fighting for his country.'[183] Denis rejoined John Farmer and Nancy, heartbroken. 'I had loved him as I had never loved anyone before.' It is too easy to mock Denis's mawkish prose, but there is no reason to doubt he meant what he wrote – every time he wrote it.

Nancy's version is less circumstantial and certainly less sugary but once again memory has played havoc with the dates. She moves us forward in time. In the middle of a makeshift but lavish dinner party in a commandeered château celebrating the liberation of Paris (25 August) and her birthday (30 August), the daughter of a Madame Renaud, a Montluçon shopkeeper who was one of the most active Resistance supporters, unaware of the relationship with Denis, announced that Alex had been killed. Denis was pole-axed. 'We had to console him as best we could, but I'm afraid we were all too busy to sympathise with appropriate dignity', Nancy comments briskly.

What actually happened? Alex's own personal file will soon tell us.

---

[183] *As we shall see, this is not correct, though it is certainly possible that it is what Denis was told in the fog of war*

18

The Scent of Battle

It is hard to balance Denis's affection for Alex with Nancy's portrayal, years later, of his predatory side, but it is pointless to ignore it, as it is part of our attempt to understand Denis's character. She writes that she had managed to calm down one furious Auvergnat farmer who had stormed in to complain about an 'advance' that Denis had allegedly made to his son. It was a delicate balancing act. Denis was itching to rejoin Alex. Nancy and John Farmer did not want to be left without an operator if he flounced off in a pique, but they could not ignore the risk to their efforts if 'we let him run wild among the good-looking men of the Maquis. The trouble with DenDen was that he actually believed most men were homosexual, and that if they were not, then they should be.'

Looking back later, Nancy concludes that it was only because the team kept a close but discreet eye on Denis that he 'was not torn to pieces or alternatively, shot by an irate father' and that no aggrieved parents sued after the war. She even tells us that a new team member, René Dusacq, code-named *Anselme* who had been dropped in early June to reinforce the FREELANCE team as a weapons instructor, was also given the parallel task of helping Nancy keep Denis out of trouble. He once had to hover protectively when the team were staying at a farmhouse, whose owners had a good-looking son on whom Denis 'had designs'.

A former Hollywood stunt man described by Denis as 'handsome, debonair and tough', Dusacq was a good choice for both roles. He was a man of action who had jumped even though confusion over the signals from the ground threatened that the mission might be aborted. He was immediately nicknamed 'Bazooka' for his skill with the shoulder-fired anti-armour rocket launcher, a soubriquet reinforced by his insistence on never being parted from his Colt .45 pistol.

Denis makes no mention of any such awkward moments, though he does refer to one altercation with a group of grumpy old men, from which Nancy and Dusacq extricated him and which, seen through the prism of Nancy's comments, may perhaps have been sparked in this way. Again we can only offer by way of balance that had Denis been questing after loamy farm girls, the potential parental problems might have been the same, though only up to a point; the gnarled French farmer of the 1940s was not in the avant-garde of liberal thinking on sexual preferences.[184] We also have to remember that despite his bantering bravery, if we add up all the blows Denis's nervous system had taken since the *Lancastria* went down, it is only surprising that he wasn't a gibbering wreck, and understandable that with death hanging over his head he might well abandon any discretion, and heed Horace's injunction to 'seize the day, put no trust in the future'. As the summer moved on, the future looked to be nasty, brutish and short.

On 20 May Coulaudon had sent out the rallying call from his isolated château. For the next two weeks young men made their way to the Massif on foot, on bicycles, in the backs of lorries and by slow local train, 2700 of them to Mont Mouchet and 1500 to Chaudes-Aigues. So many were avoiding the labour draft that Fritz Sauckel, Hitler's Plenipotentiary for Labour, who was making ever increasing demands on Vichy for men, was said jokingly to be the Maquis' best recruiting sergeant. If the mass movement did not attract German attention, the poster outside the village of Clavière proclaiming in French 'Free France Begins Here' would hardly have escaped their notice.

Coulaudon – one of whose close colleagues was the deceptively named *Monique*, in fact Gabriel Montpied, a trades union activist from Clermont Ferrand,[185] sought to impose a military command structure on his men. They were divided into Companies and as far as supplies allowed, issued with uniforms – khaki shorts, a brown or black battledress blouse, boots and a red armband with the Free

[184] *Even in politically correct 2007 one local countryman made heavy use of the pejorative 'pédé' when talking about Denis, rather than 'gay' or even 'homo'*
[185] *1903-1991, Mayor of Clermont from 1944 to 1973; the major local hospital bears his name*

French emblem of the Cross of Lorraine. In one French account the boots are described as 'English' but it seems likely that the khaki shorts and perhaps the blouses were also parachuted in from London. This initiative was probably what led to a Vichy edict a short while later warning that whatever uniform they wore and whatever military status the Allies or de Gaulle might claim for them, the Maquis were 'terrorists' who were not covered by the Geneva Convention and would be shot out of hand.

Certainly most of their weapons were British though these were little enough compared to Wehrmacht's arsenal – the heaviest weapons were Dusacq's beloved 'bazookas', and for the most part the Maquisards fought with light machine guns (probably Brens), Sten submachine guns and grenades.

Through their spotter planes, implacable interrogation of Maquisard prisoners and infiltration of Resistance groups, von Brodowsky's HQ in Clermont Ferrand had built up a clear picture of the Resistance. It did not lack local knowledge; the staff of the counter-intelligence Sonderkommando there included at least six Frenchmen.[186]

As his official War Diary recorded, von Brodowsky, a veteran of the First World War, had been given the task on 6 June to 'restore the authority of the Occupation forces in the Département du Cantal and neighbouring areas'. The Resistance, those 'disorderly gatherings of terrorist gangs' assembling in the mountains were to be fought by all possible means. This was not just for the direct threat they represented but also because the Germans feared that one of the Maquis objectives was to secure the mountain plateaux for Allied paratroop landings. The regional SIPO and SD (two of the many Hydra heads of the German security police) were put under his command for the purpose. Hugo Geissler, the 36-year-old senior SD officer in the area, drove across from his comfortable office in Vichy to St Flour to be close to the action, a move he would regret. In a career change that rivalled Denis's, Geissler had been a concierge at the Grand Hotel in Paris before joining the Nazi Party and the SD.

[186] *Martres p. 25*

Vehicle movements were virtually banned, and unauthorised cars seen on the street would be fired on without warning. The Germans took control of all petrol and oil stocks, and the population was reminded that any Resistance 'active or passive' would be severely punished. In Montluçon they had seen more than enough black-bordered notices in the strongly Vichyite local newspaper *le Centre* to know that meant a firing squad.

It was as this whirlwind accelerated, with nerves on both sides stretched to breaking point, fingers twitching on triggers and fiddling edgily with the pins on their hand grenades, that Alex was killed. The entries on his personal file are brief but clear. He died on 7 June 1944 in a shoot out at a German roadblock near the massive Éguzon dam, across the Creuse, about fifty miles west of Montluçon. Maybe it was as Denis remembered, and the Germans had spotted his car, grown suspicious and doubled back to intercept him. Maybe he just took a wrong turning. The 300 foot high dam, built in the 1920s as a triumph of hydroelectric engineering, was such a prime sabotage target that the Germans were bound to have guarded it heavily. Whatever the reason he was there, Alex's car was flagged down and whether out of impulse or a real sense of imminent danger, he tried to shoot his way through, killing a German corporal. There was a firefight and in the blaze of bullets, Alex was cut down. The personal file is silent on whether Denis was there or not but it is unlikely that Alex was alone.

Alex is buried near where he died, in the communal cemetery at Éguzon-Chantôme, in the quiet heart of his adopted country. Denis would be pleased and proud to know that his name is also recorded on the SOE Memorial at Valençay, together with those of the many other brave men and women who died for the same cause. We quoted earlier the observations of an SOE appraiser on Alex's love of danger. It is timely to add here the last line of that note, '[He is] motivated by intense hate *which might end in his unnecessary self destruction*'. But it would be unfair to the memory of a man of courage to write him off as reckless. After the war he was 'Mentioned In Dispatches' for 'outstanding diligence' in executing his landing operations. He worked hard to identify landing sites and 'took great pains to ensure, often at great risk to his own life, the safety of all who passed through his hands'.

We can pick holes in the various accounts and discrepancies, and speculate whether Denis again exaggerated the retelling of the physical side of their relationship. The only certainty is that Alex died and Denis grieved; a note on Alex's personal file describes Denis as his 'closest friend'.

Denis's grief comes through in a letter he wrote to Vera Atkins in March 1945 when what would prove fruitless efforts were being made to track down Alex's family, and even to provide financial support for that unseen son. He wrote: 'If only I had been taken instead of Alex, I feel things would really have been as arranged in my mind', private words which tell us far more clearly what he felt than the rather rose-tinted phrases he uses in his memoirs.

But the gods of battle had bigger things on their mind than the fate of one brave man. If von Brodowsky needed more evidence of the build up, and if the Maquis needed more proof of the ferocity of the German response, it came at around 2 a.m. on 9 June. A carefree and careless convoy of eleven Maquis trucks carrying some 400-500 men to Mont Mouchet took a wrong turn in the dark and ran smack into a heavily armoured German column halted near Giat waiting for movement orders. The Germans reacted before the Maquis could turn around and flee. Seven of the trucks were burned and some of the Maquis thrown into the blazing wreckage. Others were shot on the spot. The Resistance lost thirty-three men.

The same day the Wehrmacht cordoned off the area around Mont Mouchet and began moving their forces forward. The attack began the next afternoon. Two Luftwaffe flights from the specialist 'anti-partisan' squadron, and the Geschwäder Bongart (named for its aristocratic leader Hermann-Jozef Freiherr von dem Bongart) provided air support in Italian built Reggiane fighters to a dangerous, if rather mixed, agglomeration of ground units. These included motorised artillery, armoured cars, the SS, the Feldgendarmerie, a searchlight battalion and a detachment from 'the Legion of Volga Tatars'. This group was closer in spirit to the hordes of Genghis Khan than the worst elements of the Wehrmacht, who were not above hacking fingers from French corpses in the heat of battle or tugging off the gold wedding rings later when there was a lull in the fighting.

On both sides the estimated number of men involved and the subsequent casualties vary; what is not in doubt is the ferocity of the fighting and the bravery of the outnumbered and outgunned Maquisards. General Jesser, the local German commander, had made a tactical error by waiting until the afternoon to launch his attack, leaving himself short of time to press home his advantage and surround the mountain before night fell. He withdrew to a safe distance, and under cover of darkness Coulaudon began to pull his men back to la Truyère.

The next morning Jesser threw in everything he had. Artillery pounded the hillside while Bongart's aircraft strafed and bombed anything that moved. But by the time the Germans fought their way to the summit after nightfall, the Maquis had vanished, leaving their comrades' corpses, some burned out vehicles, but taking away most of their weapons. Again the German revenge was visceral. Villages were sacked, hostages shot, and more than a hundred local civilians deported to Germany.

Also on 10 June at 2 p.m. on a quiet country afternoon, some 150 miles north of Chaudes-Aigues, tanks and personnel carriers loaded with troops from the 'Der Führer' Regiment of the SS 'Das Reich' Panzer Division roared in to the peaceful hamlet of Oradour-sur-Glane. Ostensibly they were hunting for a kidnapped officer, but in truth were simply bent on terror. Of the villagers 642 were massacred. Over 500 of them were women and children. They were herded into the church at bayonet point, the doors were chained up and the Germans set the building on fire. The few who managed to scramble through the windows, hair and dresses smouldering, were machine-gunned. When ripples of the bloodbath reached Denis he must have had shivery memories of those Belgian towns in the First World War, that were devastated by an earlier generation of men in field grey; the weapons of war had not perished.[187]

---

[187] *Though the War Diary was prima facie evidence that von Brodowsky was ultimately responsible for this operation, he never faced a War Crimes trial. The French Army caught him at the end of the war and much time and trouble was saved when he was 'shot while trying to escape'*

On 12 June SD Chief Hugo Geissler and eighty men, some French, drove from St Flour to Murat to take and interrogate prisoners. On the way they shot four hostages they had brought with them. A roundup in Murat came to a bloody end when the Maquis came out of hiding and cut down Geissler and eight of his men, including two Milice in a stuttering blaze of Sten gun fire. On 13 June the teleprinter lines between Clermont and Paris clattered with messages, as the Germans debated how many hostages to shoot in reprisal. Paris demanded fifty; in the end they settled on twenty-five local men who were shot at dawn on 14 June, lined up in front of an embankment a few miles outside St Flour. Many were on the Germans' list of Maquis members, some were suspected of trying to persuade Wehrmacht soldiers to desert, and one blameless young man was picked out because the Germans could not catch his father. A few days later the Volga Tatars rounded up 115 more men from Murat who were deported to the concentration camp at Neuengamme, near Hamburg; seventy-five of them never came back.

This sad chronicle, taken from French sources, notably the work of Eugène Martres, is not just a reminder for modern readers of the savagery with which this tiny sideshow of a much larger war was being fought, but also emphasises the real perils the FREELANCE team would have faced had they been caught.

As the Mont Mouchet battle raged, Denis and FREELANCE, having done what they could to help the planning and supply of weapons, were largely spectators, waiting nervously on the other side of the River Allier at Fridefont. In reality, they were 'listeners' rather than spectators since their view of the battleground was blocked by the hills. Other than garbled messages provided by exhausted couriers, all they had to go by was the drone of German aircraft, the crump of shells and bursts of machine gun fire echoing through the valley like sticks being rattled along faraway railings.

Though again accounts vary, by 20 June some 5000 Maquis had scrambled into the la Truyère bastion. The Germans had massed a force of perhaps 10,000 men and went on the attack. Bongart's aircraft flew at tree-top height, their 20 mm cannon and .303 machine guns shredding the foliage, and Luftwaffe bombers were brought into play to back up Jesser's artillery. As night fell another withdrawal seemed to most of the Maquis leaders the only sensible course.

It was a major tactical and above all psychological victory for the Resistance. John Farmer's first report to London via Denis's radio put the Maquis losses at 1,200, though more recent French studies suggest a far lower figure. They also had to abandon badly needed vehicles and weapons. Again, though some accounts describe the German losses as 'huge', later French assessments give a far more modest toll, probably less than the Maquis. The immediate reaction in London was that the policy of concentration was wrong and that the Maquis were heavily outgunned, despite FREELANCE's efforts. Even today French analysts continue to pick away at whether the strategy of concentration was sensible, arguing that it was perhaps 'too little, too early'.

But that ignores the other benefits, which far outweighed numerical gains and losses. The initiative embodied the essence of the Resistance. Though not every faction was there at the early conference, and the Communists and the officers of the 'Secret Army' stood aside, the operation was representative of the way in which the Resistance was painfully bringing disparate groups together to shape the way France would be governed when the Germans had been driven out. It was a bravura boost to French self-respect; though they had seen their comrades die, the young men who escaped were able to say with pride 'we were there'.

They had come out of the shadows to face the invader in the heart of France, unkempt, unshaven 'Davids' in khaki shorts facing the grey-uniformed 'Goliath'. It helped the Allies by diverting important German forces at a vital time. Looking back later Coulaudon concluded that 'if we had hesitated to take the risk it would have been the death of the Resistance. If we had played a waiting game we could have seen all our forces seriously discouraged.'[188]

It is plausible to argue that the outcome also vindicated Maurice Buckmaster's selection of, and confidence in, the FREELANCE team,

---

[188] *Kedward, Maquis p. 170 citing Levy and Cordet*

individually and as a unit. Farmer was a soldier who kept his head. Nancy Wake was a tower of strength in whichever role she undertook. And Denis was not just a capable operator but irrespective of those trickily obtrusive '*tendances*', a man who kept those around him cheerful, an essential attribute for life under stress, above all a man who faced, and faced down, his fears.

In the aftermath of the Mont Mouchet battle, FREELANCE found itself plunged into even more of what Denis would later call those 'really amazing adventures'. A quarter of a century later he gave his vivid impressions of what happened. So did Nancy Wake. However, he and all those involved are probably best served if we again use John Farmer's 1944 report as our central source, simply to leave on the published record what is probably the closest we can come to an official account. But every one of those who dodged the bullets and skittered terrified up and down the rocky screes and through the chilly river waters with the Germans on their heels will have had different perspectives.

Farmer tells us that the attack lasted well into nightfall: 'When our position became untenable the order to retire in a '*sauve qui peut*' manner was given.' He does not say by whom but presumably *Gaspard*. According to Denis, the latter had initially declared that he would stay and fight to the death. He changed his mind only when at Nancy's urging, London sent him a clear order, which Denis pretended as he decoded it had been signed personally by General Koenig, the Free French Commander in London.

Farmer tells us that at this point Denis lost contact with London; Denis's version is that he had been ordered to bury his set and burn his codes. Farmer goes on '. . . at about 4 p.m. I had decided we had better make certain of getting away ourselves and had arranged for us to retire from . . . Fridefont to a small wood nearby. We had with us [Denis], four Canadian air force pilots [trying to scramble back to England] and Mrs Fournier [the sharp-tongued lady from Chaudes-Aigues]. At approximately 7p.m. [Nancy] and I came out of the wood to fetch some tea which had been left in a house', a quintessentially British gesture in the middle of a pitched battle which would have had any Maquis or Germans who saw it wondering whether it was some cunning ruse.

Farmer and Nancy were then diverted to take an urgent message to *Gaspard* at his battle HQ some six miles away. 'On the way back [Nancy] suddenly noticed four Junkers 88 following us up the road and I decided the best thing to do was to stop and get out into the ditch as quickly as possible. We made our way on foot back to Fridefont intending to join the others and depart. On arrival . . . we found a deserted village with mortar shells falling all around us and a [Maquis] patrol left behind in the hope of finding us. The patrol . . . led us away into a deep gorge where we remained until nightfall. Unfortunately [Denis] with the remainder of the party had not been able to get back to Fridefont owing to enemy shelling and troops who had come between them and the village. At night a patrol was sent back in the hope of contacting [Denis] but unfortunately they could not make contact.' (Had Denis been with them, he might have recognised the shape and noise of the marauding Junkers 88s; it was an 88 that sank the *Lancastria*.)

Nancy went on ahead with a Maquis escort to reach a Free French radio operator and tell London of their plight and ask for a new radio and codes to be sent urgently. The operator managed to raise the Free French HQ in Algiers and send a message to be passed on to Baker Street, but it was not acknowledged. Farmer and René Dusacq meanwhile retraced their steps and eventually found Denis. Farmer tells us in his matter of fact style that in this chapter of the story Nancy Wake covered a hundred miles on foot, while he, Dusacq and Denis clocked up about 130, an extraordinary accomplishment for a lame, unfit, middle-aged actor, let alone a young woman.

It is hardly surprising that looking back on all this, Denis focused on the three days of sheer hard slog up and down stony slopes and across the many streams and rivers which fissure the terrain, especially the Truyère. Its deep waters ran so fast through its rocky gorge that the Germans believed it impassable. They only posted sentries on the bridges, including the Garabit Viaduct, 400 feet above the river, designed by Eiffel of tower fame.

Again they had underestimated the ingenuity of the Maquis, who had long since laid down several 'invisible fords', narrow rock causeways, camouflaged with fallen branches, which lay just a foot or so below the Truyère's swirling surface. When Denis and his guide waded across one of the fords, spurred on by the baying of German tracker dogs in the woods, Denis lost his boots, which he had tied around his neck. The guide cut off his own jacket sleeves to make rough wrappers for Denis's troubled feet. Denis drew some comfort from nipping at a bottle of eau de Cologne, which had been dropped from London some time ago as a personal gift for Nancy and which he was carrying for her. They eventually joined up again at St Santin, a village near Aurillac, the latter a chilly town with the unusual distinction of producing over half of France's umbrellas.

There then followed one of the bolder and tougher journeys of that arduous mission. Farmer decided that Nancy should go to Châteauroux, where there was said to be another SOE operator, while he would head for Lapalisse, north-west of Vichy, where rumour had it there was an operator working for the Free French intelligence service.

He writes: 'We set off each accompanied by a companion from St Santin on a most varied journey. We travelled from St Santin to Moriat by car with four bicycles strapped to the roof. At Moriat we got into a van and travelled to the nearest railway station at Giat. From Giat we went by train to Montluçon. At Montluçon [Nancy] and her companion cycled to Châteauroux a distance of approximately fifty miles. There she was completely unable to make contact with the SHIPWRIGHT circuit. She then returned to Montluçon. I on the other hand cycled from Montluçon through Vichy to Lapalisse and there also was unsuccessful.'

Farmer was writing for the files, and thus did not dwell on the perilous background, of which some of his Baker Street readers will have been, or should have been, only too well aware. They were crossing hostile territory where in the wake of the fighting at Mont Mouchet and the resurgence of resistance, the German patrols were on edge, likely to shoot first and not even bother asking questions later. The Milice loitered like packs of teenage hoodlums at bridges and crossroads and the Gestapo and Feldengendarmerie prowled the railway stations checking every detail of identity cards and travel permits.

Montluçon itself was a major German military centre and Vichy must have been awash with alert gendarmes and plain-clothes men. Nor does he comment on the sheer physical effort, and the pain, leg muscles in spasm, thighs red raw, fingers numb from clutching the handlebars, all the more so coming as it did on the heels of their scramble to safety after Fridefont.

When they met up again 'we both rather began to despair'. It had been three weeks since they had sent word via Algiers, and still no response. They gave themselves another month; if they had still heard nothing they would try to get out via Spain, presumably, though Farmer does not say so, leaving poor Denis to his own devices. Then via a local Maquis they finally received a message from London, *en clair* rather than in code, telling them that a new radio operator was being sent out. Relief was tempered by the news that to meet him they would have to make their way back over the dangerous ground to St Santin.

19

'If You Go Down to the Woods Today'

This time they travelled in a convoy of three cars, each fitted with a Bren machine gun. As Farmer comments 'this way we were certain that at any rate one car would get through'. In fact they all made it and at 2.02 a.m. on 19 July the B24 bomber 'Varga Belle'[189] dropped Roger Faucher, '*François*', an American 'Seaman First Class' and a skilled wireless operator. He parachuted out of the sky, his radio strapped to his leg, the new codes and schedules safely tucked away inside his jumpsuit, followed by twelve containers of supplies and nine 'packages', as well as a radio and new codes for the FREELANCE group. He was just 19 years of age.

His arrival coincided with a decision to move FREELANCE base north to the tiny village of Ygrande in the forest just beyond Cosne d'Allier where they had originally parachuted in. Farmer's report is clear that the move was his initiative, though both Denis and Nancy Wake suggest that she had a powerful voice in it. In their memories it was prompted by Coulaudon, who, flushed with success after Mont Mouchet, had decided that it was time to assert himself and had declared that FREELANCE would now come under the command of one of his colonels. In fact, after D-Day Baker Street had advised its circuits that all Resistance groups were to be merged into de Gaulle's Forces Françaises de l'Intérieur under General Koenig. It was thus an 'across the board' directive not a Coulaudon diktat.

But whatever prompted it, and FREELANCE is not listed among

---

[189] *The iconic images of buxom 'pinup' girls which embellished the nosecones of the Second World War US bombers were called 'Varga Girls', after the creator of the genre, the 'Esquire' magazine artist Alberto Vargas, 1892-1982*

the missions that were amalgamated with the FFI, the battle continued. On the night of 7 August, just a day after FREELANCE and its loose fraternity of fighters had settled uneasily in the woods, a Halifax bomber from Tempsford dropped John Alsop and Reeve Schley, of the newly established US Office of Strategic Services. To the locals they were not just a surprise, they were a sensation: the first uniformed American officers to land in the Allier region. The euphoria was short-lived. The next morning they were attacked by nine truckloads of Wehrmacht headed by three scout cars. Denis was startled from sleep by the rattle of machinegun fire and grenade blasts, while the Americans struggled to pull on their much-admired riding boots.[190]

Farmer had left earlier to look for a package lost when the Americans dropped, and Nancy took command with a blaze of orders. Faucher was to take a truck and drive the radios to safety. Denis was to stay at the base, get ready to move if necessary and meanwhile tend the wounded.

Denis had a French girl to help him as the wounded staggered or were carried in on makeshift stretchers cut from brushwood. To treat them he had only medical alcohol, bandages and greyish cotton wool (perhaps reminding him of the sheets he shredded at Nurse Cavell's Clinic in Brussels). He remembers drinking 'my share' of the alcohol to get himself through it. Nancy's memory is of returning to find him 'very, very drunk', with a loaded carbine slung over his shoulder, grenades clipped to his belt and a Colt revolver on his hip. She hastily removed the grenades; the Germans were danger enough.

Recommending Nancy for a decoration Farmer records that 'She . . . led a section of ten men, after their leader had lost his head, resulting in the death of four of them. [Schley] and [Alsop] were under her command. She led the section to within range of the enemy, ordered the fire and withdrew them in good order, which showed an exceptional courage and coolness in the face of enemy fire. Her action definitely contributed to the safety of the two American

[190] When the present author asked a local farmer who had been in the Resistance how the Germans could have found their way through the thick woods, he grunted: 'They had local help, of course. Many men from round here were in the Milice'

officers who were very new to the work and rather lost', though in an earlier paragraph of his report he comments somewhat contradictorily that the two new arrivals 'behaved in an exemplary manner'.

Of Denis he was to write, 'As is well known to you, this officer has undergone considerable physical suffering in the past, and the trials which he underwent during his escape from the Fridefont attack . . . are worthy of a special mention. Although it was obvious that he was in extreme pain from his feet he never once complained and always remained cheerful in [the] face of very considerable physical trial. On each occasion we were attacked, by his personal behaviour and apparent fearlessness he contributed to a large extent to the good morale of the poorly trained Maquis.'

Whether Denis knew what Farmer thought of him, or whether he ever read this accolade, we do not know. Probably not and that's a shame. It would have been a far greater morale boost than a rave review in the *Daily Mail* for one of his stage appearances. It more than justified his determination to prove himself to his harshest critic, himself.

After a tour of the area with Coulaudon and the two Americans to hand out to Maquis groups the bundles of cash the latter had brought with them, Farmer shifted FREELANCE's HQ again, a few miles away to the even denser Forest of Troncais. Centuries of indiscriminate peasant logging had taken their toll before the forest came under the prudent management of Louis XIV's Finance Minister Jean Baptiste Colbert as part of his successful efforts to straighten out his Royal master's economy. Its 25,000 acres had become fruitful again, and provided the timber for many French ships of the line in their long running battles with the British navy. The forest suffered again when charcoal was needed to fuel the new iron foundries of the nineteenth century industrial revolution. But by the Second World War many years of careful logging and replanting had re-created a vast green umbrella, most of it oak trees. It afforded ideal shelter for men on the run, much as Sherwood had been for Robin Hood and his reputedly merry men. Even today a car parked thirty yards off one of the winding tracks is all but invisible, and the woods are so dense that cell phones do not function.

The main Maquis leader in the forest (there were several other groups) was the dashing Henri Tardivat, with whom the opportunistic Nancy rapidly swapped two Bren machine guns for a commandeered country bus on which she could move around. It also had bench seats at the rear, on which she could rest her mattress when she wanted to use it as a bedroom. Denis cut up some parachutes to make a canopy alongside the bus for himself. He cushioned the ground with leaves and brush, prompting Nancy to tease when she first looked inside 'Doing the *Desert Song* again, DenDen?' But these skirmishes were only the prelude to the bigger battle to drive the Germans out of Montluçon.

On 27 November 1942 a German officer had arrived with 300 men at the wrought iron gates of the town's Richemont Barracks. He disarmed the French garrison (whose commanding officer had gone home for lunch) and cleared them out. The Tricolour was ripped down and a Swastika flag was raised in its place and the Wehrmacht tramped in. The soldiers also took over the five-storey Hotel Terminus by the railway station as their HQ. On a recent visit, though the building was framed by scaffolding, the name could still be seen in fading whitewash on the side wall.

Meanwhile the Gestapo moved into part of the Hotel de l'Univers, incongruously sharing it for a time with the local 'Soldatenheim' or military recreation club. Active and passive resistance in Montluçon and the surrounding area increased day by day. Between February and August 1944 alone there were some fifty sabotage attacks on the railways. The pages of the pro-Vichy *le Centre* reported the inevitable aftermath: indiscriminate arrests, long prison sentences and firing squads.

It is slightly invidious to single out any one initiative, but the almost film script flavour of the goings on at the Hotel Terminus make it a story worth telling, courtesy of Andre Touret.

When the Wehrmacht took over the hotel they allowed its owner Maurice Comabanaire to go on running the restaurant. This probably suited the officers to have access to French cuisine as an alternative to sauerkraut, dumplings and boiled sausage. What they did not know was that he was an active member of the 'Marco Polo'

Resistance network, hid a radio set in his basement, sheltered Maquis on the run and even dipped into the Wehrmacht mail, partly for intelligence but mainly to divert letters from locals denouncing their neighbours. He even took steps to warn those targeted. Sadly an anonymous accusation, which slipped through his net, brought about his arrest in October 1943. He was shipped off to Germany to an unknown fate.

The weather that August was bad: Montluçon was lashed day after day by heavy rain storms and even hail. It was a fittingly grey and gloomy backcloth for the death and destruction that lay ahead as the French moved, with Farmer's encouragement, to take back the town.

On 12 August the Resistance staged a head on crash between two trains in a tunnel on the line from Montluçon to Moulins, having made sure the passengers and footplate crews had time to escape first. Andre Touret believes the incident, known as the *bataille du rail* 'which caused major damage and delay', was the most spectacular operation in the Allier region. The Resistance was growing ever more confident and the townspeople were convinced that the Occupation was on its last legs. But they were all too well aware of how the Germans operated and feared they would exact a terrible revenge before they withdrew. The fears were justified.

For weeks Feldgendarmerie and army patrols had crunched through the streets checking papers, and by the second week of August had taken some fifty men as hostages and locked them in the former French Army punishment cells at the Richemont Barracks. The oldest of the prisoners was aged 57, the youngest 19. They had mixed backgrounds. One was a Dunlop factory hand, the others were smallholders, commercial travellers, a barber, a teacher, railway men, even a confectioner.

At 5 a.m. on 14 August an open truck carrying forty-two of them, led by a scout car with Wehrmacht officers, and backed by a truckload of troops, growled out of the Barrack gates to the isolated quarry at des Grises. Trenches had already been dug and at around 6 a.m. people in the area heard a series of rifle volleys. All the men were dead, some finished off by having their skulls crushed with rifle butts.

A brave protest by Sub-Préfet Fea and Mayor Raoul Mechain to the German Kommandatur brought the stony response that the killings were 'not a Wehrmacht affair' but had been ordered by the Gestapo to punish 'the terrorists'. The town was forbidden to arrange any funerals or memorial services and the victims' bodies did not rest in a proper grave until after the war. The site of the slaughter is marked by a small stone plinth.[191]

On 15 August Allied forces landed in the south of France, in Operation Dragoon; most of the north-west of the country was already in Allied hands. (On the same day in Paris one of the last grand cocktail parties of the war was in full swing at the Auberge d'Armaillé to celebrate the publication of a new book of poems by Camille François. The last guest left at 5 a.m. Around the same time Ernst Jünger had visited the barber who had been trimming his hair throughout his time in Paris. 'He seemed to sense this was the last time I would be there, and told me 'I hope things work out OK'.') Paris was liberated on 25 August.

Hitler soon ordered the Wehrmacht to pull out of southern France, to build up resources for the last ditch defence of the Reich. They were harried by the Maquis every step of the way, their food convoys hijacked, troop lorries machine-gunned by ambushers who vanished into the woods, bridges blown, signposts turned around, and booby traps laid for the unwary.

The sabotage targets – namely telephone lines, machine tool and ball bearing factories, power plants, and fuel depots – so carefully mapped out at great risk by earlier SOE agents (and logged in the 'secret papers' Nancy guarded so closely in her handbag) were now systematically destroyed. SOE used BBC messages to give FREELANCE attack priorities to pass on to the Maquis. If London wanted them to hit roads and bridges, for example, the BBC announcer would repeat in measured tones, ' *Son récit coule de source.* ' ('His story is straight from the horse's mouth.') It is not implausible

---

[191] *After the war Dorscht, head of the Montluçon Gestapo, was sentenced to death for his role in the massacre. This was commuted in 1951 to penal servitude for life, a sentence he did not serve out in full. For this account and the story of the day that followed, I am especially indebted to the work of Andre Touret, pp 280 et seq.*

to see Leo Mark's sense of humour at work in the wording of the signal to target telephone lines. To any French-speaking German intercept operator the phrase *'L'espace vital nous manque'* had sardonic echoes of Hitler's fatal expansionist mantra that 'we need living space'.

On Saturday 19 August, Resistance leaders held another 'summit' at Hérrison, a village a few miles north-west of Cosne d'Allier, to plan the final removal of the Germans from Montluçon. With them were 'officers of the British mission operating in the area under the command of Major Farmer'. Whether Denis was there we do not know, but he was certainly aware of the meeting and the decision to move on the town, an attack in which Tardivat's Maquis were to play a central role. Though the Resistance could muster some 1300 men against 800 Germans holed up in the Richemont Barracks, the French were still lightly armed and bloody experience had shown what German firepower could do. An attempt by Farmer to get the Germans to surrender, as they had done elsewhere, met a flat refusal.

The Resistance then moved into the town and took over key buildings, but late on 20 August a German convoy from the garrison at Moulins smashed their way through to reinforce the beleaguered men in Richemont. Tardivat pulled his men back. By Tuesday the Resistance had cut off all power and water supplies to Richemont, but Wehrmacht mortars began to lob shells into their positions from the nearby hills, and the defenders made several sorties from the barracks, some to burn about a hundred houses nearby. Though seen at first as just another mindless reprisal, it had a tactical purpose. On Thursday afternoon an 800 strong convoy from the 19th Regiment of the SS, broke through the barricades and reached the Richemont gates. With men concealed in the ruined buildings providing covering fire, an SS armoured car led a convoy of sixty vehicles – scout cars, lorries and ambulances – out of the town towards Verneix and Cosne d'Allier. The last German left Montluçon at 8.30 p.m. At midnight the Tricolour, tossed into the mud in November 1942, flew again above the entrance gate of the Barracks. Today it is a training school for Warrant Officers and other NCOs of the Gendarmerie.

Some time earlier, because of the terrible weather, the forest, remote farmhouses, even the bus, had become damp and uncomfortable. With the caretaker's permission – it would have been hard to refuse – the FREELANCE team took over the Château de Fragnes, a few miles from Montluçon on the road to Cosne d'Allier. It had been abandoned, some said as far back as the First World War when its owner went off to the trenches and never returned. Its silver, ornate furniture, mirrors and artwork were untouched, but were swathed in cobwebs and a thick layer of dead flies and dust. It only needed a Miss Havisham in a tattered lace gown to convert it to a scene from *Great Expectations*. Denis fussed around with dusters and brooms to make it habitable. A recent visit showed that it had hardly changed. It is still a rambling family home, hidden and dilapidated and crying out for Denis to give it a 'bit of a tidy'.

It is incongruous that as Montluçon swayed in and out of German control just a few miles away, with retreating Germans racing down the road at the end of the drive, the château was the setting for a party to celebrate Nancy's birthday and the liberation of Paris. To borrow from songwriter Cole Porter, in the midst of war, it was truly a 'swellegant, elegant party'. Cobweb-covered bottles of vintage wine and champagne were exhumed from beneath the cellar flagstones, and despite the shortages there was suddenly enough food to make a feast. Members of the local Resistance brought little gifts and pastries for Nancy. Her bodyguards, the penniless veterans of the Civil War proffered a bunch of wild flowers wrapped in a small Spanish flag, and a poem. From somewhere, we might wonder whether it was a dim recess of the château, Schley and Alsop conjured up six etchings. As the highpoint of the day, which went on well into the night, Nancy 'took the salute' as the Maquis – Farmer had formed his own small group, mainly local gendarmes – paraded through the archway and crunched smartly across the gravelled forecourt.

Whatever was happening in the world outside there was always time for humour. Only when one marcher broke down laughing did it come to light that as they reached the corner of the château, the men were doubling across the terrace at the back and rejoining the parade, creating the impression of a never-ending flow of fighters.

But in Nancy's memory there was a spectre at the feast, poor Alex, since it was amid the merriment, toasting and speechmaking around the château dining table that she remembered that the Montluçon shopkeeper inadvertently let drop the news of his death. But a spectre of her own lurked not far away.

20

Unwinding

Like a gaggle of mustachioed ostriches, heads buried in the town's manicured flowerbeds, the wretched, misguided, politically impotent men at Vichy went on pretending they were a government until August. They spent their time vacuously shuffling papers, having ever longer lunches and *cinq à sept* sessions with their mistresses. Some cleverer senior officials had long since slipped quietly away, suddenly overcome by long-dormant, indeed hitherto invisible, Resistance sympathies. At the up-market 'Trouillet' and 'Aux Iles de Flandre' restaurants, the 'Olympique' and 'la Régence' brasseries and the 'Ambassadeurs Bar', the owners hastily took down portraits of Pétain and wrung their hands as takings plummeted. But they kept the staff busy polishing the silver, ready to bow and scrape for a new generation of clients.

In contrast to Montluçon, and due largely to the efforts of Dr Stucki, the Swiss Consul, the Wehrmacht abandoned Vichy without a fight on 19 August though the Gestapo stayed for six more days. They were busy burning some of their files in the courtyard of their main HQ at 125 Boulevard des États Unis, but were carefully packing another 150,000 to be hidden in Czechoslovakia. Laval and his Ministers fled. The SS kicked in Pétain's bedroom door and hauled the mumbling Marshal away to join them in a farcical shadow government, which rattled around like ghosts for some months in the castle of Singmaringen in southern Germany. What happened to the pretty secretary, who caught Pétain's eye in the bathroom, we shall never know.

On the night of the birthday party Denis (whose account of it makes no mention of the dreadful news about Alex) had made a scheduled contact with London, whose reply told him that Vichy was now free. He added that Coulaudon was on his way there with a group of his men to make his mark at the scene of triumph. This was despite an agreement with John Farmer that the FREELANCE team would be invited to be alongside him. Farmer, Denis, Nancy, and the two American officers hurried off to make sure the Allies were not upstaged.

It was a slow journey; every village on the way was a scrum of celebration. So was Vichy itself, when they finally got there. The last few years had been magically erased from the municipal 'hard drive', and the future embraced ecstatically.

It was in the noisy swirl and flag-waving pomp of a ceremony around the First World War memorial that Nancy's own spectre appeared. Like many such messages, the delivery was brutally banal. A woman in the crowd, who had been a receptionist at a Marseilles hotel and who recognised Nancy from those halcyon pre-war Riviera days, pushed her way towards her. Without much preamble she told her 'quite abruptly' that her husband Henri, whom she had last seen before her escape over the Pyrenees, had been taken by the Gestapo in May 1943 and had died in their hands five months later. Nancy collapsed in tears and Denis took her quietly away and held her hand.

After a diversion to Marseilles to find out what exactly had happened, and for Nancy to be reunited with her dog Picon, she, Denis and Farmer drove back to the château and then made a leisurely run through a festive France to Paris. While they waited for an RAF aircraft to carry them home Denis 'spent the whole day at the hairdresser and came out looking ten years' younger', Nancy recalled.

Appearances are often deceptive. Denis tells us that he had already been diagnosed with a form of epilepsy and had suffered a serious fit in Marseilles. Farmer, Nancy relates with an almost audible sniff, disappeared for days: '. . . he had been looking after his future and organised himself an interesting position in a Government depart-ment', which was as delicate a way as any to describe his recruitment into SIS where he did indeed have an interesting career.[192]

At this point Denis brings his story to a close with the comment

---

[192] *See, e.g. Dorril; pp 629-30 et seq.*

that he could not remember how he got back to England, and that Maurice Buckmaster had him hospitalised. 'I spent some weeks in a loony bin' before a friend found him a job in Germany.

This, as we shall see, is more shorthand from a tired man. Fortunately we can pick up the trail with the help of the personal file, Nancy's memories, the recollections of an Anglo-American film star and further research. Before we move on, though, it is sobering to reflect that Britain dealt with its heroes in wondrous ways. Denis still enjoyed the support and respect of Buckmaster and Vera Atkins, but that did not deter the accountants of SOE from launching a spiteful flurry of paperwork about a hospital charge of £ 2/12/6d probably relating to his earlier spell at Drymen; they refused to pay 10/6d to replace a pair of Army-issue spectacles Denis had lost in France.

In the last lines of his memoirs, he tells us that 'through a friend I obtained a job with the Army in Germany. But that, as they say, is another story.'

We get a more complete picture of that story from a letter to an SOE colleague, headed Army Welfare Services, Rear Headquarters, 21st Army Group and dated 1 January 1944. He was again upbeat. 'My new job is just the happiest I have ever had. I spent Christmas Day near the Dutch front line having taken a party of Belgians to entertain the troops. We had dinner in a German dugout which had only been vacated 14 hours earlier. I now go on Wednesday to the Ardennes – all very interesting and fun.'

Though the setting is very different – steamy Malaya in the 1950s rather than a wintry war-scarred Europe – Denis's description brings to mind the 1980s film of Peter Nichols's *Privates on Parade* – in which 'Captain Terri Dennis' was portrayed with high camp bravura and in 'full slap' by the late Denis Quilley. It echoes the themes of comedy and of sadness in Denis's own life, not least when the captain recounts wistfully how he was not told officially that his partner, a sailor, had been killed during the war, and only heard about it through a chance remark in a pub.

Neither the Welfare job nor his recent experiences deterred Denis Rake from seeking to go where the action was. Quite undaunted, he told SOE that he would be interested in a transfer to the Far East where the war against the Japanese was still raging, as a Jedburgh instructor. Nothing came of this, fortunately for all concerned, and he was still at 21st Army Group when Maurice Buckmaster wrote to him on 25 June 1945, to tell he had been awarded the Military Cross. 'I congratulate you most sincerely as do your many friends here.'

The lighthouse beam silhouettes him again in June 1945 a month after VE Day. Now clearly depressed and muddled 'since my accident' Denis is writing to Buckmaster, whom he has recently seen in London. He asks on the one hand if his former chief can cut through War Office red tape to allow Denis to take another job in Germany, and a few lines later asks if he can send him to France to find Alex Shaw's family. Denis says he clearly cannot go back on the stage as a 'juvenile'. He has no income and his house 'such as it was, was destroyed early in the war'. We do not know if this refers to the address in Cornwall Gardens, near Gloucester Road underground station which he gives in one SOE entry, or even that briefly glimpsed Queens Gate 'hotel' a few streets away. [193]

Buckmaster minuted on the letter 'What can we do for Denis? I would be prepared to go a long way out of my way for him.' But by September, Denis was still sliding down a snake, ending this time in the Royal Infirmary in Bradford, where he had 'arrived in state on a stretcher' after falling ill in Brussels. Writing on 6 September, this time to Vera Atkins, addressing her as 'Miss Atkins' and jokily signing himself with his workname of Denis 'Dieudonné' he tells her that he will have to stay in bed for six weeks, 'but of course they don't know that really mad people like me don't go down for so long with spinal arthritis, which they say I've got. Morale is good in parts and everyone is very kind.'

Less than a month later he is writing again, now to 'Dear Vera' from the Royal Masonic Hospital in Hammersmith, [194] reporting that he is starting a new series of treatments and asking her to visit so

---

[193] *The Post Office Directory has no entry for Denis at the Cornwall Gardens address*

[194] *In the Second World War the Hospital relaxed the rule which had limited access to Masons and their families, and admitted Allied servicemen who were 'deserving cases,' with a slight preference for officers. Denis would clearly have qualified but having a Masonic introduction would have helped*

that he can catch up, 'to ask a few questions about everyone and to know what you are becoming'. He had clearly picked up rumours about the Whitehall infighting over SOE's post-war future, a fight which ended in its brisk and brusque dissolution by a new Labour Government anxious as the Cold War loomed not to be found to be running a clandestine, politically manipulative organisation on a par with Stalin's Comintern, which was dissolved with much sycophantic publicity in 1943. His final paragraph is the essence of Denis plus an unconscious hint of Scaramouche. 'I am still completely mad and this ward does nothing else but laugh at me, all six of them. It is a lovely hospital. Hope very much you are well and happy.'

Vera Atkins replies teasingly, '. . . the fact that you are completely mad does not impress me, since I have thought so from the first day we met. If you are now coming round to this view it looks like putting me into a new mental category.' [195]

The new treatments worked since by November he was back at the Pastoria on his way to visit that tantalisingly invisible sister in Devon. In December the personal file mentions that he is starting a new job on 1 January, 1946. But there is no clue here, or in the autobiography, about what the job was. He was definitely back up a ladder, at least for a short time, though to tell the story properly we have to turn back to Nancy Wake's memories, and add in to the bouillabaisse a pinch of spice from British Intelligence history, which in Denis's case may stretch back to Belgium and Maurice Jeffes.

[195] *Denis's personal file op.cit.*

21

The Next Time They Saw Paris

The starting point is Nancy's statement to Russell Braddon, repeated in her own book, that Denis had found himself a job in the Passport Control Organisation in Paris, and that she had not taken much persuading to apply herself and join him there.

There was little that was scholastic about the Government Code and Cipher School, which intercepted and decoded foreign radio and cable transmissions and was rebranded after the Second World War as Government Communications Headquarters. Similarly the Passport Control Organisation ('PCO') had nothing to do with the humdrum business of issuing passports to British travellers. From 1920 it had been joined hip and thigh to SIS and for some years even shared the same headquarters building above St James's Park underground station. An outgrowth of the First World War efforts to control and monitor the movements of 'subversives' and 'undesirables', its circuit of overseas stations screened people wishing to travel to or through British territory, and issued visas to those it found acceptable.

The control function, the opportunity to interview and even recruit foreigners who might have useful information were attractive but equally important was the availability of a circuit of overseas bureaux to provide 'quasi-diplomatic' cover to Secret Service officers abroad. The Foreign Office was often unable and quite often unwilling, to give diplomatic posts to SIS representatives so the PCO, often housed within a Consular building, was a plausible compromise. It diligently pursued its business of issuing visas, with Examiners behind a counter dealing with harassed applicants so often tragic refugees, interviewing, filling in forms and stamping passports. Visa fees supplemented SIS's meagre budget, though the flow of ready cash and slapdash accounting occasionally led officers into temptation.

Quietly out of sight in a back room the SIS station head went about his own business. Even before the Second World War the system had been comprehensively 'blown' by indiscretion and at least one notable German coup, and in 1940 the PCO was merged back into SIS though it continued to provide cover for the latter's counter-intelligence Section V officers overseas. As we saw when looking at Denis's life in Belgium, Maurice Jeffes had joined the PCO in 1919 and was its Head from 1940 until his retirement ten years later. And we can legitimately speculate whether it was he who found Denis the job in Paris, though it might equally well have been John Farmer.

That leaves open the question of what that job was. The strong-minded Nancy might not have adapted easily to the subtleties and discipline of SIS work, and at first sight it is hard to imagine that Denis would be seen as a likely candidate. However, someone with distant but reliable memories of those strange days confirms that Denis was indeed taken on by SIS for a time after the war but his service was cut short because of his poor health.

But what were he and Nancy Wake actually doing? Nancy gives us the clue when she writes that she and Denis worked for Sir Robert Mackenzie, 'one of the most considerate and compassionate men I have ever met'.

Mackenzie had spent the war in SIS Counter-intelligence Section V, headed by Kim Philby, first of all in Spain, and later in its French subsection. In 1944 he was posted to Paris, where according to fellow SIS officer Kenneth Benton, he was 'Section V Head of Station'.[196]

We can thus conjecture that at least in post-liberation Paris, the old Passport Control system of SIS in the backroom while the clerks worked away out front, was still functioning. Counter-intelligence even, or perhaps especially, in a nation so recently a staunch ally but nursing a long history of mutual territorial challenge and hostility, was delicate work.

---

[196] Benton, p. 399. *Sir Robert Evelyn Mackenzie 1906-1990*

The de Gaulle government which had smouldered with deep distrust of the British throughout the war (as we have seen, the feeling was often heartily reciprocated) tended to see little distinction between SIS and SOE and suspected the latter of approaching its former agents in liberated France to work for 'British intelligence'. (Even the published screenplay of *le Chagrin*, a project which involved a raft of supposedly well informed people, describes SOE as 'the British espionage network'.) An SOE veterans group in Paris attracted hostile attention for its far Right-Wing orientation, while British readiness to supply the Communist Resistance with arms had not been forgotten. French suspicion that the *Entente* was not fully *Cordiale* was not misplaced. British intercept records for 1945 show that coded messages from French intelligence in London to their Paris colleagues, and 'handed to the British service for transmission' were routinely decrypted and circulated in Whitehall under 'Top Secret' cover, stamped 'TO BE KEPT UNDER LOCK AND KEY. NEVER TO BE REMOVED FROM THE OFFICE.' British intercept operators and decoders also monitored traffic between Paris and the French military mission in Washington.[197]

Bourne-Paterson's comments, with his own capital letters, about the aftermath of the war in Bordeaux are applicable more generally to the immediate post-war Anglo-French and intra-French tensions in Paris: 'Battle gave way to Intrigue, Plot and Counterplot almost overnight.'[p. 44]

Against this fractured and febrile background, what was Denis up to? He had solid Resistance 'credentials', fluent French and ready entrée to the Parisian salons, theatres and clubs, habitats of the more refined levels of the gay cultural milieu, what the French called *la grande confrérie*. Though the German menace had all but vanished save for residual fears of a Nazi 'last redoubt' and the hunt for war criminals, the reborn spectre of Soviet world ambitions and General de Gaulle's undiminished antipathy towards all things British, presented Section V with new threats to assess.

Not least there was a hostile French intelligence service and a

---

[197] *See e.g. HW 24/17, National Archives*

militant Communist Party, new sources to be nurtured and suborned, especially if their wartime record was ambivalent, and pre-war ties with the East European and White Russian émigré communities to be rebuilt. (Ironically the biggest threat of all to British secrets, Philby himself, the 'star' of Section V, would go unsuspected and undetected for several more years. Secret intelligence being a small world, Mackenzie later served as Security Officer in the British Embassy in Washington when efforts were intensifying to identify Donald MacLean as a Soviet agent, efforts mischievously muddied under Mackenzie's nose by his old colleague Philby.)[198]

With his talent to amuse, charm and flatter, Denis would have been seen as a potentially exploitable asset, albeit one whose penchant for indiscretion meant that Mackenzie would have had to run him on a tight leash.

Whatever the job, it was not arduous. Nancy's abiding memories were of laughter with Denis, and exploring Paris with him and their friend Ian Marshall to discover out of the way bistros. There were even two 'small world' coincidences rolled into one when she and Denis were reunited with their old Riviera friend Miracca from the Palm Beach, who now owned the V-Bar in the Avenue Franklin D. Roosevelt. It turned out Miracca's barman had been one of her Maquis fighters in the Forêt de Tronçais.

Her unhappier memory, shared with Denis, was the death of her old dog 'Picon', put to sleep on her lap while she and Denis sobbed and hugged one another. It is a sentimental moment, one at which a film director could dissolve and move forward. Our problem is, how far.

Apart from a mystifying glimpse of 'Greer, Captain D.J.' in a British Consular index from 1945 relating to Romania of all places (the document to which the index refers has disappeared), that malfunctioning lighthouse goes dim and does not illuminate the landscape again until sometime in the 1950s, though we know that ill health prevented Denis from taking part in one of Maurice Buckmaster's 'victory lap' missions to France. These gave him the

---

[198] *Philby p. 217*

opportunity to thank those who had helped F Section, and to receive his own share of thanks, plaudits and street–naming. It was a crowd-pulling 'walkabout' of a kind which could not fail to offend the readily offended sensibilities of the de Gaulle administration which was busily eradicating as many traces as possible of British involvement in driving the Germans out of France.

These valedictory tours were named '*Judex*', the Latin for 'Judge' but a word which to French ears conjures up the image of the mysterious adventurer who first appeared in a series of silent movies made in 1916 by Louis Feuillade and Arthur Bernéde. Whoever saw parallels with the original 'Judex', in a black cloak and slouch hat, the 'masterful fighter' and expert in disguises seeking revenge from his secret HQ in the vaults of a ruined castle, was displaying a penchant for the melodramatic rather at odds with an organisation which from its inception had displayed a vampire-like compulsion to avoid daylight.

The deep currents, which riled the Resistance, the antipathies, the resentments, the contradictions, even extended to the question of memorials to those who had fought and fallen. On 20 May 1945 Coulaudon and some of his comrades in arms, a few of whom would appear later in *le Chagrin*, placed at Mont Mouchet the first stones of a memorial to 'the Maquis of France'. Only local dignitaries attended; General de Gaulle's advisors kept him well away.[199] In his place Maurice Bourges Manoury, later de Gaulle's Minister of Defence, delivered a nuanced message about the need to work together to bring France back to normal. The Memorial was built to its present impressive bulk over the next years but the annual Remembrance ceremonies were generally low key. The General did not show up until 1959 by which time he had decided it was also safe to single out Coulaudon for unstinted praise.

Back in London the SOE was summarily disbanded early in 1946. Despite the mistakes, the carping, the infighting, it had served the nation well.

Bourne-Paterson records that SOE sent 393 officers into France.

---

[199] *Dictionnaire p. 1008*

Of them 119 were arrested or killed by the Germans. Of those captured only seventeen came back. These are statistics Denis would not have known. Nor can we imagine him indulging in historical or philosophical debates about the value of SOE in regaining France and on a wider scale, winning the war. Some have sought to measure its contribution as the equivalent of several Army divisions, or as shortening the war in Europe by many months. Others see it less quantitatively as maintaining Britain as a force to be reckoned with by the Nazis and the wider world, as an aggressive presence on enemy-held terrain in the darkest days of the fight, enabling the country to 'punch above its weight', in the cant phrase much beloved by modern diplomats.

Perhaps because its top ranks included many shrewd bankers, it also seems to have been more of a financial success than most other public sector ventures. One of the more surprising comments in William Mackenzie's History[200] is the throw-away line that 'SOE's cash expenditure on subsidies to Resistance was probably no greater than its cash gains as a dealer in the European currency black markets'.[201]

It is interesting to see Lord Selborne making a similar point to the Prime Minister in January 1945 in a shorthand version of the extraordinary Far East business venture, far removed from sabotage, mayhem or propaganda, known as 'Operation REMORSE. An SOE black market trading organisation provides currency at a low rate of exchange for all British establishments in China. So far some £10 million has been saved to the Treasury by these methods and as part of the trade, considerable quantities of quinine have been procured.' In fact quinine and cash were only some of the scarce goods from machine tools to medicines traded against foreign currencies and Swiss watches by the adroit merchants and bankers who ramped up REMORSE into a major secret success, whose profits some estimate to have been far higher than Selborne's figure.

Whatever factors are put into the equation, Denis and his SOE colleagues made a war-winning difference.

---

[200] *p.745*

[201] *The surprise is all the greater given the large amounts of cash which, along with many containers of stores, SOE dropped into the Germans eager hands in the course of their penetration of the PROSPER circuit*

22

A Gentleman's Gentleman

Even though we have met a cast of entertaining and extraordinary characters already, the lighthouse now surprises us by picking out the man who probably did more than most to persuade Denis to write *Rake's Progress.*

Remembered when he died in 2000, aged 90 as 'rakishly handsome, swashbuckling, with overwhelming charm and an incandescent smile', Douglas Fairbanks Jr was the well-known son of a famous father, a star in his own right of seventy-five less than classic movies. But today he is perhaps better remembered by British TV viewers of a certain age as the suave host of *Douglas Fairbanks Presents*, a drama series that ran from the early days of UK commercial television well into the 1970s. He was awarded the British Distinguished Service Cross and a string of US and other decorations for his work in the Second World War, not least as the inspiration of the US Navy's 'Beach Jumpers' whose mission was to mount amphibious diversionary and deception operations. When the Allies landed on the French Riviera in August 1944, which the FREELANCE team celebrated by raiding Montluçon, Fairbanks was on board the USS *Endicott* as Commander of the Special Operations Eastern Diversion Unit.

An Anglophile, who spent much of his life in England, he was appointed an Honorary KBE, (Knight Commander of The Most Excellent Order of the British Empire), in 1949.[202] His London home was a large house in the leafy, monied enclave of The Boltons in South Kensington.

---

[202] *On the other side of the coin, he was 'mentioned in dispatches' in 1963 as one of the alleged high society patrons of Christine Keeler and Mandy Rice-Davies, when the well-connected London osteopath Stephen Ward, was charged with living off their earnings*

The story of how Douglas Fairbanks met Denis opens with a scene that is almost a parody of one of those not entirely mythical SIS and SOE recruitments. It is set some time in 1950.

A group of well-dressed, well-heeled and well-connected men are propping up the bar of a gentleman's club in St James's, tradition dripping rustily from its ancient toilet cisterns. Depending on the time of year they might have been 'harrumphing' about the Labour Government's precarious hold on power, the England cricket team's demolition by the West Indian spin bowlers Ramadhin and Valentine, or the Korean War. Whatever the season, the weather would also have loomed large.

One of them is Fairbanks, whose account of events is taken from his Introduction to Denis's book. He threw in the casual comment that his wife Mary Lee was finding it hard to get good staff, much as in days gone by, 'C' might have let slip that he was looking for a good man for Gdansk. One of Fairbanks' friends said he knew 'just the right chap'. There was one condition. Fairbanks could not expect to see any references, nor could he ask about the man's past, though there was nothing criminal in it. On the contrary, the War Office rated him highly, and he was 'very intelligent and highly resourceful. He's sober and honest too'. 'A topnotch chap', the friend concluded with a fine Bulldog Drummond flourish.

The 'chap' was Denis, who reported to The Boltons to be interviewed. The Fairbanks liked what they saw.

Denis was good at the job as butler and valet – 'the shortened, rounded and jovial incarnation of Jeeves'. But when the last guest had gone, he became part of the family circle, chatting about everything under the sun, except himself. As a fellow professional, Fairbanks noted that Denis's greatest enthusiasm was the theatre, about which he obviously knew a great deal more than the average fan.

Much as Nancy Wake's book has countless references to laughter, so too Fairbanks, whose four page description of life with Denis is replete with words like 'jovial', 'jolly', 'humorous', 'laugh', 'amusing', 'wit' and 'chuckle'.

More of Denis's background came out when a letter arrived at the house one day addressed to 'Major Denis Rake MC', provoking modest muttering from Denis about 'all that nonsense . . . it's all in the past now'. Even then Fairbanks got only part of the story.

Denis's health then began to let him down and he felt he needed a less demanding job. Though on the face of it, it actually sounds more exacting than life *en famille* with the Fairbanks, he found work as a steward on an ocean liner on the London – Australia run. They were sorry to see him go, and he was sad to leave.

Rather like other episodes in Denis's life, quite how long Denis spent *du côté de chez Fairbanks* is unclear. It is probably shorter than the tone of Fairbanks' narrative implies since in talking to Peter Fitzsimons, Nancy Wake says it was in that same winter of 1950 that Denis arrived in Sydney. As the liner steamed slowly past her waterside home, she stood on the lawn waving, as she had promised, a large white sheet to welcome him. They spent four happy days together. 'I think we both knew each of us had experienced far better times but it wasn't the sort of thing we wanted to dwell on. It was just really good to see him.'[203]

As we have come to know, Denis was 'born under a wandering star' and it seems likely that rather than embarking on a new career he had simply signed up for a round trip to escape the English winter. Letters kept the Fairbanks in touch for a while, then as inevitably happens, they drifted out of contact and they even speculated Denis might be dead. An old friend of his, groping for a moonbeam of memory, offered the author the vague recollection that he had taken a job as an air traffic controller in the South Atlantic or Pacific, a notion that seems far-fetched and from a passenger's viewpoint, not without hazard, except when we remember his skill at grabbing signals from the crackling airwaves.

He wasn't dead, but based on one isolated sighting, things were once again not going too well. In a typewritten letter to Vera Atkins in July 1956 Denis is sad but indomitable. He writes, improbably, on the notepaper of the *Sydney Morning Herald*'s Fleet Street office. Though it would have been a happy coincidence to find him following in his father's footsteps as a journalist, someone who knew

---

[203] *Fitzsimons pp. 288-9*

228 The Shooting Star

him then thought he was probably hired as a translator of French news agency reports. The tone of the letter and the fact that he is careful to add as the return address his home in Warwick Square, back then a warren of rundown houses carved up into bed-sitting rooms for the lonely, and boarding houses for tired travellers, suggest that his Fleet Street spell was in its way another short theatrical engagement produced by Nancy Wake, one which had closed early because of poor reviews.

He laments that having finished a long translation project, 'I don't seem to have any luck getting additional work . . . I think it is best for me to stick to cooking as the odd job. You have been so good to me and I hate to tell you all this . . . things are very difficult, but when I look around I do realise that I am very lucky indeed and am very greatful [*sic*] for the mercies fate cares to through [*sic*] at me.'

We have seen Denis, figuratively, in the silk dressing gown of Noël Coward, or more pertinently the Japanese robe 'Max Halder' gave him. One can go too far in looking for parallels. He was an actor. Is there a hint in this letter of John Osborne's Archie Rice, *The Entertainer*, and his sad refrain as he shuffles off the stage for the last time?

> *'Why should I let it get me,*
> *What's the use of despair?*
> *If they see that you're blue,*
> *They'll look down on you,*
> *So why, oh why, should I bother to care?*

The answer is that Denis did bother to care, and that unlike Archie Rice, the iron had not entered his soul.

His ability to look on the bright side despite it all shines through from Douglas Fairbanks' comments when, some time in the mid 1960s, as if he had popped out on a pantomime stage through a hidden trapdoor by some artifice of the special effects manager, Denis reappeared in The Boltons 'apparently ageless and just as jolly, viewing life with the same unembittered, undaunted bubbling philosophy as ever, through his own kind of rose coloured glasses'.

It is hard to match this image to the quiet, serious, somehow one-dimensional Denis in *le Chagrin*. Maybe the camera made him nervous. Maybe, ever an actor, he felt that was the way to play his role, the way he wanted to be remembered. It was in a way the climax of his career, his starring role. In all those years of hoofing and singing on the stage he had usually been just one of the chorus, an 'additional' unnoticed by reviewers and unremembered by most in the audience. Though he would not have appreciated it at the time, Ophuls' camera was rolling, he was now one of the central characters in a film which many millions would see, and which critics, intellectuals and historians would debate for years. The celluloid equivalent of John Farmer's encomium after Mont Mouchet. Not bad for a circus lad.

23

Curtain Call

Fairbanks and some friends seized on Denis's reappearance to cajole him into writing his memoirs. One was the film producer Thomas Clyde. The latter's production company, though active in the 1960s,[204] has no discernible links with the Ophuls project, though there may be other connections for compulsive cinéastes to explore, not least that Marcel and Denis had experiences in common. His father Max, creator of *la Ronde* and many other classic movies, fled Germany for France after the Reichstag fire in 1933, when it was already clear that the Jews of Germany were doomed. He became a French citizen but when the Germans invaded France he had to flee again, with his actress wife Hilda and a teenage Marcel, three more of the long caravan of lost souls trekking across the Pyrenees to Spain and then the USA. When he reached Hollywood, his first movie was a potboiler *The Exile* for Douglas Fairbanks Jr.

Another of those friends was the late Ronald Seth, himself a prolific author on topics from espionage to witchcraft, who contributed a brief Epilogue and who is acknowledged by Denis as having 'helped me in getting my story down on paper'. According to his obituary,[205] Seth had been professor of literature at the University of Tallinn before the Second World War and was sent back into Estonia by SOE. He was betrayed into German hands and after heavy torture, escaped execution by agreeing to collaborate. His own story is replete with some extraordinary, not to say improbable, adventures, none of which concern us save that 'he worked briefly for the Luftwaffe in Paris' and wore a German uniform. There is no

---

[204] *Its four forgettable movies had intriguingly varied casts including Fairbanks' friend David Niven, James Robertson Justice, Leslie Caron, Trevor Howard, Dorothy Dandridge and Cilla Black*
[205] *The* Times, *5 February 1985*

suggestion he and Denis crossed paths, but it is an intriguing thought.

Rake's Progress was published in 1968. Douglas Fairbanks' Introduction is dated 'January 1968', *le Chagrin* was released in 1969, but obviously took many months to film and edit. We have noted that a proof copy of Denis's book figures in the foreground of one of his interviews. On 26 August 1968, someone we have lost sight of, Emma Luart, died in St Gilles, a district of Brussels celebrated for its Art Nouveau houses and cultural ambience. It is also the site of the prison where Edith Cavell was held by the Germans before they shot her. In later years Emma had been a teacher, passing on her craft to a new generation of singers.

Denis grieved heavily for his lovers. He shared Nancy's sorrow when she heard of her husband's death and wept with her when her dog died. All of this we know, but of how and where the news of Emma's death reached him, and how he reacted, not a word, anywhere.

Writing of her in *Rake's Progress*, he refers to her in the past tense, but that was not the first time. He also makes the connection between Emma and the other strong woman who so impacted on his life, Nancy Wake. 'You see, I hardly knew my mother. She was a strange woman, very like Nancy Wake . . . very beautiful, very amusing. Yes, I think amusing, a lovely sense of humour.' That and her entry in *Grove* must serve as her epitaph.

In an early passage in his autobiography, referring to his mother and his time in the circus, Denis tells his readers that 'if the mother's love is absent – and this is equally true in the case of children whose mothers have died – there is something lacking in the lives and natures of [those] deprived children. I adore small children and have friends who have wonderful little families and as I watch them I can see, oh so clearly, what part the affection of parents, and especially of mothers, plays in their formation as adults. I realise now in my old age, probably more than I ever did before, what I missed. I do not complain. I refer to it only so that if you are so minded you may understand a little better what has made me tick throughout my sixty-seven years.'

SOE friends ran in to him from time to time in the bar of the Knightsbridge club where they liked to get together. He was always quick to make them laugh, usually by saying something outrageous, but was more often on the fringe of the group rather than at its centre, and he said next to nothing about his private life.

There was to be one more public sighting. A last-minute archives search threw up his name in, of all places, the British television timetables for May 1972, when 'Major Denis Rake' was billed to appear in a ten minute interview in the *Times Remembered* series. It is an episode with several of the elements we have come to see as hallmarks of Denis's story: ambiguity, confusion, missing pieces, and fading memories.

For a start, somewhere in its thirty or more years in the BBC vaults, the original TV recording has lost its soundtrack. Not surprisingly after all this time, the interviewer, the veteran Denis Tuohy, cannot now remember what was said, or indeed where it took place, and there is no transcript. The interview begins with a montage of still photographs from Denis's pre-war and wartime album, some of which we have reproduced here; as they are without captions or voice-over we have to guess at when and where they were taken. Is the rather large lady in a rather large open touring car, her face concealed by a floppy hat brim, Emma Luart? If not why is Denis posing insouciantly alongside the car? Where was the interview? It seems to be a private home, in which Denis is flanked by two African-esque wooden figurines, with a tapestry of a similar style on the back wall.

The bespectacled Denis is a little plumper than in *le Chagrin*, his white wavy hair now receding, no jacket, but in a long-sleeved shirt, a tie, and what looks like a copper anti-rheumatism bangle. He seems poised, occasionally smoothing his hair reflexively as he ponders an answer. Tuohy was a skilled interviewer and would have been well prepared. So what did they talk about? Professional lip readers have played and replayed the videotape but cannot glean more than tiny, inconsequential shards: 'I told him . . .' '..he said . . .' 'These officers . . .'. It is like watching a plump parrotfish through the glass walls of an aquarium. His lips open and close. But all we get is silence, bubbles and bladderwrack.

Denis died on 12 September 1976. We have deployed several film and theatrical frames of reference for his story; he was after all essentially a man of the theatre. His last lap too has a screen parallel, to be viewed, with a slight lump in the throat, through the prism of a little known, but poignant piece by Noël Coward.

Me And The Girls produced for television in 1985, is one of the few Coward pieces in which he portrays his hero as openly gay rather than amusingly ambiguous. Tom Courtenay plays the song and dance trouper George Banks, dying of cancer in a Swiss clinic. As he slides in and out of consciousness, cosseted by a motherly nun, he remembers his team of temperamental but loyal showgirls, their exotic venues, and his past lovers, still able to be catty and cheerful through the pain and medication. He puts on a brilliant brittle façade of wry courage, much as Denis did in real life. At a stretch of the imagination, the devoted Mavis, pillar of the troupe, whose love George could never fully return, could be seen to be reprising a Nancy Wake role. And the wrenching flashback to a London policeman's nervous house call to break the news that George's boy-friend Harry has been killed in a motorbike accident, has even more direct echoes of the death of Alex.

Denis died rich in memories and experiences that for most would be nightmares. Rich too in the number of colleagues and friends who throughout his kaleidoscopic life had come to think of him with love and respect, even if tinged sometimes with exasperation. He was rich in the honours bestowed by two countries in recognition of what he had done for them. He might well have been amused that in another gesture of recognition he even rated a posthumous entry in *A Who's Who of the British Secret State*, one of the earlier exercises in 'spy outing' published in 1989.[206]

A more contemporary if subdued laugh might have come from knowing that his SOE work name 'Dieudonné' has been adopted by a twenty-first century French comedian, an icon of the troubled banlieux, sadly best known for the anti-Semitic tinge of his act.[207]

Denis had adopted England, made himself an Englishman and

[206] *See 'Lobster', Bibliography*
[207] *See bibliography Hussey p. 56*

steeled himself to do improbable feats for his country and for France at an age when he could have honourably spent the war in the Home Guard or as an Air Raid Warden.

Denis had known how he wanted to live and equally what should happen when he died. His will stipulated that there were to be 'no religious services whatever' and that his body was to be used for medical research.

In money terms he was poor, his net estate for probate a modest £986.45. Ronald Seth who had guided his hand through the autobiography, and who may have encouraged Denis to add a few highlights to the textual coiffure, was his executor. Richard Ellis, to whom Denis had sent greetings from Miranda, and who had his wrist slapped for recycling a garbled version of Denis's exploits within range of the flapping ears of an SIS officer, was to receive half of any income generated from a film of *Rake's Progress*.[208] There was no mention of his medals.

In one of the more placid memorials of the war, Olivia Cockett, a Civil Servant, kept a diary for the British 'Mass Observation' project. Asked in 1942 what 'Home' meant to her, she wrote 'Mother. Books. Cushions. A good bed, food, warmth, laughter. Appreciation, flattery, even. A garden, the nephew and niece. The reason for working at things I don't like. Music and friends and [*her husband*]. Housework and cooking and wearing old clothes. Quiet. Sleep.' We have no clear idea of Denis's last years and can only hope that he found a similar tranquility. But he reminds us again of the quotation from *Scaramouche* when he remarks, in that January 1944 letter about his work as a Welfare Officer that '. . . I know I'm crazy but I started life like that long ago and must end the same'.

Good men are rare. Denis was one, and one of a kind. If he had a touch of the muddled Munchausen in retelling his adventures he was hardly alone, but at worst he was an embroiderer, not a liar. In 1666 Molière, cornerstone of the *Comedie Française*, wrote the satirical *Le Médecin Malgré Lui – The Doctor Despite Himself.*

---

[208] *This raises again the question of what if any linkage there may have been between Max Ophuls'* le Chagrin, *the* FREELANCE *story as told by Denis and by Nancy Wake, who also records being approached on various film projects*

The title could be adapted for Denis's story, *L'Héros Malgré Lui – The Hero Despite Himself* though his experiences were real, not a satire. As his mentor Maurice Buckmaster (whose judgement Denis wholly vindicated) says of him in *le Chagrin*, Denis 'had faith, a sense of patriotism and a very deep sense of duty . . . we needed such people because they were the ones who had the courage to conquer their fears'.

Sources and Acknowledgements

The cornerstone for any understanding of SOE in France is Professor Michael Foot's magisterial study. That it took until 2008 for a French edition to appear may speak volumes about the sensitivities of the topic; 'you are walking on eggshells all the time' as one historian put it. Indeed in his sweeping introduction to the French edition, J-L. Cremieux-Brilhac says that sometime after the publication of the revised British version in 1967, a major Paris publishing house commissioned a translation. It was preparing to publish, only to find the project vetoed by the British Foreign Office; Professor Foot's work was 'Crown Copyright'. He speculates that Whitehall was anxious not to give General de Gaulle another ground for grievance. Maybe too there were sensitivities about the risk of upsetting French Resistance veterans with a 'Made in Britain' version of events which as we have seen, many in France looked back on through a different, Tricolour prism.

William Mackenzie's official history of the Executive as a whole, completed in 1948 but kept under a security blanket for the next fifty years, also provides essential background as does the 1946 paper on 'British' circuits in France by Maurice Buckmaster's deputy in F Section, Major, later Lt Colonel R.H. Bourne-Paterson. It was drafted as the author puts it, in 'a race against time' and he admits it is therefore not complete. But as he set himself to achieve 'complete frankness' some of the observations are more trenchant than if he had been writing for public consumption, which is no doubt why it was classified as 'Confidential' and again not released for many years. Like John Farmer's after-action report one of its values is its closeness to the events described. Bourne-Paterson also seems to have had access to message files and operational logs now long since shredded.

We have already noted that the French perspective of the same events can be rather different and the recent *Dictionnaire Historique* cited in the Bibliography is valuable in explaining the complex political background as well as presenting the results of more recent French research. Its own forty-page bibliography highlights just how extensive the French literature is on the subject. The similarly titled English language study edited by Bertram Gordon is a useful adjunct. Students of those times also owe a special debt to the work of H.R. Kedward in drilling down into the French archives, and interviewing in small communities to give a picture of what Resistance meant on the ground. French historians such as Andre Touret and Eugene Martes have given careful accounts of Resistance in their regions; their focus on the French side of the struggle is understandable. Paul McCue's work on Amedée Maingard and his circuit is compelling in itself and also because it covers operations in an area contiguous with FREELANCE.

Denis's autobiography, as we have attempted to show, was more of a blurred sketch map than a historical atlas, but no fuller exploration of Denis's life would have been possible had Douglas Fairbanks Jr not pushed him into writing it in the first place. More recently Marcus Binney neatly summarised Denis's exploits in his survey of a number of SOE heroes, though he did not have the space and time we have enjoyed to dig into the background.

The underlying 'raw material' – the personal and other files – were also essential reading in getting from the general to the specific. Despite one's reservations about what may have been weeded in years gone by, those who had responsibility for the SOE files from the 1960s until they came into the public domain, and the professionals at the National Archives, are to be commended for doing their best within the constraints of a secretive culture to preserve the essence of a unique chapter in British history, and running a highly efficient operation to make the material so easily accessible. The latter accolade also goes to the helpful curators of the Imperial War Museum, which holds the papers of Vera Atkins. These were valuable both for the glimpses they give of Denis after the war as well as highlighting her passionate commitment as the folk memory and avenging angel of F Section.

The story of Denis's waterlogged first landing in France in 1942 is taken largely from Sir Brooks Richards' important study of SOE's operations by sea. The irreverent Leo Marks is an invaluable source for a sense of what the London offices and corridors of SOE felt like, and a professional exposition (as well as a depressing exposé) of the initial fatal flaws in its code and communications systems. Among the other sources which have helped this story along in so many ways are the shelves of reminiscences and biographies of other SOE agents in France. Nancy Wake first told her story to Russell Braddon in 1956, and then recounted it in her own words in 1985, and yet another biography appeared in 2001. We also have the benefit of the memoirs and biographies of Richard Heslop as well as his personal file, Ben Cowburn and Virginia Hall, the epicentre of so much SOE and British escape line activity in France. The personal file of Alex Schwatsko helped build a picture of a brave man, despite its inconsistencies with Denis's own account. Maurice Buckmaster also recorded his recollections in two anecdotal volumes of memoirs (Denis disagreed with the account of his own exploits) as well as making a cameo appearance in *le Chagrin*, a film well worth seeing even without Denis in mind, as indeed is Melville's *L'Armée des Ombres*. These are just two of the many French attempts to capture the essence of the Resistance experience on the screen.

The theatrical archives at the University of Kent and the Victoria and Albert Museum have not thrown up many appearances by Denis, but have given valuable cross bearings on some of his shows and his friends, and have been an evocative delight. The Archives of *la Monnaie* in Brussels provided the highlights of Emma Luart's career, as well as photographs and examples of her handwriting. The archive of the *Times* was an extraordinary resource on many topics. Though this can be accessed by subscribers electronically, leafing though the huge leather backed volumes in the basement of the London Library, while physically challenging, provides an unrivalled panorama of the evolution of English life and priorities over the past one hundred years, as well as giving helpful perspectives on subjects as diverse as the Riviera and Greece in the turbulent 1920s and Emma's concert appearances. The Library itself is a facility that has been used extensively and which has always met the most arcane challenges with patience and expertise.

So much has been written about SOE in France that readers may be left with the impression, as were many Frenchmen, that it was really the only secret British organisation operating there in the Second World War. As the Polish files and the *Dictionnaire* show, its older rival SIS was also active there on a substantial and successful scale, and we have to hope its forthcoming official history will help redress the balance.

But to find these sources, understand where they fit in the overall picture and to get even after all this time some sense of what it was all like, one needs help and advice.

In the halcyon days when merchant and investment banking were professions, rather than factories for high-tech Ponzi schemes, firms used to flaunt their successful security offerings in newspaper 'tombstones'. Every house fought fiercely for its place in the listing of those involved. There were Lead Managers, Co-managers, the splendidly styled 'Bulge Bracket' and at the bottom of the pyramid, the 'selling group' – Wall Street's less exalted foot soldiers.

In thanking the many who have helped with the exploration of Denis's life, it seems invidious to create a similar hierarchy: the ordering below does not imply any gradation in the level of my most genuine gratitude to all who have helped. I apologise if I have accidentally omitted anyone – it has been a longish haul – and I thank all in equal measure. The end result, any mistakes, misjudgments, and the like are entirely of my own making.

My warm appreciation then to Mark Seaman, Cabinet Office Historian, for his knowledge of the archives and his guidance, Professor M.R.D. Foot for his enthusiasm, some particularly helpful suggestions, and the groundwork without which the SOE story in France might have gone untold or mistold, Sonya 'Toni' D'Artois MBE, for her first hand memories of Denis and her close friend Nancy Wake, to her brother Michael Butt for introducing me to her, to Maurice Buckmaster's son Tim who gave me many valuable pointers, shared memories of his father, searched the latter's diary for references to Denis and went to great lengths to arrange an unforgettable encounter, Denis Tuohy for his efforts to unearth the soundtrack of that old BBC TV interview, and to Larraine Callow of Deafworks in London, who laboured hard to snatch Denis's words from the grainy screen, to Professor K. Gavro, of the University of Athens for his wise counsel on Greece, and also to Dimitri Afendoulis , Demetri Dragazis, and Christos Triantafillidis for their help. Bob O'Hara, whose knowledge of the National Archives system is impressively encyclopedic, helped in particular with Alex's file and with the intercept material, Alan Shawcross and Grant White of Anthony Buckley & Constantine turned up the portraits of Denis with alacrity and were kind enough to give permission for their use. Ian Sayer, doyen of collectors in this field was also generous in making available and allowing me to use a copy of the letter from Denis to Geoffrey Wincott, and Denis's fake ID card. In our search for traces of Denis's late sister Geoff Browne, webmaster of the Uplyme community site, did his best with a posting on which over 1,000 people have 'clicked' so far but sadly to no avail, Jan van Goethem of *la Monnaie* who pointed me in the direction of Emma Luart, Didy Grahame MVO helped on matters of medals and Masons, and Barry Norman took as much pleasure as I did when, after much searching he found Denis's name on the *Suzanne* playbill. Vincent Dowd of the BBC was helpful in steering me towards Denis Tuohy. My appreciation too to Debbie Taylor, R.J. Haines of Ancestral Research Service, the team at G. Heywood Hill Ltd., Lynne McDougall of The Royal Star and Garter Home, Michael Petchey, Alan Renton, Manuel Rispal, Dominique Rousseau, Andre Touret, Jean Virlogeux, Dr Beverley Hart of the Theatre Museum Collection in the Victoria and Albert Museum and once again, the indomitable Chris Wheal, whose research contribution on so many fronts, and his energy, are unsurpassed.

Fay Elliott has lived and travelled Denis's life with me: the book is hers as much as mine.

With so much help there should be few errors. But there will be, and they are entirely my responsibility.

Bibliography

All books cited are published in London unless otherwise stated

SOE

Atkins V., *Papers*, Imperial War Museum GB 62 IWM Doc (SO VM Atkins)'

Binney, M., *'The Homosexual Agent'*, in *Secret War Heroes*, Hodder, 2005

Bourne-Paterson, R. A. *The 'British' Circuits In France, 1941-1944, National Archives, HS 7 1 122 305346*

Braddon, R., *Nancy Wake*, Cassell, 1956

Buckmaster, M. *They Fought Alone*, Odhams, 1958

Butler, E. *Amateur Agent*, Harrap, 1963

Colvin, I.[Ed], *Colonel Henri's Story*, Kimber 1954

Cookridge, E. *Inside SOE*, Barker, 1966

Cowburn, B. *No Cloak, No Dagger*, The Adventurers Club, n.d.

Cunningham, C. *Beaulieu – The Finishing School for Secret Agents*, Leo Cooper, 1998

Elliott G., *I Spy*, St Ermins Press, 1997

Farmer, Major J.H. MC, FREELANCE *Mission Report, October 1944, National Archives, SOE France No. 177 HS6/570*

Fayol, P. *Le Chambon-Sur –Ligon sous l'Occupation, . . . l'action de Virgina Hall OSS*, Paris, L'Harmattan 2007

Fitzsimons, P. *Nancy Wake*, Harper Collins, Sydney, 2001

Foot, M.R.D., *SOE In France*, HMSO 1966

Cremieux Brilhac J-L.[Edits], and Bouyssou R., [Translates] Foot M.R.D., *Des Anglaises dans la Résistance. Le Service Secret Brittanique d'Action (SOE) en France 1940-1944*, Paris, Tallandier 2008

Garnett, D., *The Secret History of PWE, The Political Warfare Executive*, St. Ermin's Press, 2002

Helm, S., *A Life In Secrets The Story of Vera Atkins*, Little, Brown, 2005

Heslop R., *Xavier*, Hart-Davis, 1970

Ditto *Personal File National Archives 2266A/HS9/701/1*

James, C. *In Memoriam Terence Kilmartin, on www.clivejames.com*

Mackenzie W., *The Secret History of SOE*, St. Ermins Press/Time Warner Books 2000

Marks, L. *Between Silk & Cyanide*, Harper Collins 1998

McCue, P., *Behind Enemy Lines With the SAS , The Story of Amedée Maingard SOE Agent*, Barnsley, Pen & Sword, 2006

Murphy C.J., *The Origins of 'SOE in France'*, Cambridge, The Historical Journal, Vol. 46 Issue 4, 2003

Ditto – *Security and Special Operations – SOE and MI5 during the Second World War*, Palgrave Macmillan 2006

Nouzille, V. *L'Espionne Virginia Hall, une Americaine dans la Guerre*, Paris, Fayard, 2007

Pearson, Judith L., *The Wolves At The Door, USA*, The Lyons Press. 2005

Philby, H.A.R., *My Secret War*, New York, Grove Press, 1968

Rake, D. *[With an Introduction by Douglas Fairbanks Jr. and Epilogue by Ronald Seth], Rake's Progress*, Frewin 1968

Ditto, *Personal File, National Archive HS9/1648-26121*

Richards, Sir Brooks, *Secret Flotillas, Vol. 2*, London, Whitehall History/Cass, 2004

Schwatschko, A. *Personal File, National Archives HS9/1331/1*

Stevenson, W., *Spymistress*, New York, Arcadia Press 2006

Wake, Nancy, *The White Mouse*, Sydney, Pan Macmillan, 1985

Knight, Major M., *A Report on Certain Aspect of the Investigation into Lt Barry Knight late of SOE, with Particular Reference To Problems of SOE Internal Security, October 1943, National Archives, KV 6 23, 305346*

Robertson, T.A., *SOE Course of Lectures, February 21st 1942, National Archives KV 4/171/2803*

Selborne, Lord, *Summaries for the Prime Minister, November 1943,* *National Archive HS/8/897 and January 1945 HS 899*

Ramsey, R. and Doril, S. *'A Who's Who of The British Secret State,* *in 'Lobster – a Journal of Parapolitics,'* Hull, May 1989

FRANCE

Auroy, B., Jours de Guerre, Ma vie sous l'Occupation, Montrouge, Boyard, 2008

Beevor, A. & Cooper A., *Paris After the Liberation,* Penguin, 2004

Boyd, D, *Voices of The Dark Years,* Sutton, 2007

Buisson, P., *1940-1945 Années érotiques. Vichy ou les infortunes de la vertu,* Paris, Albin Michel , 2008

Celati, J-P., and Cavillon, P. [eds] *Chronique de la rue Parisienne, les Années '40,* France, Parigramme, 2000

Chabrol, C., directs] *L'Oeil de Vichy,* First Run Features, DVD, 1993

Curtis, M., *Verdict On Vichy,* Weidenfeld & Nicolson, 2002

Daninos, P., *Le Carnets de Major W. Marmaduke Thompson,* Paris, le Livre de Poche, 1967

'Edwin', *Historique du Reseau F2, Autumn 1946, National Archives, HD5/1*

Flanner, Janet, *Paris Journal 1944-55,* New York, Harcourt Brace, 1988

Gildea, R. *Marianne In Chains,* Pan, 2003

Gordon B.M, *[ED] Historical Dictionary of World War II France,* Aldwych Press 1998

Hussey, A. *The Paris Intifada, Granta,* Vol. 101, Spring 2008

Jackson, J., France – *The Dark Years,* OUP 2001

Marcot, F. et al [Eds] *Dictionnaire Historique de la Résistance,* Paris, Robert Laffont, 2006

Ophuls., M., Directs, '*Le Chagrin et la Pitié',* ('*The Sorrow and the Pity'),* Milestone Films and Video, USA, 2000, *see also*

Hoffman S. Introduces *The Sorrow and The Pity, Complete Script with Illustrations,* New York, Berkeley Windhover, 1975

Goldhammer A., [Translates] Rousso P., *The Vichy Syndrome,* Harvard, 1991

Jones, C., *Paris, Biography of a City*, Allen Lane/Penguin, 2004

Jünger, E. *Journaux de Guerre 1939-1948*, Paris, Gallimard, 2008

Kaplan, A., *The Collaborator, Chicago*, University Press, 2000

Kedward, H.R., *Occupied France – Collaboration and Resistance 1940-44*, Oxford, Blackwell, 1985

Ibid – *In Search of The Maquis – Rural Resistance in Southern France 1942-44*, Oxford, Clarendon Press, 1993

Le Boterf, H., *La Vie Parisienne Sous L'Occupation, Vols 1-4*, Geneva, Famot,1978

Lytton, N., *Life In Unoccupied France*, Macmillan, 1942

Martres, E. *Auvergne-Bourbonnais – Les Archives Parlent*, Romagnat, France, 2004

Melville J.P. [Directs] *L'Armée des Ombres, 1969*, Re-released by Rialto Pictures US, 2006

Nora, P. [Edits] *Realms of Memory*, New York, Columbia University Press, 1996

Norwich J.J., *The Duff Cooper Diaries*, Weidenfeld & Nicolson 2005

Paxton, R., *Vichy France*, Barrie & Jenkins, 1972

Pryce-Jones, D., *Paris In The Third Reich*, New York, Holt Reinhart, 1981

Touret, A., *Montluçon 1940-1944. Les Memoires Retrouvées, Créer*, France, Nonette, 2005

Vinen, R., *The Unfree French*, Penguin/Allen Lane, 2006

Williams, C., *Pétain*, Little, Brown, 2005

Ziman, H.D., *Instructions for British Servicemen In France 1944, Prepared by The Political Warfare Executive, Issued by the Foreign Office, Oxford, Bodleian Library, 2005*

OTHER

Alfrey, A., *Man of Arms, The Life and Legend of Sir Basil Zaharoff*, Weidenfeld & Nicolson, 1989

Bauman, M., *German Urban Theatre in WW1, Humboldt University*, at *www.esh.ac.uk.urban-history*

Benton. K., *The ISOS Years –Madrid 1941-43, Journal of Contemporary History*, Vol.30, No. 3, July 1995

Cockett, O., *Love and War in London. A Woman's Diary 1939-1942*, Ontario, Wilfred Laurier University Press

Cooper, Lady D., *The Light of Common Day*, Hart-Davis, 1959

Davies, P.H.J., *MI6 and The Machinery of Spying*, Cass, 2004

Dorril, S., *MI6*, Fourth Estate, 2000

Drake, R.J., *History of Intelligence (B), British Expeditionary Force France from January 1917 to April 1919, PRO/WO 106/45 and at net.lib/byu.edu]*

Farson, D., *Soho In The Fifties*, Michael Joseph, 1987

Gay, G.I. and Fisher H.H., *Public Relations of The Commission for Relief in Belgium*, USA, Stanford, 1929

Gibson, H., A Journal From Our Legation in Belgium, 1914-1917, accessed at *http://net.lib.byu.edu/~7rdh/ww1memoir/legation/Gibson*

Houlbrook, M., *Queer London*, Chicago, University Press, 2005

Hutchins, R., *Elizabeth's Spy*, Weidenfeld & Nicholson, 1998

Lewinsohn, R., *Basil Zaharoff, Munitions King*, Lippincott, 1934

Masterman, J., *The Double-Cross System*, New Haven, Yale University Press, 1972

Mackenzie, C., *Greek Memories*, Cassell, 1932

Miller, N., *Out of The Past. Gay and Lesbian History from 1869 to The Present*, New York, Alyson Books, 2006

Morgan, J., *The Secrets of Rue St Roche*, Allen Lane, 2004

Muggeridge, M., *The Thirties*, Hamish Hamilton, 1940

Osborne, J., *The Entertainer*, Faber 1961

Pitt,C. *Brussels, Grove Music Online, Ed. L. Macy,* *http/grovemusic.com*

Play Pictorial Archives University of Kent, *at http://library.kent.ac.uk/library/special/icons/playbills/PLAYDAT3*

Priestley J.B., *The Good Companions*, Heinemann, 1929

Proctor, T., *Female Intelligence, Women and Espionage in The First World War*, New York, University Press, 2003

Ramsey R. and Dorril, S., *A Who's Who Of The British Secret State*, Hull, Lobster, 1989

Rowan R.W., *The Story of Secret Service*, New York, The Literary Guild, 1938

Sabatini, R. *Scaramouche, accessed via Project Gutenberg on hhht://promo.net.pg*

Shaw, D., *The Beginnings of Geochimica et Cosmochimica Acta*, in Newsletter of the Geochemical Society, No. 114, 2003

Soper, Richard T. *Belgian Opera Houses and Singers*, Spartanburg USA, The Reprint Company, 1999 (*see also* www.carmen.demunt.be)

Sparrow, E., *Secret Service – British Agents in France 1792-1815*, *Woodbridge*, The Boydell Press, 1999

Steane, J.B., *'Emma Luart', Grove Music on Line Ed. L. Macy, accessed July 2007.www.grove.music.com*

Stone, H., *Writing In the Shadows*, Cass, 1996

Taylor A.J.P., *English History 1914-1945*, Oxford University Press, 1965

The Times Archive, *various dates*, Courtesy The London Library

Tisdall, E.E.P., *Royal Destiny – The Royal Hellenic Cousins*, Stanley Paul, 1955

Toibin, C., *Love in A Dark Time, Gay Lives from Oscar Wilde to Almodovar*, Picador, 2006

Tombs, E., *'Scrutinizing France', Intelligence and National Security*, Vol.17, No. 2, London 2002

Trinder, I. F., *The History of The Royal Masonic Hospital*, Colchester, The Author, 1992

Waugh, E., *Brideshead Revisited*, Chapman & Hall, 1945

West, N. [Edits], *The Diaries of Guy Liddell, Vols 1 and 2*, Routledge, 2005

Index